"Adam Winn offers a stimulating reading Gospel in post–70 AD Rome, addressin propaganda, claims of victory, and divine bridging two emphases on Jesus' suffering and power in the key passage of 10:42-45 that presents Jesus in terms of Roman political ideology as an ideal, powerful ruler who serves and sacrifices his life for his people. In all regards Jesus is superior to Vespasian. This book adds a rich synthesis of Markan Christology in context to continuing debates about the Gospel's presentation of Jesus."

Warren Carter, professor of New Testament at Brite Divinity School, TCU

"Building upon his earlier work on Mark, Adam Winn develops a fascinating reading of Markan Christology against the backdrop of Roman imperial power and propaganda under Vespasian in the immediate aftermath of the destruction of Jerusalem and the temple in AD 70. Constantly rooted in contemporary Latin sources, this demonstration that Jesus' power is perfected in his suffering, while his passion and crucifixion demonstrate his triumph, is greatly to be welcomed."

Richard A. Burridge, dean of King's College London

"I welcome this contribution to the study of the Gospel of Mark in the context of the Roman Empire. The Jesus of the New Testament Gospels is thoroughly Jewish, to be sure, but he lived and ministered in a land that was part of the Roman world; and the evangelist Mark, the first to craft a biography of Jesus, understood this well. Mark challenges Rome and its cult of the divine emperor with a compelling portrait of the true Son of God. Adam Winn has perceptively pursued this line of inquiry shedding new light on this important field of study."

Craig A. Evans, John Bisagno Distinguished Professor of Christian Origins at Houston Baptist University

"Adam Winn has composed a careful and thoughtful study of Mark's story of Jesus, demonstrating the Markan Jesus' superlative honor and power over and against the Roman empire with its propaganda about its own 'Lord' and 'Son of God.' By reading Mark's Gospel in the context of the Roman world, Winn opens up new vistas of understanding that will truly excite and engage all readers."

Michael F. Bird, lecturer in theology at Ridley College, Melbourne, Australia

READING MARK'S CHRISTOLOGY UNDER CAESAR

JESUS THE MESSIAH AND ROMAN IMPERIAL IDEOLOGY

ADAM WINN

IVP Academic

An imprint of InterVarsity Press
Downers Grove, Illinois

InterVarsity Press
P.O. Box 1400, Downers Grove, IL 60515-1426
ivpress.com
email@ivpress.com

InterVarsity Press® is the book-publishing division of InterVarsity Christian Fellowship/USA®, a movement of
students and faculty active on campus at hundreds of universities, colleges, and schools of nursing in the United
States of America, and a member movement of the International Fellowship of Evangelical Students. For
information about local and regional activities, visit intervarsity.org.

Scripture quotations, unless otherwise noted, are from the New Revised Standard Version of the Bible, copyright
1989 by the Division of Christian Education of the National Council of the Churches of Christ in the USA. Used by
permission. All rights reserved.

Cover design: David Fassett
Interior design: Jeanna Wiggins
Images: crown of thorns: © duckycards / DigitalVision Vectors / Getty Images
        gold background: © FrankvandenBergh / E+ / Getty Images
        Roman gold coin: Ancient Rome Vespasian Gold Aureus / Hoberman/UIG / Bridgeman Images

ISBN 978-0-8308-5211-6 (print)
ISBN 978-0-8308-8562-6 (digital)

Printed in the United States of America ♾

Library of Congress Cataloging-in-Publication Data
Names: Winn, Adam, 1976- author.
Title: Reading Mark's Christology under Caesar : Jesus the Messiah and Roman
  Imperial ideology / Adam Winn.
Description: Downers Grove : InterVarsity Press, 2018. | Includes
  bibliographical references and index.
Identifiers: LCCN 2018017722 (print) | LCCN 2018027295 (ebook) | ISBN
  9780830885626 (eBook) | ISBN 9780830852116 (pbk. : alk. paper)
Subjects: LCSH: Bible. Mark--Criticism, interpretation, etc.--History. |
  Church history--Primitive and early church, ca. 30-600. | Jesus
  Christ--Person and offices. | Emperor worship--Rome. | Propaganda, Roman.
Classification: LCC BS2585.6.E46 (ebook) | LCC BS2585.6.E46 W565 2018 (print)
  | DDC 226.3/067--dc23
LC record available at https://lccn.loc.gov/2018017722

P	23	22	21	20	19	18	17	16	15	14	13	12	11	10	9	8	7	6	5	4	3	2	1
Y	38	37	36	35	34	33	32	31	30	29	28	27	26	25	24	23	22	21	20	19	18		

TO MY FATHER, DOUG WINN,

who taught me the invaluable lesson

of admitting when I was wrong.

CONTENTS

ACKNOWLEDGMENTS

I N 2008 MY DOCTORAL DISSERTATION (Fuller Theological Seminary) was published by Mohr Siebeck under the title *The Purpose of Mark's Gospel: An Early Christian Response to Roman Imperial Propaganda*. In that book I argue that Mark's Gospel was written for the purpose of responding to the propaganda of the emperor Vespasian, propaganda that had created a crisis for the Markan community. As a part of that project I argued, following the lead of Robert Gundry, that Mark's Christology was one that was characterized by power from beginning to end, and thus christological material in Mark that appeared to be related to suffering and death had to be reinterpreted or mitigated in some way. Given that I was swimming against a very strong current in Markan scholarship, it is not surprising that my book was strongly critiqued by fellow Markan interpreters. Initially this critique stung, but it was ultimately helpful and allowed me to see significant weaknesses in my reading of Mark's Christology, weaknesses I note within this book. I am particularly indebted to the SBL Mark Group that generously listened to my presentation of Mark's Christology of power and offered helpful criticism and direction. This criticism sent me back to the drawing board and led me to reconsider the nature of Mark's Christology. But instead of leading me away from reading Mark as a response to Roman imperial realities (the central argument of my earlier book), this criticism pushed me further into the Roman imperial world in search of ways to make sense out of the disparate pieces of Mark's Christology. This book is a result of that search. It is ultimately an acknowledgment that in my former work I missed the mark on Markan Christology. The present book seeks to correct my mistake, but I do so without departing from my earlier conclusions regarding Mark's setting and purpose— namely, that Mark was written to address a crisis in his church that was created by Flavian propaganda. My new understanding of Mark's Christology is closely connected to this setting and purpose, but it offers a more balanced view than what appeared in my earlier work. Thus this book is like one who brings out of the house treasures both new and old.

Like all such projects, the generosity and work of many are responsible for the final product before you. I want to thank Robert Duke, my dean at Azusa Pacific University, for granting a reduction in my teaching load so that I could devote more time to working on this project, over half of which was written while I was working at APU. I would also like to thank Tim Crawford, my current dean at the University of Mary Hardin-Baylor, for being sensitive to this writing project while putting together my teaching load. As all professors know, numerous new course preparations are the enemy of productive writing, and I am thankful to Tim for a year in which new course preparations (at a new job no less!) were minimal. As a result I was able to complete this book in my first year teaching at a new institution.

I would also like to thank Elizabeth Struthers Malbon, Tim Brookins, Mark Lamas, and David Wilhite, all of whom read portions of this book and provided invaluable feedback and editorial work along the way. Elizabeth was particularly helpful in the current shape of my work on the Markan secrecy motif. This work began as an SBL paper that Elizabeth generously took interest in and for which she offered valuable critique, all of which no doubt played a significant role in the paper being published as an article in the *Journal of Biblical Literature*. It is particularly noteworthy that Elizabeth and I often come to different conclusions in our readings of Mark's Gospel, including the Markan secrecy motif. But despite such differences Elizabeth was willing to help and encourage a young scholar. May she be a model to other senior scholars as they engage young scholars who are trying to find their way in a very difficult and at times unfriendly field. I hope to follow her example of grace, kindness, and generosity.

I would also like to thank Dan Reid, senior acquisitions editor at InterVarsity Press, for seeing the value in this project and for enthusiastically supporting it since the day I first proposed it. I also would like to thank Anna Gissing, who, upon Dan's retirement, saw this book through the production process and gave crucial guidance along the way. Along with Dan and Anna, I would like to thank the editorial review board at InterVarsity Press, who were able to see what Dan saw in this project and elected to move forward with it. I would also like to thank all at InterVarsity Press for the hard work devoted to reviewing, editing, and promoting this book—all such efforts play a significant role in the resulting final product.

As the dedication to this book indicates, I owe great thanks to my father, Doug Winn, who modeled for me the ability to admit when he was wrong. Among the many lessons he has taught me, it numbers among the greatest. I am a much better person for having learned it.

I also want to thank both my wife, Molly, and my daughter, Brennan, who are daily my joy and inspiration. Your constant love and support are a blessing, without which I could never complete such a project.

Finally, I must thank the God and Father of my Lord Jesus Christ, from whom come all of the blessings noted above and countless more beyond these. May this book bring better understanding to the Gospel of Mark's presentation of Jesus, as well as glory to the God who inspired that Gospel. For all the blessings and successes in my life, including any that might come from this book, I give him all honor, glory, and praise. Amen.

ABBREVIATIONS

Modern Sources

AB	Anchor Bible
ABD	*Anchor Bible Dictionary*. Edited by David Noel Freedman. 6 vols. New York: Doubleday, 1992
ANRW	*Aufstieg und Niedergant der römischen Welt: Geschichte und Kultur Roms im Spiegel der neueren Foschung.* Part 2, *Principat.* Edited by Hildegard Temporini and Wolfgang Haase. Berlin: de Gruyter, 1972–
CBQ	*Catholic Biblical Quarterly*
CIL	*Corpus Inscriptionum Semiticarum.* Paris, 1881–
ET	English translation
JBL	*Journal of Biblical Literature*
JRS	*Journal of Religious Thought*
JSNT	*Journal for the Study of the New Testament*
JSNTSup	Journal for the Study of the New Testament Supplement Series
LCL	Loeb Classical Library
LNTS	Library of New Testament Studies
NIGTC	New International Greek Testament Commentary
NTL	New Testament Library
NTS	*New Testament Studies*
TDNT	*Theological Dictionary of the New Testament*
WBC	Word Biblical Commentary
WUNT	Wissenschaftliche Untersuchungen zum Neuen Testament

Ancient Sources

Ann.	Tacitus, *Annales*
Aug.	Suetonius, *Divus Augustus*
Cal.	Suetonius, *Gaius Caligula*
Claud.	Suetonius, *Divus Claudius*
Hist.	Tacitus, *Historiae*
Inv. Od.	Plutarch, *De invidia et odio*
J.W.	Josephus, *Jewish War*
Or.	Cicero, *De oratore*
Tib.	Suetonius, *Tiberius*
Vesp.	Suetonius, *Vespasianus*

INTRODUCTION

I N THE LAST CENTURY, few issues have vexed Markan interpreters more
than the nature of Mark's Christology.[1] Interpretations have run the gamut
from a Gospel that primarily presents Jesus as the all-powerful "divine man" to
a Gospel that primarily presents Jesus as the suffering and dying Messiah, one
who shuns power and embraces weakness. For some Mark clearly presents Jesus
as God's messianic king, while others reject any such royal or messianic associa-
tions. Such diversity of scholarly opinion might lead casual observers to question
whether these interpreters were in fact reading the same text. But these diverse
interpretations do find their origins in the Markan text, a text full of diverse and
at times apparently contradictory christological material. Explaining such diverse material with a single comprehensive theory is notoriously difficult and
thus has led to interpretations that are as divergent and contradictory as the

---

[1]When referring to "Mark's Christology," this study refers to the way that Mark presents the
central character of the narrative, Jesus, including the ways the Gospel identifies Jesus, the roles
and functions attributed to Jesus, and the ultimate significance given to Jesus as God's agent. I
will consider all of these realities in light of Mark's entire narrative and not as separate pieces to
be examined in isolation. Mark's Christology is indeed a "narrative Christology" and will be
treated as such in this study, i.e., this study is not simply sifting Mark for theological nuggets.
This note is a response to Elizabeth Struthers Malbon's critique of previous studies on Mark's
Christology that are primarily interested in how Mark's presentation of Jesus fits into anachro-
nistic theological categories or systems and that trend toward propositional language (see *Mark's
Jesus: Characterization as Narrative Christology* [Waco, TX: Baylor University Press, 2009], 3-4,
16-19). Here I use *Christology* simply as a reference to how Jesus is presented or understood in
Mark's narrative.

material itself. Some interpreters have thrown up their hands, claiming irresolvable tension in Mark's christological material and that such was the intention of the Evangelist.

The question of how to assemble the disparate pieces of Mark's Christology is the very question this study intends to pursue. What are these disparate pieces? Is any particular set of pieces primary? Is Mark's Christology intentionally locked in irresolvable tension? And where might we look for answers? Should we limit ourselves to the text itself? Or might a reconstruction of Mark's setting provide a way forward? The present introduction will address these questions by outlining the christological pieces of Mark's Gospel, considering the various ways these pieces have been assembled in the field of Markan interpretation, and proposing a new way forward.[2]

THE DIVERSE PIECES OF MARK'S CHRISTOLOGICAL PUZZLE

Before considering the way in which the pieces of Mark's christological puzzle have been assembled, I will first outline the differing sets of pieces that must be accounted for.

Considering titles. The first set of pieces to be considered are the various ways that Mark identifies Jesus or the titles that the Evangelist attributes to Jesus. These titles include Messiah, Son of God, Son of Man, Son of David, teacher, king of the Jews, and perhaps Lord. Throughout much of the twentieth century, studies on Mark's Christology focused heavily on these christological titles, assessing which titles were primary in the Gospel, which titles might be in tension, what such titles might have meant in light of Mark's *Sitz im Leben*, and then adducing from such analysis the Christology of the Gospel. Narrative critics have strongly critiqued such an approach to Mark's Christology. They have made a strong case that Mark's Christology is a narrative Christology and that Mark's christological titles only have meaning in the context of the Markan narrative. While Mark might proclaim from the outset that Jesus is God's Messiah or Son, only Mark's narrative can tell us what kind of Messiah he is or what Jesus' identity as "Son of God" might mean for the Markan Evangelist.

This corrective offered by narrative critics is an important one indeed, but I would argue that it does not altogether mitigate the role that christological titles

---

[2]Unless otherwise noted I use "Mark" to refer to the Gospel so named rather than the Evangelist. The arguments herein do not rest on the identity of the historical author of the Gospel.

in and of themselves play in assessing and understanding Mark's Christology. While it is true that Mark's narrative shapes the way one must understand its christological titles, these titles also help shape the way one understands Mark's narrative. The titles themselves carry with them various meanings for Mark's first-century readers, and while Mark's narrative can emphasize certain aspects of those meanings or redefine those meanings in certain ways, the inherited meanings of these titles always play a role in understanding Mark's Christology. Thus any study of Mark's Christology must pay attention to these titles, giving attention to both the meanings these titles might have had in the minds of Mark's first-century readers, and also to how Mark's narrative employs, redefines, affirms, or critiques such titles. To ignore either aspect of these titles would lead to an inadequate understanding of them.

Considering power. Through numerous narrative elements, Mark clearly presents Jesus as a figure of supreme power. A brief catalog of these elements is provided here.

Healings and exorcism. The Markan narrative clearly presents Jesus as a powerful healer, recording nine specific healing episodes (Mk 1:29-31, 40-45; 2:1-12; 3:1-6; 5:21-43; 7:31-37; 8:22-26; 10:46-52) and referencing Jesus' general healing activity on three separate occasions for which no specific details are offered (Mk 1:32-34; 3:10; 6:53-56). Jesus' healings include the restoration of hearing, the restoration of sight, the reversal of paralysis, the healing of deformity, the healing of skin disease, and even the raising of the dead. Alongside such healings Jesus is frequently presented as an exorcist. The Markan Evangelist records four detailed episodes in which Jesus exorcizes a demon or demons (Mk 1:23-28; 5:1-20; 7:24-30; 9:14-29). The Evangelist offers four additional references to Jesus' success as an exorcist without recording any specific details (Mk 1:32-34, 39; 3:11-12, 20-30).

Power over the natural world. In addition to exorcisms and healings, the Markan Jesus also demonstrates power over nature. In Mark 4:35-41 Jesus calms a raging sea storm with simply an audible command. And in Mark 6:45-52 Jesus walks on a stormy sea and presumably calms it by his mere presence. Additionally, on two occasions Mark presents Jesus as one who is able to feed thousands with a minimal amount of food. In Mark 6:30-44 Jesus feeds five thousand with five loaves of bread and two fish—twelve baskets of food are left over. In Mark 8:1-10 Jesus feeds four thousand with seven loaves of bread and a few small fish—seven baskets of food are left over.

Revelations by supernatural beings. Throughout Mark's Gospel supernatural beings declare Jesus' powerful identity. On two occasions it is God himself who declares Jesus to be his son (Mk 1:11; 9:7). The second occasion occurs after Jesus is transfigured before three of his disciples, and his glorious (heavenly?) identity is revealed. On three occasions demons make pronouncements about Jesus' identity, declaring him to be the "Holy One of God" (Mk 1:24), "Son of God" (Mk 3:11), and "Son of the Most High God" (Mk 5:7). For Mark's first-century audience, such supernatural declarations would certainly have identified Jesus as an extremely powerful figure.

Popularity and proclamations. At many points in Mark's Gospel, Jesus is presented as being wildly popular among the people. On many occasions the reader is told of Jesus' fame spreading (Mk 1:28, 32-33, 45), of people coming long distances to see and hear him (Mk 3:7-8; 6:33, 55), and of large crowds gathering around him (Mk 2:2, 13; 3:9; 4:1; 5:21, 24, 31; 6:34; 8:1; 9:14-15; 10:1). Mark often notes the amazement of the people and records proclamations of the crowd that are evoked by Jesus' power (Mk 1:27; 2:12; 7:37). Those who are the beneficiaries of Jesus' power proclaim it widely (Mk 1:45; 5:20; 7:36). Perhaps the most significant public proclamation is found at Jesus' entry into the city of Jerusalem, where he is hailed by the people as one who "comes in the name of the Lord" and is identified with the coming kingdom of David (Mk 11:7-10). Through such mediums the power and glory of the Markan Jesus is magnified.

Divine knowledge and prerogative. Throughout Mark's Gospel, Jesus possesses divine knowledge and often exercises a divine prerogative. Jesus supernaturally knows the thoughts of others (Mk 2:8; 3:5; 9:33-35; 12:15) and successfully foretells future events, including his own death (Mk 8:31; 9:31; 10:33-34; 11:2-3; 13:2-9; 14:13-15, 18, 27, 30).[3] He claims both the divine right to forgive sins (Mk 2:5-10) and lordship over the Sabbath (Mk 2:28). Such demonstrations of divine knowledge and prerogative would have communicated Jesus' great power and authority to the reader.

---

[3]While some interpreters have questioned whether the knowledge of others' thoughts indicates divine knowledge (see for example Vincent Taylor, *The Gospel According to Saint Mark*, 2nd ed. [London: MacMillan, 1966], 196; Taylor also cites others), the majority of recent interpreters attribute this knowledge to supernatural power (see Joel Marcus, *Mark 1–8: A New Translation with Introduction and Commentary*, AB 27 [New York: Doubleday, 2000], 217; Adela Yarbro Collins, *Mark: A Commentary*, Hermeneia [Minneapolis: Fortress, 2007], 185-86). It should also be noted that at times the Markan Jesus lacks knowledge of future events, and thus Jesus' divine knowledge is not absolute; at times it is limited.

Authoritative teacher. In addition to exorcist, healer, and miracle worker, Mark presents Jesus as a powerful and authoritative teacher. Mark specifically notes that "authority" distinguishes Jesus' teaching from the teaching of the scribes (Mk 1:22). It seems Mark closely associates Jesus' teaching with his work as an exorcist and healer, and by doing so magnifies the authority of the teaching and the teacher (Mk 1:22-28; 2:1-12; 3:1-6). There also seems to be a strong link between Jesus' teaching and the kingdom of God (Mk 4:1-20, 26-32; 9:1; 10:13-31; 12:28-34), further evincing Jesus' power and authority. Additionally, Mark presents Jesus as thwarting the Jewish religious authorities through superior wisdom and knowledge of Israel's Scriptures (Mk 2:18-22, 25; 7:1-15; 12:13-34).

To the first-century reader, Mark's Jesus stands as an impressive figure indeed, one with power that was virtually unparalleled in the ancient world.

Considering suffering. While Mark clearly presents Jesus as a powerful and glorious figure, he also presents him as a suffering figure. Here I catalog the narrative features that contribute to this presentation of the Markan Jesus.

Foreboding foreshadowing. It has long been noted that a "suffering" motif is relatively absent in the first half of Mark (Mk 1–8), where instead the motifs of power and glory predominate. Though such a claim is true, there are a handful of narrative elements that ominously foreshadow Jesus' future suffering and death.[4] The first example of such foreshadowing comes in Jesus' answer regarding why his disciples do not fast. In Jesus' reply he says, "The wedding guests cannot fast while the bridegroom is with them, can they? As long as they have the bridegroom with them, they cannot fast. The days will come when the bridegroom is taken away from them, and then they will fast on that day" (Mk 2:19-20). Presumably Jesus is to be understood as the bridegroom, who will at some point be taken away from the wedding guests (his disciples). This removal of the bridegroom is presumably an allusion to Jesus' death, a sorrowful event that will result in his disciples' fasting.

The second foreshadowing follows Jesus' healing of a man on the Sabbath (Mk 3:1-6). Mark notes that, after witnessing this healing, the Pharisees and the Herodians conspire to kill Jesus. It is difficult to deny that this episode foreshadows

---

[4]In my former work I mistakenly sought to downplay the significance of this foreshadowing in Mark's Gospel (see *The Purpose of Mark's Gospel: An Early Christian Response to Roman Imperial Propaganda*, WUNT II/245 [Tübingen: Mohr Siebeck, 2008], 114-15). I offer my appreciation to the critics of this earlier work, who noted the weaknesses in my attempts to marginalize this Markan foreshadowing and encouraged me to reconsider its importance.

Jesus' future death at the hands of Jewish religious leaders and Roman authorities. Though less conspicuous, Jesus' rejection in his hometown of Nazareth (Mk 6:1-6) may also foreshadow Jesus' future rejection by his own people. Finally, Mark's narration of John the Baptist's death at the hands of the Roman client king Herod Antipas seems to foreshadow Jesus' own death at the hands of Roman authorities (Mk 6:14-29)—as they do to the forerunner, so will they do to Jesus.

Passion predictions. Mark's first explicit reference to Jesus' suffering and death comes on the lips of Jesus himself, who prophesies these events to his disciples at Caesarea Philippi (Mk 8:31). This prophecy is the first of three "passion predictions" made by the Markan Jesus to his disciples (Mk 9:31; 10:33-34). It should be noted that each one of these passion predictions also includes a prediction that Jesus will rise from the dead after three days. The ominous foreshadowing in the first half of Mark finds its first explicit expression in Jesus' own prophecies.

Service, humility, and suffering. After each Markan passion prediction Jesus' teaching addresses the themes of service, humility, and suffering. As Jesus willingly suffers, so also must his disciples (Mk 8:34). Likewise, as their master humbly serves and sacrifices himself for others, so also must his disciples (Mk 9:35; 10:42-45). In fact only those who possess the humility of a child are able to receive the kingdom of God (Mk 10:14-15). All such teaching is grounded in the example of Jesus himself, giving it christological significance.

A prophetic parable. Mark 12:1-12 presents an allegorical parable in which Jesus is to be identified with the vineyard owner's (God's) son. The tenants seizing and executing this son is therefore an explicit prediction of Jesus' impending arrest and execution. Here the Markan Evangelist ties together Jesus' identity as God's Son with his suffering and death—giving christological significance to the latter.

A burial anointing. In Mark 14:3-9 a woman anoints Jesus' head with oil, an anointing that parallels the anointing of a royal figure.[5] However, Jesus redefines the anointing as one for his burial, a reference to Jesus' impending death. By bringing together Jesus' royal identity and his impending death, Mark gives christological import to the latter.

Passion narrative. The Markan motif of christological suffering reaches its zenith in the Markan passion narrative. In the celebration of the Passover meal, Jesus' death takes center stage and is presented as a sacrifice for many (Mk 14:18-25).

---

[5]For example, see Francis J. Moloney, *The Gospel of Mark: A Commentary* (Peabody, MA: Hendrickson, 2002), 280-81.

Following this meal he is betrayed by one from his inner circle (Mk 14:10-11, 43-45), pleads with God to remove his cup of suffering (Mk 14:36), is arrested by armed men (Mk 14:43-49), is abandoned by his followers (Mk 14:50), is falsely accused (Mk 14:55-59), is spat on and beaten (Mk 14:65), is denied three times by Peter (Mk 14:66-72), is flogged and mocked by Roman soldiers (Mk 15:16-20), and is sentenced to crucifixion by Pontius Pilate (Mk 15:15). During his crucifixion his clothes are divided among his executioners (Mk 15:24), he is mocked by onlookers (Mk 15:29-31), and he is executed alongside criminals (Mk 15:27). His cry from the cross might even suggest divine abandonment (Mk 15:34). That Mark's passion narrative presents the reader with a suffering Jesus is undeniable.

Considering the narrative arrangement of power and suffering. After outlining the Markan material that illustrates Jesus as both a figure of extreme power and a figure of suffering, it is important to comment on how these two sets of christological pieces are arranged. As noted above, the Jesus of power dominates the first half of Mark, with only a handful of details that foreshadow Jesus' suffering. And though such foreshadowing is present, it is seemingly overshadowed by a narrative of the supremely powerful Jesus. But at the end of Mark 8, the tenor of the narrative takes a dramatic turn in regard to the nature of its christological material. While the powerful Jesus of the first half of Mark does not disappear entirely, he seems to take a backseat to the suffering Jesus. Thus it seems the first eight chapters of Mark emphasize Jesus' power, while the last eight emphasize Jesus' suffering. Such an organization of christological material should play a significant role in the assessment of Mark's Christology.

Considering secrecy. The Markan secrecy motif was first identified by William Wrede in his landmark book, *The Messianic Secret*.[6] Wrede argued for a unified (and unifying) motif of secrecy that ran throughout Mark's Gospel. This motif included (1) Jesus' commands for silence both to the beneficiaries of miracles (Mk 1:43-44; 5:43; 7:36; 8:26) and to those who spoke of his identity (Mk 1:25, 34; 3:12; 8:30; 9:9); (2) Jesus' attempts to conceal his whereabouts (Mk 7:24; 9:30-31); and (3) the secret nature of Jesus' teaching, often called the "parable theory" (Mk 4:11-12). Subsequently, interpreters have debated whether these three elements are unified at all, with many suggesting that each functions

---

[6]William Wrede, *Das Messiasgeheimnis in den Evangelien: Zugleich ein Beitrag zum Verständnis des Markusevangeliums* (Göttingen: Vandenhoeck & Ruprecht, 1901); ET, *The Messianic Secret*, trans. J. C. G. Greig (Cambridge: James Clarke, 1971). For a helpful discussion of the history of the messianic secret in New Testament interpretation, see Collins, *Mark*, 170-72.

differently in Mark's Gospel.[7] While resolving this debate is not my present purpose, I do note that the first element, that is, Jesus concealing who he is and what he does, has a more clear connection to Mark's Christology than the latter two elements. Therefore it is this element that I put forward as the fourth significant piece of Mark's christological puzzle—one that has been widely recognized by Markan interpreters for the past century. How do Jesus' attempts to conceal his identity and his miracles fit together with the christological pieces already identified, that is, with titles, power, and suffering?

PUTTING THE PIECES TOGETHER

Over the past century of Markan scholarship, these pieces have been considered and evaluated in a variety of ways, through a variety of methods, with a variety of presuppositions and conclusions. Here I briefly discuss the major ways in which interpreters from various methodological schools have assembled the pieces of Mark's christological puzzle.

Form critics: No assembly required. Generally speaking, form critics saw the Gospels as unsophisticated compilations of Christian traditions, with the Gospel authors as mere compilers who strung these traditions together like pearls on a string.[8] As such, form critics (e.g., Rudolf Bultmann, Martin Dibelius, Karl Ludwig Schmidt) felt little need to assemble the pieces of Mark's Christology into a coherent whole—in their estimation, such a whole was never the Evangelist's purpose. However, one form critic's assessment of Mark's Christology, that of Bultmann, had a major impact on Markan studies until the late twentieth century. Bultmann argued that Mark presented a θεῖος ἀνήρ or "divine man"

---

[7]For such arguments, see Ulrich Luz, "Das Geheimnismotiv und die markinische Christologie," *Zeitschrift für die Neutestamentliche Wissenschaft und die Kunde der Älteren Kirche* 56 (1965): 9-30; ET, "The Secrecy Motif and the Marcan Christology," in *The Messianic Secret*, ed. Christopher Tuckett (Philadelphia: Fortress, 1983), 75-96; Heikki Räisänen, *The "Messianic Secret" in Mark's Gospel*, trans. Christopher Tuckett (Edinburgh: T&T Clark, 1990), 242-43; Schuyler Brown, "'The Secret of the Kingdom of God' (Mark 4:11)," *JBL* 92 (1973): 60-74; Andreas Bedenbender, "Das 'Messiasgeheimnis' im Markusevangelium," *Texte und Kontexte* 27, nos. 3-4 (2004): 1-96, esp. 35. For those who still hold that all three elements form a unified theme, see Gerd Theissen, "Die pragmatische Bedeutung der Geheimnismotive im Markusevangelium: Ein wissenssoziologischer Versuch," in *Secrecy and Concealment: Studies in the History of Mediterranean and Near Eastern Religions*, ed. Hans G. Kippenberg and Guy G. Stroumsa, Studies in the History of Religions 65 (Leiden: Brill, 1995), 225-45; Collins, *Mark*, 172.

[8]K. L. Schmidt uses the language of placing pearls on a string (*Der Rahmen der Geschichte Jesu* [Berlin: Trowitzsch und Sohn, 1919]).

Christology.[9] The "divine man" was the power of the divine coming on and re-siding in the human; as such the divine man possessed supernatural abilities as well as divine knowledge and wisdom. For Bultmann, Mark was a representative Gospel for Pauline Hellenistic churches, churches where the concept of the divine man was borrowed from the Hellenistic religious world and imported into Christianity. "Son of God," a title that Bultmann recognized as prominent in Mark, was synonymous with this concept of the divine man, a title with or-igins solely in the Hellenistic rather than Jewish world. Therefore Bultmann locked on to one set of Markan christological pieces, those that emphasized Jesus' power, and understood those pieces to be the predominant christological orientation of Mark's Gospel. Because he understood the Gospels as many parts haphazardly strung together into a whole, he had no interest in how the other christological pieces of Mark—pieces that emphasized suffering, for example—fit together with this predominant Christology of power.

Redaction critics: Suffering pieces "correct" power pieces? The eventual eclipsing of form criticism by redaction criticism had a significant impact on Markan scholarship in general and assessments of Markan Christology in par-ticular. Redaction critics rejected the form-critical conclusion that the Gospel authors were mere compilers of early tradition and instead identified them as creative authors and theologians who were intentional in the way they constructed their respective Gospels. Such a conclusion pushed Markan interpreters to find coherence in Mark's christological material. Virtually all early redaction critics accepted (rather uncritically) Bultmann's assessment of the power pieces in Mark's Gospel, pieces that were understood to reflect a "divine man" Christology that found its origins not in Judaism but in the Hellenistic world. The task at hand was to figure out the relationship between this divine man Christology and the pieces of Mark's Christology that Bultmann and the form critics had largely ignored—namely, pieces that emphasized Jesus' suffering and death. With the redaction-critical emphasis on identifying Gospel source material and the way in which that source material was used, the door was opened for scholars to see conflict between the Gospel authors and the material they received and edited. Scholars recognized that the Markan Evangelist could take source material toward which he had a

---

[9]Rudolf Bultmann, *Theology of the New Testament*, trans. Kendrick Grobel (New York: Scribner's, 1951), 131-32. For the concept of the "divine man," Bultmann relied heavily on the work of Ludwig Bieler, *Theios Anēr: Das Bild des "Göttlichen Menschen" in Spätantike und Frühchristentum* (Vienna: Höfels, 1935), vol. 1.

negative disposition and edit or arrange that material in a way to bring it in line with his own theological position. What emerged as a result of this development were studies that tended to pit one group of christological pieces against another, either an emphasis on power or divine man Christology over a Christology of suffering and the cross, or vice versa. While a few interpreters held to the Bultmannian position that a divine man Christology was the dominant christological orientation of Mark's Gospel, the vast majority favored a Christology of suffering and death—a Christology of the cross.[10] These studies of Mark's Christology placed significant emphasis on the Gospel's christological titles. Understanding Mark's Christology often meant understanding the correct or primary christological title in Mark. Those who advanced a "corrective" Christology generally favored "Son of Man" as Mark's primary christological title, though some redaction-critical studies favored "Son of God."[11]

A central tool of the redaction critics was the reconstruction of the *Sitz im Leben* of a Gospel's author and community, and redaction critics turned to this tool in order to understand the relationship between the disparate pieces of Mark's Christology. Though reconstructions of such communities varied in specifics, their general contours were quite similar. These communities were believed to have had an unhealthy esteem for power and glory, an esteem driven in part by a divine man Christology that emphasized Jesus' power and glory. Paul's opponents in 2 Corinthians often served as a basis for the existence of such communities. It was then proposed that Mark was written to address this unhealthy or imbalanced Christology. In the first half of the Gospel, the Evangelist presents the errant or imbalanced christological perspective of his community, tempers it

---

[10]For examples of this sort of "corrective" Christology among redaction critics, see Norman Perrin, "The Creative Use of the Son of Man Traditions by Mark" and "The Christology of Mark: A Study in Methodology," in *A Modern Pilgrimage in New Testament Christology* (Philadelphia: Fortress, 1974), 84-93 and 104-21, respectively; Ludger Schenke, *Die Wundererzählungen des Markusevangeliums* (Stuttgart: Katholisches Bibelwerk, 1974), esp. 393-95; Theodore J. Weeden, *Mark—Traditions in Conflict* (Philadelphia: Fortress, 1971); Leander Keck, "Mark 3:7-12 and Mark's Christology," *JBL* 84 (1965): 341-58, esp. 349-51, 354, 357-58; Paul J. Achtemeier, *Mark*, Proclamation Commentary (Philadelphia: Fortress, 1975), esp. 41-47; Achtemeier, "Gospel Miracle Tradition and the Divine Man," *Interpretation* 26 (1972): 174-97; Achtemeier, "Origin and Function of the Pre-Markan Miracle Catenae," *JBL* 91 (1972): 198-221, esp. 198, 220-21; Ralph P. Martin, *Mark—Evangelist and Theologian* (Exeter, UK: Paternoster, 1972), esp. 153-62.

[11]For example, see P. Vielhauer, "Erwägungen zur Christolgie des Markusevangeliums," in *Zeit und Geschichte. Dankesgabe an Rudolf Bultmann zum 80. Geburtstag*, ed. E. Dinkler (Tübingen: J. C. B. Mohr, 1964), 155-69; H. J. Steichele, *Der Leidende Sohn Gottes: Eine Untersuchung einiger alttestamentlicher Motive in der Christologie des Markuseangeliums*, Biblische Untersuchungen 14 (Regensburg: Pustet, 1980).

with the motif of the messianic secret, and then corrects it with the second half of the Gospel, which emphasizes Jesus' suffering and death. Thus, for the Markan Evangelist, Jesus' primary christological identity is that of a suffering Messiah and not that of power and glory. This way of reading Mark dominated the work of many redaction critics from the 1950s to the 1980s.

This redaction-critical reading of Mark's Christology was critiqued on a number of grounds. First, the concept of the Hellenistic "divine man," a concept that sat at the heart of both form- and redaction-critical readings of Mark, was shown to be a rather vague and unsubstantiated one, as the term *divine man* itself never functioned as a fixed expression in either Hellenism or Hellenistic Judaism. As such it was an inadequate way of describing the "power pieces" of Mark's Christology or the Gospel's use of "Son of God." Second, once the divine man piece was removed, the historical reconstructions of Mark's *Sitz im Leben* fell apart, leaving the notion of a corrective Markan Christology without any historical grounding or explanation. Third, greater attention to the Markan narrative itself demonstrated that the power pieces of Mark were presented positively and thus were unlikely to represent a Christology opposed by the Markan Evangelist. There is virtually nothing in the Markan narrative itself that would lead the reader to a negative assessment of the powerful Jesus. Fourth, the work of redaction critics to separate Markan material from pre-Markan material, a foundational move that allowed interpreters to perceive competing traditions in Mark, was demonstrated to be highly subjective, with little consistency in either methods or results.[12] The weight of these critiques ultimately led to an abandonment of redaction criticism as the primary method for engaging Mark's Gospel, as well as to an abandonment of the christological conclusions this method had produced.

Moving toward narrative criticism: Considering the narrative arrangement of the pieces. One of the most vocal and prominent critics of the "corrective" reading of Markan Christology was Jack Dean Kingsbury, perhaps best represented in his monograph *The Christology of Mark's Gospel.*[13] Kingsbury levels many of the critiques noted above and offers a new reading of Mark's Christology that (1) makes no distinction between Markan and pre-Markan traditions, (2) locates the meaning of Mark's Christology within the Gospel of Mark

---

[12]C. Clifton Black, "The Quest of the Markan Redactor: Why Has It Been Pursued and What Has It Taught Us?," *JSNT* 33 (1988): 19-39; Black, *The Disciples According to Mark: Markan Redaction in Current Debate,* JSNTSup (Sheffield, UK: JSOT Press, 1989).

[13]Jack Dean Kingsbury, *The Christology of Mark's Gospel* (Philadelphia: Fortress, 1983).

itself and gives no consideration of a reconstructed Markan community, and (3) pays closer attention to the Markan narrative. For Kingsbury the Markan secrecy motif is primary in Mark and plays a central role in understanding the Gospel's Christology.

Also important for Kingsbury are the christological titles in Mark's Gospel, particularly to understand how they are used throughout the Markan narrative and their relationship to the Markan secrecy motif. Through his analysis of the Markan narrative, Kingsbury argues that "Messiah/Christ," "Son of God," "Son of David," and "King of the Jews" are all correct and appropriate christological titles for Jesus, though not all carry the same christological weight. Throughout the narrative the Evangelist demonstrates that "Messiah/Christ," "Son of David," and "King of the Jews" are correct christological titles that reveal certain truths of Jesus' identity, but they are ultimately insufficient and represent an incomplete understanding of Jesus. As insufficient titles, they are not kept secret but are made known throughout the Gospel. In contrast to these titles is the title "Son of God," the title that Kingsbury argues is the central christological identification of Mark's Gospel. It is this title and this title alone that is the subject of the Markan secrecy motif, and Kingsbury argues that this title is kept a secret in Mark until after Jesus' crucifixion, where it is proclaimed by a Roman centurion. For Kingsbury, the significance of Mark's "Son of God" secret is that Jesus' identity as "Son of God" can only be understood in terms of Jesus' suffering and death. Any understanding of Jesus as the Messiah apart from his death (understandings conveyed in Mark by the correct yet insufficient titles "Messiah/Christ," "Son of David," or "King of the Jews") is incomplete. Closely associated with this analysis is Kingsbury's assessment of the Markan use of "Son of Man." He argues that "Son of Man" stands in contrast to the other Markan christological titles, as, unlike these titles, "Son of Man," though a "title of majesty," is not messianic.[14] For Kingsbury "Son of Man" is a technical term that points to Jesus' divine authority in the face of opposition, with one significance of that term being Jesus' judgment of opposition at the parousia.

When it comes to the assembling of the christological pieces of Mark's Gospel, Kingsbury takes a decisive step away from the redaction critics who preceded him. Unlike these predecessors, Kingsbury gives attention to the final form of

---

[14]Kingsbury says "Son of Man" "is neither 'messianic' in nature nor is it used to inform the reader or any character in Mark of the identity of Jesus." Ibid., 174.

Mark and the narrative of that final form. Such attention allows him to abandon notions of competing christological material in Mark that played a central role in redaction-critical assessments of Mark's Christology. However, like many redaction critics, Kingsbury still seems to give priority to Mark's messianic titles in the assessment of Mark's Christology. Though he gives more attention to the way those titles are arranged in the Markan narrative than earlier redaction critics, that assessment focuses primarily on the arrangement of these titles in relationship to one another and the Markan secrecy motif—relatively little attention is given to the structure and development of the Markan narrative itself. Joel Williams characterizes Kingsbury's work well when he says, "Kingsbury's goal was to examine how Mark's narrative discloses the most correct title for Jesus rather than to explore how Mark's narrative as a whole characterizes Jesus."[15]

In his assessment of the pieces of Mark's Christology characterized by power and those characterized by suffering, Kingsbury does not pit one against the other like the redaction critics to whom he responds. Both sets of pieces accurately depict Jesus' identity, though Kingsbury seems to give priority to the pieces characterized by suffering. Yet Kingsbury does not address the oft-perceived tension between these two groups of pieces, and like most narrative critics who followed him, he is presumably content to let these two sets of christological pieces sit in tension.

A number of additional critical observations must be made. (1) The distinction that Kingsbury makes between Mark's christological titles is indeed questionable, particularly the sharp distinction that is made between "Son of God" and "Son of Man." Can it truly be said that "Son of Man" is not messianic in nature or that it does not inform the identity of the Markan Jesus? Also, is the title "Messiah" truly less important than the title "Son of God"? (2) Kingsbury's reading of Mark's Christology is largely contingent on his assessment of the Markan secrecy motif. But what if his assessment is misguided? What if, as has recently been proposed, the material commonly attributed to this motif has nothing to do with secrecy?[16] (3) While Kingsbury claims to pay close attention to the Markan narrative (something he certainly does far better than his redaction-critic predecessors), there

---

[15]Joel F. Williams, "The Characterization of Jesus as Lord in Mark's Gospel," in *Character Studies and the Gospel of Mark*, ed. Christopher W. Skinner and Matthew R. Hauge, LNTS 483 (London: T&T Clark, 2014), 107-26.

[16]See David F. Watson, *Honor Among Christians: The Cultural Key to the Messianic Secret* (Minneapolis: Fortress, 2010), and Adam Winn, "The Markan Secrecy Motif and Roman Political Ideology," *JBL* 133, no. 3 (2014): 583-601.

are many narrative features that Kingsbury fails to recognize, features that likely play a role in the construction of the Gospel's Christology (e.g., Mk 8:22–10:52 as a distinctly crafted literary unit that includes teaching about Jesus' suffering and death that is bookended by pericopes in which Jesus heals the blind). While Kingsbury's work might be a helpful step forward from that of redaction critics, in my estimation it ultimately does not account for all of the narrative pieces of Mark's Christology, nor does it seek to resolve the apparent tension that exists between the suffering and powerful Jesus.

Narrative criticism: The pieces can only make sense in the narrative. In many ways narrative criticism of the Gospels emerged as a response and corrective to the interests and methods of modern critical biblical interpretation. The driving interests of modern critical biblical interpretation were primarily historical and theological. Source critics were interested in the earliest source so that they might reconstruct the history behind the Gospel narratives. Form critics were interested in the early Christian communities and the way they shaped and used the text (or the traditions behind the text). Redaction critics were interested in the historical author and how the historical author, in response to his context (often thought in theological terms), shaped and edited his sources to address that context. In one way or another, these interpretive methods were seeking to answer *what* the text meant, particularly in light of its history of development. But criticisms of these methods began to emerge. Theories regarding how Gospel traditions were used throughout the stages of oral transmission were highly speculative and led to conflicting results. The same was demonstrated about the efforts of redaction critics to reconstruct the historical author or the community that the author was addressing. Too often the meaning and/or theological content of the Gospel narratives was conditioned by realities lying outside the text rather than those within. Such criticisms were reinforced by developments in the world of literary criticism (New Criticism and structuralism) that challenged the ability to reconstruct "authorial intent" and the validity of finding a single authoritative meaning in such reconstructions.

As a result of these criticisms and developments, a paradigm shift began to take place in Gospel scholarship. Interpreters transitioned from asking questions about how the history of a text's composition conveyed meaning to asking how the current composition of the text as a narrative conveyed meaning. Attention shifted from the reconstruction of historical authors and audiences, theological titles, and redaction of hypothetical sources to analysis of a Gospel's narrative setting, characters, and plot—with the interpreter's primary interest being the way in which the arrangement of these features by the (implied) author generates meaning. While issues of historical context are not completely ignored, they are limited to historical knowledge demanded by the text itself (e.g., the meaning of a Greek word, the significance of a Greco-Roman custom, the location of a noted city), and no attempt is made to read the text in light of a more specific historical situation, one that would require historical reconstruction by the interpreter. And while narrative critics do not ignore the theological character of the Gospels, they are adamant that the theological message of the Gospels must be generated by a close reading of the Gospel narratives themselves and not by preexisting theological commitments and/or categories that exist outside the narrative.

Such developments in Gospel scholarship have had a significant impact on the study of Mark's Christology. Perhaps the most significant development is a transition from title-focused studies of Mark's Christology—that is, studies primarily focused on christological titles used in Mark—to studies that focus on the totality of Mark's narrative presentation of Jesus. While christological titles are still significant for these studies, how those titles are used, shaped, and given meaning by the Markan narrative becomes paramount for the interpreter. Another development is the limiting of one's understanding of Mark's Christology to the text of Mark alone and the rejection of any dependence on reconstructions of the Evangelist's specific historical setting (as noted previously, attention to the general setting of the first-century Mediterranean world is always considered). Particular attention is paid to Mark's characterization of Jesus through what Jesus says and does as well as what is said about and done to Jesus. Attention is also paid to the plot and structure of Mark's narrative and its impact on characterization. Such developments have led to many fruitful studies in Mark's Christology over the last thirty years.[17]

One of the more recent and most significant narrative studies on Mark's Christology is that of a leading Markan narrative critic, Elizabeth Struthers

---

[17]For example, see Robert C. Tannehill, "The Gospel of Mark as Narrative Christology," *Semeia* 16 (1979): 57-95; M. E. Boring, "The Christology of Mark: Hermeneutical Issues for Systematic Theology," *Semeia* 30 (1984): 143-44; Moloney, *Gospel of Mark*; Francis J. Moloney, *Mark: Storyteller, Interpreter, Evangelist* (Peabody, MA: Hendrickson, 2004); David Rhoads, Joanna Dewey, and Donald Michie, *Mark as Story: An Introduction to the Narrative of a Gospel*, 2nd ed. (Minneapolis: Fortress, 1999).

Malbon, in her work titled *Mark's Jesus: Characterization as Narrative Christology*.[18] Malbon divides her study of Mark's narrative Christology into five different categories: (1) enacted Christology, or what Jesus does; (2) projected Christology, or what others say about Jesus; (3) deflected Christology, or what Jesus says in response to what others say about him; (4) refracted Christology, or what Jesus says instead of what others say about him; and (5) reflected Christology, that is, the significance of Jesus reflected through exemplary characters in Mark. Through the analysis of these various categories, Malbon seeks to demonstrate different layers of Mark's narrative Christology, layers that are at the same time mutually interpreting and in tension with one another.

Perhaps a good example of this phenomenon is the relationship that Malbon sees between the Markan narrator and the Markan Jesus. Malbon argues that the Markan narrator should be understood as a distinct character in Mark's Gospel, one created by the implied author. For Malbon the Markan narrator and the Markan Jesus both view Jesus as the Christ, but the Markan narrator is bold in this affirmation, while the Markan Jesus is reticent. While the Markan narrator and other characters boldly proclaim and/or show Jesus as the powerful Son of God, the Markan Jesus boldly proclaims the kingdom of God and the powerful but suffering "Son of Humanity." While the Markan narrator continually directs attention to Jesus, Jesus continually directs attention away from himself to God. Thus while Malbon does not see the Markan narrator and the Markan Jesus at complete odds with each other, she does see them in tension with each other, a tension that she perceives as purposefully created by the implied author. Unlike many Markan interpreters, Malbon does not clearly distinguish between christological material that emphasizes Jesus' power and material that emphasizes Jesus death. However, it is noteworthy that the Markan narrator certainly seems to emphasize Jesus' power (without ignoring his suffering and death), particularly when contrasted with the Markan Jesus, who downplays his own power and emphasizes both his service and suffering.

While I will engage Malbon's work more thoroughly at different points throughout this study, it is the tension that Malbon perceives within Mark's christological material that I want to note here. When redaction critics faced similar tension, the solution was to pit one set of christological material (e.g., material related to power) over against another set of material (e.g., material

---

[18]Elizabeth Struthers Malbon, *Mark's Jesus: Characterization as Narrative Christology* (Waco, TX: Baylor University Press, 2009).

related to suffering), with one seen as correcting the other. But Malbon strongly resists any such attempt, claiming that "the implied author of Mark sets up this tension to draw in the implied audience—not to resolve the tension but to see the story of Jesus in its full spectral colors of commitment to God and God's rule, to hear the story of Jesus in its full complexity and mystery."[19]

Recognizing such tension in Mark's Christology is a common feature in narrative-critical assessments of Mark's Christology, though not all such assessments formulate or articulate that tension in the same way as Malbon.[20] The following assessment from Eugene Boring reflects this narrative-critical tendency:

> Mark's narrative mode of expressing his Christology allows him to juxtapose images of Jesus that, if expressed in discursive language, would be radical contraries. Some Markan images and languages for Jesus portray him as the truly divine agent of God's salvation, acting in the place of God and doing what only God can do. . . . Other images portray Jesus as truly human, fully identified with human weakness and victimization. . . . Conceptually, the two types of christological imagery cannot be combined without compromising one or the other or both. . . . Mark affirms both Christologies, and devised a narrative mode of claiming and explicating them both. The narrative juxtaposes the conflicting imagery without synthesizing it. . . . Mark should not be considered a "synthesis" or "integration" of opposing views: his narrative includes each perspective without adjusting it to the other.[21]

Here Boring recognizes conflicting christological material in Mark's Gospel but claims that this material stands in paradoxical tension and that no effort should be made to resolve that tension.

It must be noted that not all narrative critics directly identify or address this christological tension in Mark's Gospel.[22] Some simply allow the Markan

---

[19]Ibid., 210.

[20]For examples of narrative-critical studies that perceive tension between Mark's presentation of both a powerful and a suffering Jesus, see Werner H. Kelber, "Conclusion: From Passion to Gospel," in *The Passion in Mark: Studies on Mark 14–16*, ed. Werner H. Kelber (Philadelphia: Fortress, 1976); Dorothy A. Lee-Pollard, "Powerlessness as Power: A Key Emphasis in the Gospel of Mark," *Scottish Journal of Theology* 40 (1987): 73-88; Francis Watson, "Ambiguity in the Markan Narrative," *Kings Theological Review* 10 (1987): 11-12; Philip G. Davies, "Mark's Christological Paradox," *JSNT* 35 (1989): 3-18; Mark I. Wegener, *Cruciformed: The Literary Impact of Mark's Story of Jesus and His Disciples* (Lanham, MD: University Press of America, 1995), esp. 154-57; Narry F. Santos, *Slave of All: The Paradox of Authority and Servanthood in the Gospel of Mark*, JSNTSup 237 (London: Sheffield, 2003); 16-18; Laura C. Sweat, *The Theological Role of Paradox in the Gospel of Mark*, LNTS 224 (London: T&T Clark, 2013), esp. 4-5.

[21]M. E. Boring, *Mark*, NTL (Minneapolis: Fortress, 2006), 258.

[22]For example, see Rhoads, Dewey, and Michie, *Mark as Story*.

presentation of Jesus as a powerful divine agent of God to sit in tension with Mark's presentation of the suffering and dying Jesus. Little effort is made to resolve this paradoxical tension, as it is understood to be inherent to Mark's narrative. Seemingly, the resolution of this christological paradox would be undermining the Markan narrative itself and thus the entire enterprise of narrative criticism.

Yet, while most narrative critics are reluctant to relieve this tension by sacrificing power for suffering or vice versa, there seems to be trend among prominent narrative critics to emphasize or give greater narrative priority to the christological pieces in Mark that are associated with suffering over against those associated with power. In what is seen as the seminal work on Mark as narrative Christology, Robert Tannehill claims, "Although the healing and exorcism stories make up an important part of Mark, they have a different status from the material that emphasizes the disciples and those who try to oppose Jesus. The disciple and 'opponent' material is part of developing narrative lines that come to a climax in the passion story."[23] For Tannehill the narrative climax of Mark, and thus the christological climax, is Jesus' passion. As such, Jesus' powerful miraculous deeds take a backseat to "passion material" in Tannehill's assessment and assembly of Mark's christological pieces: "Since they [healings and exorcisms] do not form a sequence leading toward the passion story, the narrative climax of the Gospel, they are subordinate material to the material that does."[24] For Tannehill it seems that Jesus' powerful miracles are primarily a conduit for the Evangelist to focus on Jesus' relationship to other characters in the Markan narrative and have little inherent christological significance. Francis J. Moloney reflects a similar attitude in *Mark: Storyteller, Interpreter, Evangelist*, a work that is clearly narrative critical:

> Miracles are important. They demonstrate the reigning presence of God in Jesus as he sweeps away the evils of sickness, demon possession, taboo, angry nature, and untimely death. The miracles are a means to an end, not an end in themselves. To understand Jesus as a miracle worker is to misunderstand Jesus—and Jesus' commands to silence regularly remind the reader that, however badly the secret is kept, miracles do not explain who he is.[25]

---

[23]Tannehill, "Gospel of Mark as Narrative Christology," 67.
[24]Ibid.
[25]Moloney, *Mark: Storyteller, Interpreter, Evangelist*, 133.

Thus for Moloney Jesus' miracles demonstrate God's reign through Jesus, but they play a minor role in understanding who the Markan Jesus is or the significance of the Markan Jesus. In fact Moloney claims that "Mark, as interpreter, wishes to disassociate all worldly success and honor from his presentation of Jesus of Nazareth. He must be understood as Christ and Son of God insofar as he is the crucified one."[26] In Moloney's assembly of Mark's christological puzzle the "power pieces" play a relatively significant christological role.[27]

While Malbon does not make a clear distinction between christological material that emphasizes power and that which emphasizes suffering and service, it is noteworthy that her reconstruction of both the narrator's view of Jesus and Jesus' view of himself fall roughly along these lines of power and suffering. It is the narrator who proclaims Jesus as Messiah and Son of God, and it is the narrator who "shows" his reader the power of Jesus through Jesus' mighty deeds. In contrast the Markan Jesus seeks to distance himself from such identities and mighty deeds. Instead he directs attention to God and away from himself, and he chooses to identify himself primarily through service, sacrifice, and suffering, over against power and glory. And while Malbon certainly grants that Jesus' great deeds of power play a role in Mark's narrative Christology, they get little exegetical attention, relative to other narrative features in Mark. To be fair to Malbon, she never privileges the Markan Jesus over the Markan narrator, and as noted above, desires to hold both in tension. But one is left to wonder how a reader might resolve that tension. Would not Jesus' view of himself take precedent over that of the Markan narrator? And might the lack of attention that Malbon gives to Jesus' deeds of power lead the reader to conclude that such deeds are relatively unimportant in the process of assembling the pieces of Mark's Christology?

Narrative critics have taken an important step forward for Markan studies in general and in assessments of Markan Christology in particular. The recognition that Mark is a unified narrative and that any assessment of Mark's Christology must pay close attention to that narrative is an indispensable contribution that cannot be ignored. But here I note two weaknesses that I perceive in many narrative assessments of Mark's Christology. The first regards the common conclusion that inherent to Mark's Christology is an intentional and unresolvable

---

26Ibid., 151.

27See Rhoads, Dewey, and Michie, *Mark as Story*, 103-15, who primarily understand Jesus in terms of service, suffering, and death, and give very little attention to Jesus' power, glory, or authority. See also Lee-Pollard, "Powerlessness as Power."

tension between the powerful Jesus and the suffering Jesus. Most narrative critics will affirm that the Markan Jesus is both a powerful and a suffering figure, but outside understanding this Christology in paradoxical terms, rarely is there an attempt to ascertain how these two christological motifs are united in Mark's Gospel. While such a conclusion is possible, I question whether it is necessary or even preferable. If Mark is a unified narrative, might we not expect to find in this narrative a unified Christology? Might there be a way to resolve this perceived christological tension and read Mark's Christology in a unified manner?

The second weakness regards the tendency among some narrative critics to emphasize or prioritize the christological pieces that emphasize suffering and minimize the christological pieces that emphasize power.[28] While Markan narrative critics certainly decry the "corrective" Christology proposed by Markan redaction critics, ironically, their assessments of Mark's Christology are strikingly similar. Granted, these narrative critics do not see the implied author "correcting" a Christology of power, and they are willing to give Jesus' deeds of power a place in their assessment of Mark's Christology, but that place is regularly quite minor in comparison to the place given Jesus' suffering and death. Moloney goes as far as to say that the Markan Evangelist disassociates Jesus from all "worldly success and honor."[29] Such a claim sounds strikingly similar to that of Markan redaction critics who proposed that Mark's Christology was rejecting a Christology of power and replacing it with a Christology of the cross. Jesus' great and powerful deeds in the Markan narrative are all too often treated as if they were simply hors d'oeuvres before the main course of Mark's Christology of a suffering Messiah. This marginalization is all the more striking when one considers that the first half of Mark's narrative is dominated by Jesus' deeds of tremendous power, immense popularity, and regular glorification, features that do not disappear in the second half of the narrative. It seems to me that many narrative critics are not paying as close attention to Mark's narrative as they claim, because if they were, the powerful Jesus who dominates the first half of Mark would play a much greater role in their assessments of Mark's Christology.

Considering an outlier: Power pieces trump suffering pieces. While the vast majority of studies on Mark's Christology have, in various ways and to varying degrees, emphasized the suffering Jesus over the powerful Jesus, one Markan

---

[28]See discussion of Tannehill, Moloney, and Malbon above as examples of this tendency.
[29]Moloney, *Mark: Storyteller, Interpreter, Evangelist*, 133.

interpreter, Robert Gundry, has argued strongly in the opposite direction.[30] While Gundry sees two sets of competing christological material in Mark, that which presents a powerful and successful Jesus and that which presents a suffering Jesus, he argues that the Markan Evangelist uses the former to mitigate the shame and weakness of the latter. For Gundry, Mark's Christology is wholly a Christology of power that functions as an apology for Jesus' shameful crucifixion. According to Gundry, Mark is writing to a non-Christian audience for whom the cross is a significant barrier to faith. To overcome this barrier Mark emphasizes the power of Jesus from beginning to end, even throughout the passion narrative itself. In a sense Gundry proposes a "corrective" Christology of his own, only Mark's Christology is seeking to correct the misguided assumptions of non-Christians about Jesus' shameful death. To this end Gundry spends a significant amount of time explaining how pieces of Mark's Christology that appear to emphasize suffering are actually not doing so at all but are rather being used in service to a Christology of power. For example, Gundry argues that Jesus' passion predictions are signs of his power alone, as the ability to predict one's death and the details of that death was seen as a divine power. Thus, by introducing Jesus' suffering and death through a prediction formula, the Evangelist removes their sting and emphasizes Jesus' power.

While working on my doctoral dissertation I found much in Gundry's presentation of Mark's Christology to be compelling, and to this day I continue to see many important contributions. In the last fifty years of scholarship on Mark's Christology, Gundry virtually stands alone in recognizing the christological importance of the powerful Jesus who dominates the first half of Mark's narrative. He also offers important exegetical insights that demonstrate that the powerful Jesus does not disappear in the second half of Mark's Gospel, and that where christological pieces emphasizing suffering are present, pieces that emphasize power are often close at hand. As noted above, these insights are often ignored by Markan interpreters who seek to emphasize Jesus' suffering and death in their assessment of Mark's Christology at the expense of Jesus' great power. For these reasons, I initially followed Gundry quite closely in my own analysis of Mark's Christology, arguing that Mark's presentation of Jesus is characterized by power from beginning to end.[31]

---

[30] Robert H. Gundry, *Mark: A Commentary on His Apology for the Cross* (Grand Rapids: Eerdmans, 1993); see in particular his introduction, 1-26.

[31] Adam Winn, *The Purpose of Mark's Gospel: An Early Christian Response to Roman Imperial Propaganda*, WUNT II/245 (Tübingen: Mohr Siebeck, 2008), 108-36.

But as important as some of Gundry's insight into Mark's Christology might be, criticisms of both his work and my own have demonstrated that both Gundry and I have swung the pendulum too far in the opposite direction.[32] Critics have argued that there are many features in the Markan narrative that demonstrate that Jesus' suffering and death play a significant role in Mark's Christology and that they are not simply obstacles to be overcome. Throughout the first half of Mark's Gospel, while power may dominate, as noted above, there is intentional foreshadowing of Jesus' impending suffering and death. Such foreshadowing is hard to explain if Jesus' suffering and death are seen by the Evangelist as a problem that needs to be solved. It is also hard to deny a literary relationship between the two-stage healing of a blind man in Mark 8:22-26 and Peter's confession and subsequent correction at Caesarea Philippi in Mark 8:27–9:1. Peter's confession of Jesus as the Messiah seems to closely parallel the partial healing of the blind man that immediately precedes it. As the blind man needs further action by Jesus to see clearly, so Peter needs further instruction from Jesus, that is, instruction on Jesus' necessary suffering and death, in order to see his identity clearly. These are simply two examples among many (e.g., Mk 10:42-45; 14:3-9, 22-25) that strongly undermine the conclusions of both Gundry and myself, and demonstrate that Jesus' suffering and death play a central role in Mark's Christology.

Gundry's work is important, as it rightly recognizes that a Jesus of extreme power plays a significant role in Mark's Christology and that this powerful Jesus should not be subordinate to the suffering Jesus. Yet Gundry goes too far in the opposite direction and wrongfully marginalizes the role of Jesus' suffering and death. For this reason I can no longer follow Gundry as far as I did in my previous work, but I do remain influenced by his important contributions to the understanding of Mark's Christology.

THREE DRIVING QUESTIONS, METHOD, AND OUTLINE: MY APPROACH TO ASSEMBLING THE PIECES

As the above review of research on Markan Christology has shown, one's method of engaging the Markan text plays a significant role in the results one produces.

---

[32]While some of these criticisms can be found in formal reviews of both Gundry's commentary and my own volume on Mark, I am particularly indebted to the SBL Mark Group and the helpful criticism they offered in response to a paper I presented on Mark's Christology at the 2009 annual meeting in New Orleans. In particular I would like to thank Joel Williams for his poignant questions regarding Mark's presentation of Peter and the disciples in the Caesarea Philippi pericope, questions that played a significant role in softening my stubborn stance on Mark's Christology.

And one's method is closely tied to the interpretive questions that drive the interpretive task. Until the rise of narrative criticism, the questions that drove most New Testament interpreters were primarily historical questions—namely, what did the text mean in its original context, with various methods employed to arrive at answers to this driving question. As we have noted above, narrative criticism developed in part as a reaction against the prioritizing of historical questions among biblical interpreters, with narrative critics shifting their interests to *how* the text means as opposed to *what* the text meant.[33] Thus narrative critics were (and continue to be) much more interested in reading New Testament Gospels as timeless narratives, though first-century narratives to be sure, than texts located in a particular sociocultural and historical setting (e.g., written in a particular city, addressing a specific event(s), at a particular time). This study reflects an attempt to swing the pendulum back toward asking historical questions about the text and returning to a pursuit of what the text might have meant in its original setting. I make this attempt with full awareness of the critiques leveled against previous enterprises of this nature, and as such I must make a number of important comments.

First, this attempt to read the Gospel of Mark in light of its original context does not in any way presuppose that such a reading is superior to other readings of the Gospel. Other reading strategies for Mark, strategies that are uninterested (as least primarily) in Mark as a historical phenomenon, are both valid and important, and should be conversation partners with studies on Mark that are more historically inclined. Here I recognize that historical readings of Mark have much to learn from strict narrative readings of Mark as well as from strict reader-response readings of Mark, and perhaps vice versa. But I strongly assert that despite the existing limitations, seeking to understand Mark as a historical phenomenon and a text that originated in a particular sociohistorical setting is a valid enterprise and one that can and should be pursued.

Second, the historical concerns of modern biblical interpretation have too often been accompanied by a misguided belief that if historical methodology were rigorously followed, certain historical results could be assured. I undertake the present study with full awareness of the uncertainty inherent in any historical enterprise in general and in the pursuit of ancient history in particular.

---

[33]For this description of a difference between narrative-critical studies of the Gospels and their redaction-critical predecessors, see Malbon, *Mark's Jesus*, 1-16.

But the inherent uncertainty of historical analysis should not (and regularly does not) prevent us from attempting such analysis; rather, it should caution us to recognize our results for what they are: plausible interpretations and reconstructions of the existing historical data. Though inherently uncertain, historical analysis and research can produce good and useful results, results that help us better understand the ancient world and the ancient texts it produced.

Third, historical research should always be seeking to improve its methods, correct misguided practices, and abandon flawed results. With this awareness in mind, this project will seek to improve on the methods and practices of previous attempts to understand Mark's text (and its Christology) within a particular historical setting. Such improvements will ultimately lead to greater confidence in the results of historical analysis.

With these considerations in mind, I now turn my attention to the method of the present project, a method that might be described as historical-narratival. Unlike the historically minded work of many redaction critics, this study will focus on the final form of Mark's Gospel—specifically, the Gospel as a unified narrative from beginning to end, with the commitment that it was intended to be read as such. Thus I will make virtually no distinction between Markan and pre-Markan material, nor will I offer any analysis of Markan redactional activity, an enterprise that has been demonstrated to be highly speculative.[34] And while I recognize the Gospels as theological in character and as having theological concerns, contra the commitments of many redaction critics, I am committed to the notion that the theological content of Mark is embedded in and inseparable from the narrative itself. No attempt will be made to understand Mark's theology apart from the Markan narrative. Thus in these regards my work shares strong sympathies with the work of narrative critics.

With that said, my work is distinct from narrative critics in at least one crucial way—it seeks to read Mark's narrative from a particular sociocultural and historical setting. A major part of this work will involve offering a historical reconstruction of the situation in which Mark was written, to which it sought to respond, and in which it was intended to be read. As acknowledged above, any historical reconstruction is inherently uncertain, but certain reconstructions are better grounded and more reliable than others. Of the utmost importance is grounding the Gospel in a historically verifiable setting, one that can be

---

[34]Black, "Quest of the Markan Redactor"; Black, *Disciples According to Mark*.

supported by dense historical data. On this front redaction critics frequently failed, as their reconstructions of Mark's setting were hypothetical historical situations that lacked supporting data. Demonstrating that Mark wrote in any *one* particular setting can never be done with certainty (though evidence can be put forward to support certain settings over others), but if one intends to place Mark in a particular setting, strong historical evidence is needed to validate the existence of the proposed setting.

Given my desire to understand Mark in light of a particular historical context, some brief comments should be made regarding my interest in Mark's author. Some might perceive an attempt on my part to identify the original author of Mark and to in some way grasp the authorial intent behind Mark's Gospel. While my work here might provide a window into the intents of an original author of Mark's Gospel, I have little interest in reconstructing what a particular historical figure intended to communicate. For the most part I believe that such realities lie beyond our grasp. Instead my conception of the Markan author is in some ways similar to the literary concept of the implied author, though one that pushes beyond the strict limits of the implied author that exist within the field of narrative criticism. Within the field of narrative criticism the implied author is the author implied by the text itself, the author that is perceived by any reader of the text apart from any knowledge of the historical author. Like the concept of the implied author, my conception of "author" is also interested in what one might infer about the author from the Markan text; however, it also includes what one might infer about the author from the reconstructed historical context in which I will situate the composition of the Gospel. Such a conception of authorship allows the interpreter to expand the parameters of the knowledge, aims, and goals of the narrative-critical implied author, but at the same time also allows the interpreter to maintain a distance from any need to reconstruct the mind, personality, or values of an original or historical author(s) of Mark's Gospel. Thus whenever I directly or indirectly reference the author of Mark's Gospel, it is this expanded conception of "authorship" that I am using.

The method outlined here addresses some of the critiques leveled against redaction critics and their efforts to understand what Mark meant in its original context, and it offers some important correctives to such efforts. Despite such corrective efforts, many of my colleagues who are strongly committed to narrative criticism will no doubt point out that, like the redaction critics before me, my reading of Mark will remain contingent on historical reconstruction, a reality their approach to Mark is able to avoid. Clearly I cannot avoid such an objection, and I openly recognize this limitation of the present work. I would respond to this objection in two ways. One, such a critique can be offered against any analysis of ancient history. The reconstruction of any ancient historical reality (and many that are not ancient) or any attempt to understand such realities will always be, to varying degrees, speculative in nature. But the contingent or speculative nature of historical work should never stop us from engaging in it or from pursuing historical knowledge. As imperfect as such knowledge may be, there is still value in seeking it. This present project seeks the value in that knowledge.

Two, attempts to read Mark apart from consideration of its particular socio-historical setting, such as the attempts of strict narrative critics, have their own undeniable limitations. Mark was undoubtedly written in a particular context, and that context both shaped the writing of the Gospel and the way in which that Gospel would have been read and heard by its earliest audience. As such there are certain features of the Gospel that we certainly misunderstand or mis-interpret because we lack knowledge of this particular context. In this regard the analogy of a puzzle is helpful for comparing the narrative-critical approach to Mark's Christology with the present approach.[35] Narrative critics are assem-bling Mark's christological puzzle using only the pieces available, the pieces of Mark's text.[36] As such they are assembling the puzzle without all of the available pieces. Undeniably they are missing the pieces of Mark's particular historical context. While this method allows interpreters to be confident in the pieces that they have, they run the significant risk of forcing pieces together in a way that do not actually fit. Thus, while narrative critics work with the narrative alone, speculation still remains regarding the meaning and significance of the nar-rative they reconstruct. Might the apparent tension that narrative critics per-ceive within Mark's Christology be a result of constructing Mark's christological

---

[35]I fully understand that this analogy is in many ways simplistic and crude as a means of under-standing something as complex as written communication—and, like most analogies, ultimately breaks down when pushed too far. However, here I use this simple analogy as a way of compar-ing and contrasting the strengths and weaknesses of two approaches to reading Mark's Gospel.

[36]Here I would note that even the existing pieces of Mark's text are in and of themselves opaque and require some level of context to be understood, e.g., knowledge of Greek grammar, syntax, and vocabulary, and knowledge of first-century Jewish and Greco-Roman culture. Narrative critics are fully aware of the need for such context, and thus, in describing their use of "existing pieces," such broad issues of historical context are implied.

puzzle without all of the necessary pieces? Might knowledge of additional pieces, such as those related to Mark's particular historical context, reveal that no such tension actually exists in the narrative?

In contrast, I am seeking to reconstruct the missing pieces of Mark's Gospel, that is, the pieces of Mark's particular historical context, and fit those pieces together with the existing pieces of Mark's narrative. While this enterprise has the disadvantage of using uncertain pieces, it has the advantage of potentially offering a more complete picture of both Mark's narrative and the Christology communicated through that narrative. And I would propose that if the reconstructed pieces can be firmly grounded in a well-established historical context and can be shown to fit well with and to make sense of the existing pieces of Mark's narrative, a high level of confidence in the reconstructed pieces can be achieved.

In light of this methodology, the project will begin by locating Mark in a particular historical setting. Chapter one will make an argument for a plausible date and provenance for Mark's Gospel, and from that information it will offer a reconstruction of the Gospel's historical setting. The subsequent chapters will seek to understand the pieces of Mark's Christology from the perspective of this reconstructed setting. Chapter two will address the christological titles of Mark's Gospel. Chapter three will address the first half of Mark's narrative, the prologue and Galilean ministry, in which a Jesus of extreme power dominates the narrative. Chapter four will address the central section of Mark's Gospel, where Jesus' death and suffering are first explicitly introduced to the reader—particular attention will be given to the way in which this section functions to unify the christological pieces that present a powerful Jesus with the christological pieces that present a suffering Jesus. Chapter five will address the motif of secrecy in Mark's Gospel. Chapter six will consider Jesus' ministry in Jerusalem, with particular attention given to Jesus' relationship to the Jerusalem temple. Finally, chapter seven will consider the christological significance of Mark's passion narrative.

ONE

RECONSTRUCTING MARK'S HISTORICAL SETTING

THE PURPOSE OF THIS CHAPTER IS TWOFOLD: (1) to make a plausible and well-grounded case for the date and provenance of Mark's Gospel, and (2) to reconstruct the historical setting of Mark based on the proposed date and provenance. The language of plausibility regarding the Gospel's date and provenance is intentional, as I recognize the uncertain nature of such an enterprise. Yet despite such uncertainty, arguments can be put forward that can increase our confidence in a particular date and provenance for the composition of Mark's Gospel.

A ROMAN GOSPEL

Over the past century in Markan scholarship, there has been significant debate regarding the provenance of Mark's Gospel, with Rome, the traditional position, being pitted against relatively recent propositions of the eastern provenances, Syria and Galilee. It is not my intention to repeat the details of this debate here. For the purpose of this project it is only necessary to demonstrate the existence of strong evidence for a Roman provenance and thus establish Rome as a historically plausible provenance for the composition of Mark's Gospel.[1]

---

[1]Hendrika N. Roskam provides a thorough argument for a Galilean provenance in *The Purpose of the Gospel of Mark in Its Historical and Social Context*, Novum Testamentum Supplements 114

For the past two millennia Rome has been widely accepted as the place of Mark's composition. Such acceptance likely finds its origin in the traditions of the early church fathers. Both Irenaeus (ca. 180 CE) and Clement of Alexandria (ca. 195 CE) claim that Mark wrote his Gospel in Rome, testimony that is consistent with the so-called anti-Marcionite prologue that claims the Gospel was written in the "regions of Italy."[2] Later witnesses such as Origen, Eusebius, the Monarchian Gospel prologue, and Jerome affirm this position. Aside from the late fourth-century witness of John Chrysostom, who claims the Gospel was written in Alexandria, the external witness of the early church unanimously supports a Roman provenance for Mark's Gospel.[3] While the reliability of this tradition has not gone unchallenged, the majority of modern scholars accepted it, as it seemed to fit well with the internal evidence of the Gospel.[4] The most significant and most oft-cited internal evidence in support of a Roman provenance is the numerous Latinisms in Mark's Gospel. The Gospel contains numerous Greek transliterations of Latin words (*caesar, census, denarius, flagellare, grabatus, legio, modius, praetorium, sextarius, quadrans*, et al.), and scholars have argued that such transcriptions suggest a western rather than eastern provenance. But Latin was known and used throughout the empire. Many of these transcribed Latin words are related to the economy, military, or political administration, and thus do not require a Roman provenance to explain their presence in Mark's Gospel.

Not all Latinisms in Mark are explained so easily. Martin Hengel has noted Mark's use of Graecized Latin expressions to explain common Greek words.[5]

(Leiden: Brill, 2004). For arguments for a Syrian provenance see Joel Marcus, *Mark 1–8: A New Translation with Introduction and Commentary*, AB 27 (New York: Doubleday, 2000), and Gerd Theissen, *The Gospels in Context: Social and Political History in the Synoptic Tradition* (Minneapolis: Fortress, 1991), 236-45. For arguments against both a Galilean and a Syrian provenance, see my own work, *The Purpose of Mark's Gospel: An Early Christian Response to Roman Imperial Propaganda*, WUNT II/245 (Tübingen: Mohr Siebeck, 2008), 83-91.

[2] The date of the "anti-Marcionite" prologue is debated, with some dating the prologue to as early as 150 CE and others dating it as late as 350 CE. For discussion on the date of the prologue see Jürgen Regul, *Die antimarcionitischen Evangelienprologe*, Vetus Latina: Die Reste der altlateinischen Bibel 6 (Freiburg: Herder, 1969), esp. 266-67; Wilbert Francis Howard, "The Anti-Marcionite Prologues to the Gospels," *Expository Times* 47 (1935–1936): 534-38; Richard G. Heard, "The Old Gospel Prologues," *Journal of Theological Studies* 6 (1955): 1-16.

[3] The witness of John Chrysostom (*Homily on Matthew 1:7*) is almost certainly connected to the early tradition that John Mark was the bishop in Alexandria.

[4] For a challenge to the early traditions supporting a Roman provenance for Mark's Gospel, see C. Clifton Black, *Mark: Images of an Apostolic Interpreter* (Minneapolis: Fortress, 2001), 224-25. For a thorough response to Black, see my previous work, *Purpose of Mark's Gospel*, 77-80.

[5] Martin Hengel, *Studies in the Gospel of Mark*, trans. J. Bowden (Philadelphia: Fortress, 1995), 29-30.

Mark 12:42 uses the phrase ὅ ἐστιν κοδράντης ("which is a quadrans") to explain the Greek word λεπτός (a small copper coin). Mark 15:16 uses the Graecized Latin phrase ὅ ἐστιν πραιτώριον ("which is the praetorium") to explain the Greek word αὐλή (courtyard/palace). These examples suggest that Mark was writing to an audience that had a greater knowledge of Latin than Greek. Additionally, Bas van Iersel has demonstrated that Mark also includes Latin idioms that are translated into unnatural Greek word combinations (ὁδόν ποιεῖν = *viam facere*, Mk 2:23; ἐσχάτως ἔχει = *ultimum habere*, Mk 5:23; κατακρινοῦσιν θανάτῳ = *capite damnare*, Mk 10:33).[6] Perhaps even more telling are Latinisms that are embedded in the very structure of the author's language.[7] Van Iersel argues that these Latinisms reflect the influence of a "Latin-speaking milieu on speakers whose mother-tongue was not Latin."[8]

Another piece of internal evidence that is consistent with a Roman provenance is the Markan motif of suffering disciples. Many Markan interpreters have noted that Mark seems to be addressing readers who are or have recently experienced persecution or the threat of it. While there is evidence of sporadic persecution of Christians in the first decades of the church's existence, the first formal persecution that we have certain knowledge of is that of Roman Christians at the hands of Nero in 64 CE. Roman historian Tacitus provides us with vivid details about this persecution: "And derision accompanied their end: they were covered with wild beasts' skins and torn to death by dogs; or they were fastened on crosses, and, when daylight failed were burned to serve as lamps by night."[9] Such experiences would make perfect sense of the Markan Jesus' instructions that true disciples

---

[6]For this data, see Bas M. F. van Iersel, *Mark: A Reader-Response Commentary*, trans. W. H. Bisscheroux (London: T&T Clark, 1998), 34.

[7]One such Latinism is related to the word order of substantives and verbs. In Greek an accusative or dative noun follows a verb, but in Latin the order is reversed. In Mark's Gospel, this Latin word order occurs thirty-seven times, compared to only two such occurrences in Luke and Matthew when they are not following Mark. And in most instances Luke and Matthew reverse the Latin word order of their Markan source. A second Latinism concerns the word ἵνα when it is used with words related to speaking, asking, or commanding. Mark's use of ἵνα often parallels the way in which the Latin word *ut* is used with such verbs. This Latin construction appears thirty-one times in Mark's Gospel, of which Matthew preserves only eight and Luke only four. When not following Mark, Luke only uses this construction four times and Matthew only twice. While certain Markan Latinisms are easily explained by their common use in the market or by Roman political or military officials, many are not, and instead point to a Western provenance in which Latin was spoken. A Roman provenance for Mark is consistent with (and supported by?) this evidence. For this information, see van Iersel, *Mark*, 34-35.

[8]Van Iersel, *Mark*, 34.

[9]Tacitus, *Ann.* 15.44, trans. John Jackson, LCL, 4 vols. (Cambridge: Harvard University Press, 1937).

must take up their cross and give up their lives for the sake of Jesus and the Gospel (Mk 8:34-35). Tacitus's claim that Christians turned on other Christians to save their lives provides an excellent context for understanding the Markan Jesus' promise that "brother will betray brother to death, and a father his child, and children will rise against parents and have them put to death" (Mk 13:12).[10] And Jesus' claim that believers will be "hated by all" (Mk 13:13) fits quite well with Tacitus's claim that Nero convicted Christians for "hatred of the human race."[11] There is no known persecution of the first-century church that fits Mark's motif of suffering disciples better than that of Roman Christians under Nero.

Thus the external evidence that is virtually unanimous in support of a Roman provenance, for Mark dovetails exceptionally well with the internal evidence from Mark's Gospel. In fact there is no internal evidence in Mark that is inconsistent with a Roman provenance. Thus, while certainty about Mark's provenance is elusive, there is good evidence that suggests Mark was written in Rome, presumably for a Roman audience. This study will move forward assuming such a provenance for Mark.

A POST-70 CE GOSPEL

When it comes to the date of Mark's composition, external evidence is less consistent. Irenaeus claims that Mark wrote after the deaths of Peter and Paul, while Clement of Alexandria claims that Mark wrote during the lifetime of Peter and includes a tradition in which Peter himself approved of Mark's endeavor.[12] It seems Irenaeus's claim is more reliable than Clement of Alexandria, who seems to be legitimizing Mark by tying it more closely to Peter. But a date after the death of Peter and Paul is quite open ended. Thus internal evidence has led most scholars to date Mark in close temporal proximity to the Jewish revolt, with Markan interpreters rather evenly divided over whether Mark was composed before or after the destruction of Jerusalem and its temple.[13] At the center of this

---

[10]Tacitus, *Ann.* 15.44.

[11]Tacitus, *Ann.* 15.44.

[12]Irenaeus, *Against Heresies* 3.3.1-3; Eusebius, *Ecclesiastical History* 2.15.1-2.

[13]For a breakdown of interpreters who favor a pre–70 CE date and those who favor a post–70 CE date, see Winn, *Purpose of Mark's Gospel*, 56nn32-33. While the vast majority of Markan interpreters date the Gospel between 65 and 73 CE, James Crossley has argued for a date as early as 40 CE; see James Crossley, *The Date of Mark's Gospel: Insight from the Law in Earliest Christianity*, JSNTSup 266 (London: T&T Clark, 2004). For a critique of Crossley's position see Winn, *Purpose of Mark's Gospel*, 51-56.

debate is Mark's prediction of the destruction of the Jerusalem temple (Mk 13:2) and the apocalyptic discourse that follows this prediction. Much of the debate focuses on whether the prophecy is authentic to the historical Jesus or whether it represents a *vaticinium ex eventu*. It is a commonly held assumption that if it can be demonstrated that the prophecy is an authentic saying of Jesus, then Mark should be dated prior to the temple's destruction. However, as I have argued elsewhere, the historical authenticity of Jesus' prediction of the temple's destruction is largely irrelevant to the date of Mark's Gospel, as it is equally possible for the Evangelist to have recorded an authentic prophecy of Jesus before or after the event that was prophesied.[14] Thus, for the debate regarding the date of Mark's composition, the authenticity of a particular Jesus saying is not solid ground on which to make one's case.

Others have sought to resolve the debate by pointing to details in the text that either suggest specific knowledge of the temple's destruction or lack of such knowledge. A good example is Jesus' claim that no stone will be left upon another (Mk 13:2). Gerd Theissen has argued that this claim is quite specific and suggests *vaticinium ex eventu*. He even contends that Mark's use of the word ὧδε might suggest that Mark is distinguishing between the stones of the temple, which were all torn down, and the stones of the retaining wall, many of which were left standing.[15] But ὧδε could easily be referring to both the retaining wall and the temple itself. On just such grounds, others have argued the exact opposite conclusion from Theissen—namely, that Mark lacks specific knowledge of the temple's destruction, as not *all* of the stones were overturned, that is, the stones of the retaining wall remained. But in my opinion it seems both sides are taking specific words of the Markan Jesus far too literally. I concur with Adela Yarbro Collins that the phrase is best understood as expressing the gravity of the destruction of the temple and that little information can be drawn from this phrase regarding the date of Mark's composition.[16]

Another detail commonly used to argue for a pre–70 CE dating is Jesus' statement "Pray that it may not be in winter" (Mk 13:18), describing the cataclysmic events that will either accompany or follow the desolating sacrilege of Mark 13:14. The destruction of Jerusalem occurred in the summer and not the

---

[14]Winn, *Purpose of Mark's Gospel*, 57-58.

[15]Theissen, *Gospels in Context*, 259.

[16]Adela Yarbro Collins, *The Beginning of the Gospel: Probings of Mark in Context* (Minneapolis: Fortress, 1992), 76.

winter, and thus this verse demonstrates a lack of knowledge on the part of Mark regarding the historical reality of the temple's destruction—as such, Mark must have been written before the destruction, or so the argument goes. Yet this argument is dependent on equating Mark 13:14 with the destruction of Jerusalem and not another eschatological sign that is yet to come about. Such a conclusion is far from certain, and thus Jesus' statement regarding winter could have nothing to do with the date of Mark's composition.[17]

In my previous work I argued that a more fruitful way forward in determining whether Mark was written before or after the destruction of the Jerusalem temple is consideration of the rhetorical purpose of Jesus' prophecy regarding the temple's destruction. I contended that the prophecy had a greater rhetorical impact after the fact of the temple's destruction than before that destruction. Recording the prophecy after the fact demonstrated Jesus' prophetic power to the reader, while recording the prophecy before the fact left the reader in a "wait and see" mode regarding Jesus' prophetic power. I also noted that by recording the prophecy before the fact, Mark risked a great deal, and that if the temple were not ultimately destroyed by the Roman armies that surrounded it, Mark's Jesus would have lost a great deal of credibility.[18] While I believe these arguments still have merit, I think a stronger argument for a post–70 CE dating of Mark exists. This argument still considers Markan rhetoric, but it looks beyond Jesus' prediction of the temple's destruction and considers the way in which Mark treats the temple as a whole.

Recent studies have recognized that Mark 11–12 comprises a distinct literary unit in Mark, one that includes a distinct "temple" motif.[19] At a later point I will provide a thorough narrative analysis of this motif and argue that Mark's presentation of the temple is decidedly negative. For the present moment I will briefly outline the basic contours of this motif. Jesus' triumphal entry ends at the temple, where the lack of reception by the temple authorities stands in stark contrast to his reception by the Jewish pilgrims who celebrated his entry into Jerusalem (Mk 11:1-11). The next day Jesus enters the temple, stops all of its

---

[17]For an argument that Mk 13:14 is describing a future eschatological event, see Winn, *Purpose of Mark's Gospel*, 69.

[18]Ibid., 56-67.

[19]For example, see Timothy C. Gray, *The Temple in the Gospel of Mark: A Study in Its Narrative Role*, WUNT II/242 (Tübingen: Mohr Siebeck, 2008; repr., Grand Rapids: Baker, 2010); John Paul Heil, "The Narrative Strategy and Pragmatics of the Temple Theme in Mark," *CBQ* 59 (1997): 76-100; David Seeley, "Jesus' Temple Act," *CBQ* 55 (1993): 263-83.

activities, and condemns it (Mk 11:15-19), actions that many interpreters understand as a symbolic judgment. In response to these actions, the temple authorities seek a way to kill Jesus. Jesus' symbolic judgment of the temple is intentionally sandwiched between episodes concerning a fig tree that Jesus curses (Mk 11:12-14), which withers the next day (Mk 11:20-21). The vast majority of Markan interpreters see a clear connection between the fig tree and the Jerusalem temple. As the cursed fig tree withered and died, so also will the cursed temple. Jesus' authority is then challenged by "the chief priests, the scribes, and the elders" (Mk 11:27-33), characters that the Markan Jesus has already claimed will be responsible for his death (Mk 8:31; 10:33). Jesus tells them a parable in which these temple authorities are portrayed as enemies of God, enemies that kill God's representatives, including his beloved son (Mk 12:1-12). The parable concludes with Jesus predicting the destruction of these temple authorities. Following this encounter are three subsequent encounters in which the temple authorities challenge Jesus, challenges that demonstrate their opposition to God (Mk 12:13-18, 19-27, 28-34).[20] Jesus then gives a scathing critique of the scribes, a group closely associated with the temple authorities in Mark (Mk 12:38-40). This critique is followed by a story that illustrates the scribes' "devouring" of widows, as an impoverished widow gives all she has to a corrupt temple institution (Mk 12:41-44). This thorough Markan critique of the temple and its authorities concludes with Jesus' explicit prediction that the temple will be utterly destroyed (Mk 13:2).[21]

Thus, when it comes to the date of Mark's Gospel, instead of simply asking about the rhetorical purpose of Jesus' prediction of the temple's destruction, one must ask about the rhetorical purpose of Mark's entire antitemple motif. In what way is this antitemple motif functioning for Mark's readers? Given that the Evangelist devotes two chapters to this motif, it must be of great importance and may in some way address the situation of Mark's audience.

To answer this question a related question becomes relevant concerning the ethnic makeup of Mark's audience. Scholars have long argued that Mark was written for a primarily Gentile audience. Mark 7:3-4 offers a detailed explanation

---

[20]Note that in Mk 12:13-18 it is Pharisees and Herodians who approach Jesus, groups that are not accurately identified as temple authorities. Yet the text indicates that these groups are sent by the temple authorities (Mk 12:13).

[21]A more thorough treatment of Mk 11–12 and the antitemple motif therein can be found below in chapter six.

of Jewish purity rituals, something one would expect in a Gospel written for Gentiles rather than Jews, who would not require such an explanation. Additionally, in this passage Mark specifically refers to "all the Jews," a reference that seems to suggest a separation between his intended audience and those who are Jews. Mark also explains for his readers that Sadducees do not believe in the resurrection (Mk 12:18), something that Jews, even Hellenistic Jews, would have already known. That the "Day of Preparation" is the day before the Sabbath is also explained for Mark's readers (Mk 15:42). Again, this fact would have been well known by all Jews and would not require explanation if Mark were writing to a predominantly Jewish audience. The prominence of a Gentile mission in Mark (Mk 11:17; 13:10; 14:9) might also suggest a Gentile audience. When one compares the Matthean parallels to Mark 11:17; 13:10, one sees that the Matthean Evangelist, commonly recognized as writing to a Jewish audience, removes these references to a Gentile mission. Thus there is compelling evidence that the Markan Evangelist is writing for an audience that is primarily Gentile rather than Jewish.

If a Gentile audience for Mark is granted, the question of Gentile Christian interest in the Jewish temple becomes significant. The amount of attention the Markan Evangelist gives to the Jewish temple surely indicates that Mark's Gentile audience is interested in it. But such an interest is strikingly absent in the New Testament. Our best window into the concerns of the early Gentile churches is no doubt the undisputed letters of Paul. But in these letters we see no interest in the Jerusalem temple. Any Pauline reference to the "temple" is a reference to the church itself and not the physical temple in Jerusalem. For Paul it is the church and not the cultic center in Jerusalem that is God's temple. Perhaps even more significant is that when Paul identifies the church as the temple, the physical temple in Jerusalem plays no role. Paul never argues that the Jerusalem temple is corrupt and that it needs to be replaced. Nor does Paul argue that the temple has been replaced by the church. Paul never associates the cultic functions of the former temple with the church as God's temple in a way that would suggest such replacement. The language of "newness" never accompanies Paul's description of the church as the temple. For example, he never identifies the church as the "new" temple of God that replaces the Jerusalem temple. In light of this evidence it seems that the Jerusalem temple played no role in Paul's pastoral and missional work among Gentile churches. Even in the book of Acts, the preaching of Paul among the Gentiles is completely void of any reference to the Jerusalem temple—

a reality that is perhaps surprising given the prominent role given to the temple in other parts of the book. Thus all the existing evidence portrays an early Gentile Christian church that has no interest in the Jerusalem temple.[22]

I propose that the sharp contrast between the apparent lack of interest in the Jewish temple among Gentile Christians and Mark's clear interest in that same temple suggest that a significant development has taken place, something that has led otherwise uninterested Gentile Christians to care about the Jewish temple. Two obvious and related possibilities for such a development emerge: the Jewish revolt against Rome and the destruction of the Jewish temple itself. I contend that the latter option has far greater explanatory power than the former. Certainly the Jewish revolt might garner the interest of Gentile Christians in the events occurring in Judea and Galilee, as truly these were major world events in the place of Christian origins. Yet it is hard to see how the revolt itself would increase interest in the temple specifically. The fate of the temple itself was uncertain until the end of the revolt—even in the mind of Rome. Roman victory was by no means assurance of the temple's destruction. Perhaps it could be argued that the Evangelist was prophetically looking forward to the temple's destruction and offering an explanation for that destruction to his community. But to what purpose is such an explanation given? Why does an audience with little concern for or interest in the Jerusalem temple need such an explanation? And given such a lack of need, why would the Evangelist devote so much attention to such an explanation? Why would a Gentile audience care? And if the temple were still standing, the rhetorical power of such an antitemple motif is significantly weakened, as the reader undoubtedly would have taken a "wait and see" approach. Ultimately the rhetorical value of such a motif would have been minimal.

A far better option seems to be the destruction of Jerusalem itself. This destruction played a central role in the propaganda of the Flavian family and in its attempt to legitimize its power. It was featured in a massive triumph celebrating Vespasian and Titus's military accomplishments. It was also featured prominently on Roman architecture and coins.[23] The message of this propaganda was quite clear: the Flavian family was a recipient of divine favor and that

---

[22]This paragraph and the following are reworked from material published in my essay "'No Stone Left upon Another': Considering Mark's Anti-Temple Motif in Both Narrative and History," in *Christian Origins and the Formation of the Early Church*, ed. Stanley E. Porter and Andrew W. Pitts, Early Christianity in Its Hellenistic Context Series 4 (Leiden: Brill, forthcoming).

[23]For discussion of material evidence see Jason A. Whitlark, *Resisting Empire: Rethinking the Purpose of the Letter to "the Hebrews*," LNTS 484 (London: T&T Clark, 2014), 160-88.

the gods who favored it, the Roman gods, were greater than the God of the Jews. Such propaganda would have almost certainly raised challenges for Gentile Christians, in particular recent converts from Roman paganism. Such Flavian propaganda would likely have led to serious questions among fledgling Christians about the legitimacy of their new faith. Perhaps a commitment to one crucified by Roman power was indeed misguided, particularly since the God of that crucified savior had just been defeated by that same power. Pagan family and friends would no doubt have used Rome's destruction of the Jewish temple as evidence to persuade Gentile Christians that they were indeed on the wrong side and that they should return to their former, and clearly superior, religion. Such questions and circumstances would have required a strong answer in order to keep these Christians from abandoning their new faith and returning to the familiar gospel of Roman *pax et securitas*.[24]

Another challenge created by the Roman destruction of the Jerusalem temple was that facing Christian mission among Gentiles. Gentile mission was seemingly important to the author and audience of Mark (e.g., Mk 13:10). But Vespasian's propaganda regarding the destruction of both Jerusalem and the Jewish temple would undeniably have been a major obstacle to Christians who were attempting to persuade Gentiles to devote their lives to the Jewish Messiah Jesus and the Jewish God. Even for those interested in converting to Christianity, no doubt a strong response to Flavian propaganda would have been required. In his treatise against heretics Irenaeus is still responding to pagan claims that Roman destruction of the Jerusalem temple undermined the honor and power of the God of Israel.[25] If Christians a century later had to provide an apologetic for the destruction of the Jerusalem temple, how much more would such an apologetic have been needed for Christians living in the immediate aftermath of that destruction? Thus Irenaeus is strong evidence for the existence of the crisis I have outlined here.

Thus the destruction of the Jewish temple offers the best explanation for an increased interest among Gentile Christian communities in that temple. In light of this conclusion the best explanation for the rhetorical purpose of Mark's anti-temple motif comes into focus. The motif functions as a response to the crisis that the Roman destruction of the Jewish temple created among Gentile Christians.

---

[24]Much of this paragraph and the following are also reworked from my essay "'No Stone Left upon Another.'"

[25]Irenaeus, *Against Heresies* 4.4.

Like the Jewish prophets explaining the destruction of the first temple and like Jewish contemporaries explaining the destruction of the second temple, Mark claims that the Roman destruction of the temple was a result of its corruption, that it occurred according to God's purpose and was predicted by God's appointed ruler, Jesus. Through this move Mark disarmed Flavian propaganda and made Rome a pawn in the plans of Israel's God and Messiah.

The implications of this analysis for Mark's date of composition are quite clear. Explanations for the rhetorical function of Mark's antitemple motif in pre–70 CE Gentile Christian communities are wanting, while an obvious and compelling explanation of the motif's rhetorical function can be found in post–70 CE Gentile Christian communities. In light of this argumentation the present study will move forward under the conclusion that Mark was written after the destruction of the Jerusalem temple.

RECONSTRUCTING THE SETTING OF POST-70 ROME

Having established a date and location for the composition of Mark's Gospel, I now offer a reconstruction of the historical realities present in Rome in the years immediately following Rome's victory over Jerusalem. I will give particular attention to the rise of the new imperial dynasty, the Flavian family, and the means by which this dynasty sought to legitimize its power. I will then consider the potential impact of this new dynasty on the Christians living in Rome, for whom I contend the Gospel of Mark was written.

Rome's political turmoil and Vespasian's rise to power. After the death of Nero the Roman Empire experienced extreme political chaos and civil war. Nero had no successor, and thus control of the empire could be gained by military power. Many suitors for the Principate emerged and battled with one another for supremacy. As a result Rome experienced four successive emperors in a single year. Galba, a Roman governor who had rebelled against Nero, was the first appointed to the Principate. After a short time he was replaced by one of his fellow conspirators, Otho, who betrayed him. Otho was then opposed and defeated by the general Vitellius. Vitellius was then opposed and defeated by the general Vespasian, who had been serving in Galilee and Judea, putting down the Jewish revolt per the appointment of Nero in 66 CE. When Vespasian assumed the Principate, he inherited an empire with enormous problems. Due to Nero's irresponsible fiscal policies, Rome's economy was in shambles, as was its infrastructure. The food supply in the city of Rome was extremely low, with an estimated ten-day supply of grain remaining. Vespasian himself estimated that rehabilitation of the state would require forty thousand million *sestertii*, an exorbitant number when compared to the average revenue of eight hundred million *sestertii*.[26]

But perhaps the greatest problem facing Vespasian was his own ignoble birth. Vespasian was from the plebeian class, and he was the first from this class to rise to the Principate.[27] This identity made Vespasian a "new man" in Roman politics and an upstart in the eyes of senatorial families that had enjoyed political privilege for centuries. Having a lower-class citizen such as Vespasian now ruling over them certainly did not sit well with the social and political sensibilities of these elite families. Such sociopolitical tensions made Vespasian vulnerable to political opponents seeking to overthrow him. While Vespasian had the backing of powerful legions, he was still fighting in the provinces to secure his power. If the right political families conspired against him, he could have found himself fighting in the city of Rome as well. In light of these challenges related to his ignoble birth, Vespasian began an extensive propaganda campaign to legitimize his reign. Here I will outline the significant pieces of Flavian propaganda.[28]

Destruction of Jerusalem and the temple.[29] As noted above, a major piece of this propaganda was Vespasian's victory against the Jewish rebellion and the destruction of both Jerusalem and the Jewish temple.[30] Understanding the propagandistic value of these events requires consideration of what J. Rufus Fears calls the "theology of Victory," that is, the way in which ancients understood

---

[26]Some argue the number should read four thousand million *sestertii*. For a brief discussion and bibliography, see Winn, *Purpose of Mark's Gospel*, 157n19.

[27]Suetonius suggests that Octavian's family was patrician from the time of the kings but then fell to the rank of plebeian for a time, until Julius Caesar elevated it once again. Suetonius, *Aug.* 2.

[28]For a more thorough discussion of Vespasian's rise to power, the challenges he faced after securing power, and the means by which he sought to secure power, see Barbara Levick, *Vespasian* (New York: Routledge, 1999), 43-123.

[29]Much of the material in this section is revised material from my essay "'No Stone Left upon Another.'"

[30]Almost the entirety of this section is a reworking of material from ibid. and is used with permission from the publisher. This discussion of the destruction of Jerusalem and the temple owes a great debt to the excellent work of Jason Whitlark, found in his monograph *Resisting Empire*, especially 160-88. My thanks to Jason not only for this work but also for a handful of informal conversations regarding this material.

the religious significance of victory in battle.[31] Traditional means of succession or power transitions were perceived to be sanctioned by the gods, as the right to rule the world was granted by divine prerogative. When these established means failed, an alternative means was needed for the gods to communicate their will. Quite often military victory was perceived as just such an alternative means. For example, military victory legitimized the reigns of Alexander and even Rome's first emperor, Augustus. Theology of Victory was understood in the following way. To those who demonstrated the virtue of *virtus*, or courage and aggression, the gods would grant the virtue of *felicitas*, or good fortune. But excessive *virtus*, perhaps granted by the gods, would lead to the manifestation of the goddess Victory, a manifestation that resulted in actual military victory. Therefore victory in battle represented the gods' choice of one potential ruler over another—specifically, the victor over the vanquished. But winning in battle was only part of the equation in the theology of Victory. Such victory needed to be followed by peace and prosperity in order to legitimize a claimant's divinely sanctioned power.[32]

In order to legitimize his reign, Vespasian presented his success over the Jews as a major victory, one that ended a major threat to the stability of Rome's empire and brought to it peace and prosperity. In this way the new Flavian emperor cleverly employed the theology of Victory by promoting his victory over the Jews in a variety of ways. The first and perhaps most noteworthy expression of the theology of Victory was the massive triumph that celebrated both Vespasian and his son Titus's victory over the Jews.[33] Josephus offers a vivid description of this triumph.[34] The triumphant procession began with both Vespasian and Titus emerging from the temple of Isis while wearing purple imperial robes and laurel crowns and sitting on ivory thrones. The following procession was a display of the theology of Victory writ large, as it included seven hundred captive Jewish soldiers, scenes from the war itself dramatically and extravagantly reenacted, spoils of war prominently displayed (including sacred vessels from the Jewish temple), and enormous statues of Roman gods signaling the source

---

[31] See J. Rufus Fears, "Theology of Victory at Rome: Approaches and Problems," *ANRW* 17.2:736-826.

[32] The description in this paragraph of Rome's theology of Victory is greatly indebted to both Whitlark, *Resisting Empire*, 167-68, and Fears, "Theology of Victory at Rome."

[33] A *triumph* was a traditional Roman celebration of a major military victory of a general or emperor. For a thorough discussion of his tradition, see Mary Beard, *The Roman Triumph* (Cambridge, MA: Harvard University Press, 2007).

[34] Josephus, *J. W.* 7.117-159. For a more detailed summary, see Winn, *Purpose of Mark's Gospel*, 164-65.

of Roman power and greatness, the vast wealth that this victory had brought the Roman people. Josephus concludes his description of the triumph by saying, "For the city of Rome kept festival that day for her victory in the campaign against her enemies, for the termination of her civil dissensions, and for her dawning hopes of felicity."[35] With these words Josephus is drawing on the theology of Victory, as he recognizes this military victory over the rebellious Jews and the hope and prosperity that it created. The clear implication is the divinely legitimized reign of Vespasian.

In addition to this triumph, Vespasian promoted the theology of Victory through numerous building projects. Not long after celebrating his triumph, Vespasian began construction on the Temple of Peace, a project he funded with the spoils taken from the Jewish war. When completed, this temple housed the sacred vessels from the Jewish temple that had been paraded in Vespasian's triumph, including a golden table, candlesticks, and lampstands.[36] Thus the Temple of Peace was a constant reminder that the Jewish revolt was a threat to Rome's peace and prosperity and that through his victory Vespasian had secured both. The Arch of Titus, though completed an entire decade after the Jewish war, contains panels that depict the triumph of Titus, his crowning by the goddess Victory, and the spoils of war taken from the Jewish temple.[37] The arch functioned to commemorate the military victory that legitimized the Flavian dynasty. Presumably another arch located in the Circus Maximus, no longer extant, was dedicated to Titus (81 CE) as a commemoration of his defeat of the Jews. This arch supposedly claimed that Titus and Vespasian were the first to conquer Jerusalem.[38] Though such claim is patently false, it establishes the importance attributed to this event by the Flavian family. Given the prominent role the destruction of Jerusalem and its temple played in the Flavian dynasty even a decade after the event itself, it seems safe to conclude that this event played a prominent role at the outset of Vespasian's reign—when the need to legitimize his power was at its greatest.

Coinage was a common way for a ruler to promote particular political narratives, and Vespasian certainly used the minting of coins to promote his narrative of the theology of Victory. After his victory over the Jews, Vespasian

---

[35]Josephus, *J. W.* 7.157.
[36]Whitlark, *Resisting Empire*, 164.
[37]Ibid., 165.
[38]Ibid.

reinstituted the *capta*-type coin, which commemorated military victory. Augustus, who like Vespasian obtained power through military victory, instituted such coins.[39] They were abandoned by Augustus's Julian-Claudian successors, since these were able to legitimize their power through familial connection to Augustus. Perhaps most significant was Vespasian's minting of the *Judaea Capta* coins, designed to specifically commemorate Roman victory over the Jews. A variety of images are displayed on these coins, including Romans towering over and ignoring captive Jews, captive Jews chained to a palm tree, and the winged goddess Victory nailing a Roman shield to a palm tree (the Roman symbol for Judea).[40] Inscribed on this last coin are the words OB CIVES SER(VATOS), "for the security of the citizens." This inscription expresses the belief that Roman victory over the Jews was not an insignificant military accomplishment but served to secure the *pax et securitas* of the empire.[41] These coins were minted throughout Vespasian's reign, and thus they evince the prominent role that Vespasian's victory over the Jews played in the Flavian foundation myth.[42]

Vespasian also promoted his victory over the Jews by transforming the "temple tax" into the *fiscus Judaicus*. Thus the tax paid by every Jewish male for the upkeep of the Jewish temple became a tax that would now be paid by all Jewish males for the rebuilding and upkeep of the Temple of Jupiter. This move provided a constant reminder to all Jews not only of Roman power but also of the superiority of Jupiter Maximus to the God of Israel.

Healings, prophecies, and portents. Vespasian's propaganda also included the performance of miraculous healings. While Vespasian was in Alexandria, prior to taking up his duties as Principate in Rome, two individuals requested healing from him, both claiming that they were told to do so by the god Serapis through a dream.[43] The first individual was blind, and Vespasian applied his own spittle to the man's eyes, which resulted in the man's sight being restored. The second man had a disfigured hand, which was restored after Vespasian touched

---

[39]For discussion on these coins see ibid., 166-67, and Jane M. Cody, "Conquerors and Conquered on Flavian Coins," in *Flavian Rome: Culture, Image, Text*, ed. A. Boyle and W. Dominik (Leiden: Brill, 2003), 103-23.

[40]See Whitlark, *Resisting Empire*, 166.

[41]Ibid.

[42]For a list of these coins see ibid., 166n27.

[43]For these stories see Tacitus, *Hist.* 4.81.1-3; Suetonius, *Vesp.* 7.2; Cassius Dio, *Roman History* 66.8.1.

it with his foot. Such healings demonstrated that Serapis had granted Vespasian the power to heal, a power that further legitimized Vespasian's divine right to rule. Tacitus's claim that eyewitnesses still talked about these miraculous healings some thirty years after the fact demonstrates that this propaganda was indeed quite powerful and likely had the effect the Flavian family desired.

In addition to these healings, numerous portents and prophecies were put forward in order to provide divine legitimization for Vespasian's reign. Suetonius lists eleven portents, a number of which are also recorded by Tacitus and Cassius Dio.[44] These include the story of a dog bringing a human hand to Vespasian while he was eating breakfast. The hand was a body part associated with power, and thus the event was interpreted as a sign of future power being granted to Vespasian. Another story recounts an ox escaping its yoke, running into Vespasian's dining room, and bowing before the future emperor. It was claimed that Nero himself had premonitions of Vespasian's rise to power, as he had a dream in which he was instructed to move the sacred chariot of Jupiter from his own house to that of Vespasian. It was also claimed that while Vespasian was fighting in the Roman East, a statue of Julius Caesar turned from facing west to facing east, an omen indicating the origin of the next Roman ruler. And after Vitellius had defeated Otho at Betriacum, people witnessed two eagles fighting in the sky. The victorious eagle was then attacked and defeated by a third eagle that flew in from the east—the parallels between those vying for the Principate in 69 CE are quite obvious.

More examples can be added to these eleven. While Vespasian was in Palestine (presumably in 68 CE, when he was considering his bid for the Principate), he visited an oracle on Mount Carmel who told him that he would be successful at whatever he attempted to do. Similarly, when Vespasian was in Alexandria, he visited a famous temple of the god Serapis. While alone in this temple Vespasian had a vision of a man named Basilides who at the time was sick and a long way from Alexandria. Basilides gave Vespasian "sacred boughs, garlands, and loaves," items best identified as signs of royalty.[45] These portents, most of which are either legendary or creatively embellished, function to demonstrate that Vespasian's rise to power was the will of the gods. The use of such *omina imperii* to establish one's divine right to rule had a long precedent,

---

[44]See Suetonius, *Vesp.* 5.
[45]See A. Henrichs, "Vespasian's Visit to Alexandria," *Zeitschrift für Papyrologie und Epigraphik* 3 (1968): 62-63.

including Alexander and his successors, leaders of the late Republic, and even the first emperor, Augustus.[46]

But perhaps the most important piece of propaganda for my purposes is Vespasian's claim to be the true fulfillment of Jewish messianic prophecies and expectations. Three different Roman historians claim that Jews rebelled against Rome because of misguided expectations that a world ruler would arise from among them, expectations that find their origin in the prophecies of Jewish Scripture. All three of these historians claim that the true fulfillment of such prophecies was the political rise of Vespasian, who became ruler of the world while in the Roman East.

The first and earliest Roman historian to make such a claim is Josephus:

> But what more than all else incited them [the Jews] to the war was an ambiguous oracle, likewise found in their sacred writings, to the effect that about that time some one from their country should become ruler of the world. This they understood to mean some one of their own race, and many of their wise men went astray in their interpretation of it. The oracle, however, in reality signified the sovereignty of Vespasian, who was proclaimed Emperor on Jewish soil.[47]

While Josephus does not identify a specific scripture, he clearly references Jewish messianic hopes grounded in Jewish Scriptures. He also claims that such hopes were misguided and that the scripture these hopes were based on found their true fulfillment in Vespasian. Tacitus offers a similar analysis:

> Few [Jews] interpreted these omens as fearful; the majority firmly believed that their ancient priestly writings contained the prophecy that this was the very time when the East should grow strong and that men starting from Judea should possess the world. This mysterious prophecy had in reality pointed to Vespasian and Titus, but the common people, as is the way of human ambition, interpreted these great destinies in their own favor, and could not be turned to the truth even by adversity.[48]

Suetonius offers a very similar tradition, but unlike Josephus and Tacitus, he does not specifically reference Jewish Scriptures.

---

[46]See J. Rufus Fears, *Princeps a Diis Electus: The Divine Election of the Emperor as a Political Concept at Rome*, Papers and Monographs of the American Academy in Rome 26 (Rome: American Academy in Rome, 1977), 171.

[47]Josephus, *J.W.* 6.312-613, trans. H. St. J. Thackeray, LCL, vol. 3 (Cambridge, MA: Harvard University Press, 1928).

[48]Tacitus, *Hist.* 5.13.1-2, trans. C. H. Moore and John Jackson, LCL (Cambridge, MA: Harvard University Press, 1931).

There had spread over all the Orient an old and established belief, that it was fated at that time for men coming from Judaea to rule the world. This prediction, referring to the emperor of Rome, as afterwards appeared from the event, the people of Judaea took to themselves; accordingly they revolted and after killing their governor, they routed the consular ruler of Syria as well.[49]

In light of these three testimonies, there seems to be a clear and unmistakable Roman tradition that Vespasian fulfilled Jewish messianic prophecy.[50] But what is the likely origin of this tradition? Some have argued that the tradition was created by Josephus himself, and that it dates to the late 70s, the time in which Josephus was composing his *Jewish War*.[51] But Eduard Norden has argued that Tacitus does not seem to be dependent on Josephus but rather has an independent source, undermining the conclusion that Josephus has created this tradition.[52] Christian Sauliner has argued that this section of Josephus's work is an erratic block of text, oddly placed, and as such appears to be lifted directly from a different source and forced into the larger narrative.[53] Thus it appears the tradition was not created by Josephus but was an independent tradition that existed prior to the composition of his *Jewish War*. In my estimation the most likely origin for the tradition, and that which seems to be recognized by most classicists, is the Flavian family itself, as it was the greatest beneficiaries of the tradition.[54] In all likelihood the tradition developed alongside the propagandistic portents, healings, and prophecies noted above and was used to legitimize Vespasian's reign. This piece of propaganda was indeed cleverly crafted, as it simultaneously accomplished multiple purposes: (1) it pointed to Vespasian's military victory and the divine legitimization such victory communicated; (2) it tied Vespasian to the prophecies from sacred texts, furthering his case of divine

---

[49]Suetonius, *Vesp.* 4.5, trans. J. C. Rolfe, LCL, vol. 2 (Cambridge, MA: Harvard University Press, 1914).

[50]To be clear, I am not arguing that Josephus (or others) perceived Vespasian to be the Jewish Messiah; rather, he was claiming that Jews were mistaken to expect a Messiah at all, as their Scriptures truly pointed to Vespasian. The tradition is inherently antimessianic, as is Josephus's entire presentation of Judaism.

[51]Steve Mason, "Josephus, Daniel and the Flavian House," in *Josephus and the History of the Greco-Roman Period: Essays in Memory of Morton Smith*, ed. Fausto Parente and Joseph Sievers (Leiden: Brill, 1994), 188-90; Tessa Rajak, *Josephus: The Historian and His Society* (Philadelphia: Fortress, 1984), 193.

[52]For discussion see E. Norden, "Josephus und Tacitus über Jesus Christus und eine Messianische Prophetie," in *Zur Josephus Forschung*, ed. Abraham Schalit (Darmstadt: Wissenschaftliche Buchgesellschaft, 1973), 27-69.

[53]Christiane Saulnier, "Flavius Josèphe et la Propagande Flavienne," *Revue Biblique* 96, no. 4 (1989): 550.

[54]See J. Nicols, *Vespasian and the Partes Flavianae*, Historia Einzelschriften 28 (Wiesbaden: Franze Steiner, 1978), 96.

legitimization; and (3) it sent an ominous warning to any Jewish group that might consider using its sacred Scriptures to justify rebellion.[55] Such a claim by the Flavian family would certainly have had implications for Roman Christians, implications I consider below.

Generous benefaction. Vespasian paired this case for divine legitimization with strong efforts to restore the prosperity of Rome itself, using his own resources in such efforts. When he received the Principate, he sent grain from Alexandria—the entirety of which was regarded as the emperor's personal property—to address a grave food shortage in the capital city.[56] Some of this grain was distributed directly to the urban plebs.[57] When Vespasian arrived in Rome, he gave monetary gifts to its citizens, three hundred *sestertii* apiece.[58] He used his personal finances to repair the city's infrastructure, including the restoration of needed aqueducts and city streets.[59] He devoted funds to building projects, refurbishing parts of the city destroyed in the fire of Nero's reign, restoring sacred temples (most noteworthy being the Capitol), and starting construction on the famous Colosseum. In these ways Vespasian presented himself as a generous benefactor to the people of Rome, much like the first and ideal emperor, Augustus.

The impact of Vespasian's propaganda on Roman Christians. Over the past two decades of New Testament scholarship, there has been a growing recognition of the Roman imperial world as an important foreground for reading New Testament texts, and that New Testament authors were quite intentional about responding to the realities of the Roman Empire that challenged Christian commitments and practices. In the propaganda of Vespasian, I see two significant challenges to the faith commitments of early Christians. The first challenge is the implications regarding Vespasian's defeat of Jerusalem and the destruction of the Jewish temple. Vespasian's promotion of his victory over the Jews and his destruction of their deity's temple communicates not only divine support of

---

[55]For further discussion regarding this prophecy and its connection Flavian propaganda, see Winn, *Purpose of Mark's Gospel*, 160-64.

[56]P. Garnsey, *Famine and Food Supply in the Graeco-Roman World: Responses to Risk and Crisis* (Cambridge: Cambridge University Press, 1988), 218-27; cf. Levick, *Vespasian*, 124-25.

[57]Levick notes that the urban plebs made dedications to Vespasian in thanks for the receipt of grain he gave to them; *Vespasian*, 124n2; cf. *CIL* 6, 3747; M. McCrum and A. G. Woodhead, *Select Documents of the Principates of the Flavian Emperors: Including the Year of Revolution: A.D. 68–96* (Cambridge: Cambridge University Press, 1961), 141n468.

[58]Levick, *Vespasian*, 125.

[59]Ibid., 125, 130; McCrum and Woodhead, *Select Documents*, 115-16, nos. 408, 412; cf. H. R. Graf, *Kaiser Vespasian, Untersuchungen zu Suetons Vita Divi Vespasiani* (Stuttgart: Kohlhammer, 1937), 135.

Vespasian himself but also the superiority of Roman gods over the God of Israel. Such a challenge strikes at the fundamental Christian belief in the God of Israel and Jesus Christ as sovereign ruler over the entire world. While such a challenge is indeed significant, the second challenge strikes even closer to the heart of Christian faith—namely, that Jewish Scriptures did not point to a Jewish Messiah but rather to the rise of the emperor Vespasian. If this Flavian claim is true, then the Christian claim that Jesus was the prophesied Jewish Messiah is false.

Such challenges to fundamental Christian faith commitments would certainly have impacted Roman Christians. As noted, Rome's destruction of the Jerusalem temple would likely have raised doubts in the minds of some Gentile converts to Christianity, particularly recent converts. Vespasian's claim to be the true fulfillment of Jewish messianic prophecies would only have heightened such doubts. Vespasian would have offered fledgling Roman Christians a compelling resume. He had been victorious in battle over the Jews and had destroyed the temple of the Jewish God. He currently commanded the powerful legions of Rome and held power over the entire known world. He had performed miraculous healings that demonstrated divine favor and legitimization. He could point to numerous portents and prophecies that foretold his rise to power, including prophecy from Jewish Scripture. And he was able to offer tangible blessings to the people of Rome. Certainly some Roman converts to Christianity, converts who had committed themselves to a crucified world ruler who currently reigned in the heavens and for whom they faced possible persecution, might have questioned whether they were actually on the right side. It seems highly plausible that concerned family and friends would have used such Roman propaganda to convince conflicted Christians that they indeed were not. Quite likely Christian missionary efforts would also have been hindered by this Flavian propaganda. For potential Gentile converts to Christianity, a crucified Jewish lord and savior would have paled in comparison to the impressive resume of Vespasian. Thus Flavian propaganda would have created a significant crisis for Roman Christians, one that was at its core christological. Such a crisis would require a strong pastoral response that undermined Flavian propaganda and made a convincing case that Jesus was God's Messiah and the true ruler of the world.

It is from within this historical situation that I propose Mark's narrative be read and from which I draw the necessary pieces to complete Mark's christological puzzle. What follows is an assessment of Mark's narrative and christological pieces from this distinct historical vantage point. Throughout this assessment I will consider the ways in which Markan material in general and Markan Christology in particular fit this proposed historical reconstruction, as strong coherence between the text and historical reconstruction should function to increase the plausibility of the proposed reading.

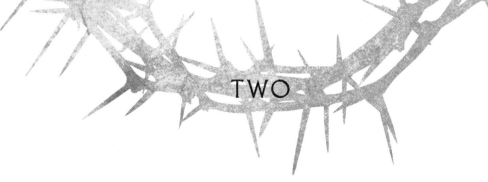

TWO

MARK'S
CHRISTOLOGICAL TITLES

A S I NOTED IN THE INTRODUCTION, form and redaction critics often reduced Mark's Christology to an assessment of the Gospel's use of titles. Often misguided understandings of those titles and their role in the development of early Christianity led to misguided conclusions about Mark's Christology. Narrative critics offered a sharp critique of this approach, noting that the christological titles of Mark are embedded in a larger narrative and that as such they must be understood within the context of that narrative. Mark's Christology is thus narrative Christology and cannot be reduced to the meaning of particular titles. While narrative critics offer an important corrective to the study of Mark's Christology, one I fully embrace, it is important to clarify that the meaning of christological titles in Mark is not solely determined by the Markan narrative. The first-century readers of Mark did not come to these titles with a blank slate but already had an understanding of their meaning and significance. It is just such meanings that the Markan narrative assumes but is then free to reshape, redefine, or perhaps even affirm in part or in whole. Thus the meaning and significance of Mark's christological titles can only be found through the interplay between the titles' meanings for first-century readers and the way in which such meanings are influenced by the Markan narrative.

Thus, in assessing the meaning and significance of these titles, I propose that three steps are necessary. First, the possible ways first-century readers (particularly those likely reading Mark) could have understood Mark's christological titles apart from the narrative itself must be addressed. Second, those possible meanings should be narrowed in light of clues from Mark's text (e.g., references to Jewish Scripture and who applies a title to Jesus), particularly when there are multiple ways in which a title might have been understood by a first-century reader. Third, consideration should be given to the way the narrative of Mark shapes our understanding of these christological titles.[1] In this chapter I will address steps one and two, with step three addressed in the following chapters that address the narrative features of Mark's Christology. As a part of my consideration of steps one and two, I will also consider the way in which the proposed historical setting for Mark might influence the reader's understanding of Mark's christological titles.

CHRIST / MESSIAH

From the outset of Mark, Jesus is clearly identified as the Jewish Messiah or "anointed one" (Mk 1:1), with the title directly attributed to Jesus at three different points (Mk 8:29; 9:41; 14:61-62).[2] Thus virtually all Markan interpreters recognize that Mark understands Jesus to be God's Messiah.[3] Despite the great variety in Jewish messianic thought, because Mark is best identified as a Christian text, one can be fairly confident that the title implies that Jesus is God's sole eschatological agent. But what type of eschatological agent does Mark understand Jesus to be? The title "Messiah" alone does not answer this question, and thus we must consider both additional christological titles and the way the Markan narrative shapes Jesus' messianic identity.

---

[1]While the features noted under step two are indeed features of Mark's narrative, here I am distinguishing between details within the narrative and larger aspects of narrative such as plot progression and characterization.

[2]There has been some debate as to whether "Christ" should be understood as a title or as a part of Jesus' name. For discussion of this debate and justification of seeing "Christ" as a title, see Adam Winn, *The Purpose of Mark's Gospel: An Early Christian Response to Roman Imperial Propaganda*, WUNT II/245 (Tübingen: Mohr Siebeck, 2008), 93-94. A fourth passage that clearly indicates Jesus' identity as God's Messiah is Mk 13:21-22, where Jesus warns against "false christs." This text implies that Jesus is the true Christ.

[3]For a rare exception see Richard Horsley, *Hearing the Whole Story: The Politics of Plot in Mark* (Louisville: Westminster John Knox, 2001), 250-51. For a response to Horsley's position, see Robert Gundry's thorough review of Horsley's work, "Richard A. Horsley's *Hearing the Whole Story*: A Critical Review of Its Postcolonial Slant," *JSNT* 26 (2003): 131-49; see also Winn, *Purpose of Mark's Gospel*, 35-41.

SON OF GOD

Many interpreters have argued that "Son of God" (or "Son") is the preeminent christological title in Mark.[4] Jesus is identified as God's Son as many as seven times in Mark (Mk 1:1, 11; 3:11; 5:7; 9:7; 14:61; 15:39).[5] Twice God directly affirms Jesus as his son (Mk 1:11; 9:7). Twice more demons, who presumably have supernatural knowledge, declare Jesus to be God's son. And Jesus himself affirms this identity when he responds to the high priest's question, "Are you the Messiah, the Son of the Blessed One?" affirmatively (Mk 14:61). Many interpreters have noted that the Evangelist strategically places this title at the beginning (Mk 1:1, 11), middle (Mk 9:7), and end of the narrative (Mk 15:39), and in doing so communicates the title's importance.[6] But what significance does this title hold in Mark?

Perhaps most telling are the two instances in which God declares Jesus to be his Son: "You are my Son, the beloved; with you I am well pleased" (Mk 1:11); and "This is my Son, the Beloved; listen to him!" (Mk 9:7). These divine affirmations of Jesus' sonship seemingly echo Psalm 2:7, a royal coronation psalm, and thus establish a clear context for understanding Jesus' sonship in Mark; namely, that Jesus' divine sonship expresses his identity as God's appointed ruler. The kings of Israel were regularly identified as God's sons, and Mark draws on this background in its presentation of Jesus' divine sonship. As such, Mark's use of "Son of God" helps us better understand Jesus' identification as God's Messiah. Amid the myriad understandings of Messiah in Second Temple Judaism, it seems that Mark's understanding aligns well with the popular notion of the Messiah as an eschatological ruler or king.[7] Thus Mark's use of Messiah and "Son of God" finds unity in the notion of God's appointed eschatological ruler.

---

[4]See for example Jack Dean Kingsbury, *The Christology of Mark's Gospel* (Philadelphia: Fortress, 1983); Craig A. Evans, *Mark 8:27–16:20*, WBC 34B (Nashville: Thomas Nelson, 2001), lxxii-lxxiii; W. R. Telford, *The Theology of the Gospel of Mark* (Cambridge: Cambridge University Press, 1999); Larry Hurtado, *Mark*, New International Biblical Commentary 2 (Peabody, MA: Hendrickson, 1989), 10-11; P. J. Achtemeier, "Mark, Gospel of," *ABD* 4:551-53.

[5]The use of "Son of God" in Mark's incipit is textually uncertain, with interpreters relatively evenly split on its originality to the Markan text. For a discussion of relevant data and arguments regarding this text-critical issue, see Winn, *Purpose of Mark's Gospel*, 94-95 (see note 11 for a relevant bibliography on this issue).

[6]For example, see Evans, *Mark 8:27–16:20*, lxxix-lxxx; Telford, *Theology of the Gospel of Mark*, 38-39; Adam Winn, "Son of God," in *Dictionary of Jesus and the Gospels*, 2nd ed., ed. Joel B. Green, Jeannine K. Brown, and Nicholas Perrin (Downers Grove, IL: InterVarsity Press, 2013), 890.

[7]For discussion see John J. Collins, *The Scepter and the Star: The Messiahs of the Dead Sea Scrolls and Other Ancient Literature* (New York: Doubleday, 1995), 49-68.

But while a Jewish context is significant for understanding Mark's employment of "Son of God," the Greco-Roman context for this title must also be
considered. Both Roman and Greek rulers were commonly identified as sons of
gods. Alexander the Great was identified as "son of Ammon" by an oracle in
Egypt (Ammon being the equivalent to the Greek god Zeus), and his Ptolemaic
successors embraced this identity as well.[8] More importantly for our purposes
is the use of the title "Son of God" in the Roman imperial cult. Octavian (later
Augustus) took for himself the title *divi filius* ("God's son" or "son of God"), as
he was the adopted son of the deified Julius Caesar. *Divi filius* was translated
into Greek as θεοῦ υἱός ("son of god"). This title, appearing in both languages,
was regularly used of Augustus (e.g., καίσαρος θεοῦ υἱός αὐτοκράτω, "Caesar,
Son of God, Emperor").[9] Claims to divine sonship were also used by many of
Augustus's successors, including Tiberius, Germanicus, and Nero.[10]

It seems quite likely that Greek and Roman readers of Mark would have been
influenced by this close association between "Son of God" and the powerful rulers
of their world, and thus would likely bring such a background to their understanding of Mark's identification of Jesus as "Son of God." But does such a conclusion negate the kingly or messianic implications of the title in a Jewish context,
a context that Mark clearly draws on? Must the interpreter choose one context over
the other for understanding the significance of this title in Mark? Would a first-
century reader be forced to make such a choice? I would argue that the multiva-
lence of language allows both contexts, Jewish and Greco-Roman, to coexist at the
same time for the reader. Thus Mark would have been able to draw on both contexts, using divine sonship to affirm Jesus' identity as God's messianic ruler but also
using divine sonship to place Jesus in the same category as the great rulers of the
world. This type of "double coding" would have allowed the Markan Evangelist a
wide range of options for how the title "Son of God" might be employed. Such a
tool that would be particularly useful if realities grounded in a Jewish context were
perceived to be in conflict with realities grounded in a Greco-Roman one.[11]

---

[8]W. von Martitz, "υἱός," *TDNT* 8:336. See also A. Y. Collins, "Mark and His Readers: The Son of
God Among Greeks and Romans," *Harvard Theological Review* 93, no. 2 (2000): 87; Winn, *Purpose of Mark's Gospel*, 101; Winn, "Son of God," 886-87.

[9]See Tae Hun Kim, "The Anarthrous υἱός θεοῦ in Mark 15,39 and the Roman Imperial Cult,"
Biblica 79 (1998): 221-41.

[10]See Evans, *Mark 8:27–16:20*, lxxxii-lxxxiii; Winn, *Purpose of Mark's Gospel*, 101-2.

[11]For the concept of double coding, see J. M. Scott, "Gods, Greek and Roman," in *Dictionary of
Jesus and the Gospels*, ed. Green, Brown, and Perrin, 330.

SON OF MAN

"Son of Man" is the primary way in which the Markan Jesus identifies himself and the most prevalent title for Jesus in Mark. Significant debate has surrounded the meaning of this title in Mark. Many commentators and interpreters who either preceded the advancement of narrative criticism or have not fully engaged in it have concluded that "Son of Man" is not a christological title in Mark.[12] For many of these interpreters, the conclusion is based on two related pieces of evidence: (1) there is little evidence that "Son of Man" was a christological title in early first-century CE Judaism, and thus the historical Jesus did not employ it as such; and (2) "Son of Man" is never used as a christological confession of Jesus' identity in Mark; that is, no characters in Mark declare Jesus to be "Son of Man" in the way that they declare him to be Christ and Son of God. It is then concluded that "Son of Man" is a generic idiomatic form of self-reference rather than a title that conveys christological identity, though some might allow that "Son of Man" at certain points might find continuity with Markan christological titles.

A number of criticisms can be levied against such argumentation regarding Mark's use of "Son of Man." The first claim, that "Son of Man" was not used as a messianic title in the early part of the first century CE, is far from certain. "Son of Man" certainly seems to be used as such a title in the Similitudes of Enoch (see 48.1-10; cf. 46.2-4; 62.7, 9, 14; 63.11; 69.26-27, 29), which Adela Yarbro Collins dates to the late first century BCE or early first century CE.[13] While the prevalence of such a messianic use of "Son of Man" is uncertain, its use in 1 Enoch demonstrates that at least some of Jesus' contemporaries could have understood the title messianically. But perhaps more importantly, the way in which this title could have been understood by the historical Jesus should have little bearing on how the title is understood in Mark, as significant developments of the title's meaning could have taken place between the life of Jesus and the Evangelist's narration of it. What is truly pressing is whether Christians in the late first century (i.e., potential readers of Mark) understood "Son of Man" as a title that conveyed messianic significance.

---

[12]For interpreters who reject "Son of Man" as a christological title in Mark, see Evans, *Mark 8:27–16:20*, lxxv; Kingsbury, *Christology of Mark's Gospel*, 157-76; Douglas R. A. Hare, *The Son of Man Tradition* (Minneapolis: Fortress, 1990), 183-211; Martin Hengel, *Studies in Early Christology* (Edinburgh: T&T Clark, 1995), 104-8.

[13]See Adela Yarbro Collins, *Mark: A Commentary*, Hermeneia (Minneapolis: Fortress, 2007), 58.

This assessment brings us to the second claim: that no character in Mark uses this title as a means of confessing Jesus' identity, and thus "Son of Man" should not be understood as a christological title. I contend that such an argument presumes far too much about the christological commitments of the early church and the manner in which early Christians expressed those commitments. First, it presumes that the confession of christological titles encompasses the totality of christological thought and expression among early Christians. Surely early Christians expressed christological commitments in numerous ways beyond simple declarative confessions. Such thought could have been conveyed through hymns, exegesis of Hebrew Scripture, and even the oral reporting, writing, and reading of Jesus traditions. If "Son of Man" played a prominent role in any of these forms of christological expression, it could carry significance as a christological title regardless of whether it played a prominent role in the declarative christological confessions of early Christians.

Second, this argument ignores plausible reasons for why Christians might have excluded "Son of Man" from such christological confessions. It is widely recognized that the historical Jesus used "Son of Man" as his primary means of self-identification.[14] This form of self-reference is found in virtually every layer of Gospel tradition.[15] Compare this frequency to the scarcity of traditions in which Jesus identifies himself as Christ or "Son of God," particularly in the Synoptic Gospels. That the title "Son of Man" was not picked up by the early church as a common christological confession (apart from the lips of Jesus, the title only appears four times in the New Testament, Acts 7:52; Heb 2:6; Rev 1:13; 14:14, with three of these four being direct citations of Old Testament texts) strongly suggests that Jesus' use of the title was not created by the early church but was original to Jesus himself.[16] Given that the church remembered Jesus' use of this title but never incorporated it into its own christological confessions, a strong case can be made that the church guarded this tradition carefully and was extremely reluctant either to put other christological titles on the lips of Jesus or to place the title "Son of

---

[14]The significance the historical Jesus attributed to this title is hotly debated (as an idiomatic form of self-reference or a reference to the apocalyptic Son of Man in Dan 7), but the majority of scholars affirm that the historical Jesus did apply this phrase to himself. For discussion, see James Dunn, *Jesus Remembered,* vol. 1 of *Christianity in the Making* (Grand Rapids: Eerdmans, 2003), 1:724-62.

[15]"Son of Man" can be found in Mark, material commonly called Q (that shared by Matthew and Luke), unique Matthean material, unique Lukan material, and in John's Gospel.

[16]For example, see Dunn's strong conclusions in *Jesus Remembered,* 737-39, 759.

Man" on anyone's lips but Jesus".[17] If this was indeed the way in which the church treated the title "Son of Man," it would not be surprising that no Markan character uses this title in a christological confession. Thus the absence of such a confession in no way demonstrates that the Evangelist rejected "Son of Man" as a christological title or denied it christological significance—rather, it may merely evince the church's protection of this title as one used by Jesus himself.

In conclusion, I contend that neither the historical Jesus' intended use of "Son of Man" nor the absence of "Son of Man" in the christological confessions of Mark (or of the early church, for that matter) necessarily leads to the conclusion that "Son of Man" is not a christological title in Mark. In assessing Mark's use of "Son of Man," one must pay careful attention to the function of the title in Mark's narrative, as well as the understanding of the title that Mark's readers would have brought to that narrative, both of which I will now consider.

As noted above, "Son of Man" is the most common descriptor of Jesus in Mark (14x), and it is used explicitly by Jesus in reference to himself.[18] Both of these facts strongly suggest that this descriptor of Jesus carries great significance in Mark—certainly Jesus' assessment of himself plays a crucial role in Mark's presentation of Jesus' identity and significance.[19] But what significance does this descriptor bear? The first two instances of Jesus' use of "Son of Man" come in the context of Jesus' claiming significant power (i.e., the power to forgive sins [Mk 2:10] and lordship over the Sabbath [Mk 2:28]). Thus it seems the title is closely associated with unique powers possessed by Jesus. It is noteworthy that no explanation is given to the reader of Jesus' identity as "Son of Man" or of why that identity might bring with it these unique powers. One might then conclude that either the readers are expected to already possess knowledge that will enable them to understand the significance of these claims or they are expected to look for such knowledge as they encounter the rest of the narrative.

---

[17]The only other character in the New Testament who uses this title to describe Jesus is Stephen (Acts 7:52). This instance is best explained by the author of Acts drawing an intentional connection between Stephen and the discipleship described in Lk 9:23-27, i.e., the Son of Man is depicted as "not being ashamed" of the martyr Stephen.

[18]While some interpreters have argued that Jesus may have used "Son of Man" to refer to someone other than himself (see Rudolf Bultmann, *The History of the Synoptic Tradition*, trans. John Marsh [Oxford: Basil Blackwell, 1963]), 112; H. E. Tödt, *The Son of Man in the Synoptic Tradition*, trans. Dorothea M. Barton [London: SCM Press, 1965], 55-60), it is quite clear that the Markan Jesus uses this phrase as a form of self-reference.

[19]See Elizabeth Struthers Malbon, *Mark's Jesus: Characterization as Narrative Christology* (Waco, TX: Baylor University Press, 2009), 196-210.

The vast majority of the subsequent uses of the "Son of Man" are in the context of Jesus' coming suffering and death, including the passion predictions (Mk 8:31; 9:31; 10:33-34), his purpose to give his life as a ransom for humanity (Mk 10:45), and his betrayal (Mk 14:21, 41). Again, no explanation for the title's meaning and significance is given to the reader, and the Evangelist makes no attempt to explain how the great power that was previously associated with Jesus' identity as "Son of Man" is related to the suffering and death that is seemingly associated with these latter uses.

There are also three uses of "Son of Man" that identify Jesus with the apocalyptic "Son of Man" in Daniel 7:13-14, a figure to whom God grants eternal dominion over the entire world (Mk 8:38; 13:26; 14:62). Such a use of "Son of Man" seemingly brings this title into close relationship with the Markan titles "Messiah" and "Son of God," as all three are associated with God's eschatological agent and ruler. Yet Mark's use of "Son of Man" expands the scope of this ruler's power to include the entire world. Additionally, this use of "Son of Man" gives additional meaning to the previous uses of "Son of Man" that attribute to Jesus the power to forgive sins as well as lordship over the Sabbath. These citations of Daniel 7 also give additional meaning to Jesus' suffering and death, as they point to future vindication of Jesus and a coming judgment that will follow his death.

It seems clear that as the Son of Man the Markan Jesus is understood as God's appointed ruler of the world who, though he bears tremendous power and authority on earth, will also suffer and die. Yet both suffering and death will ultimately result in vindication and Jesus' enduring reign as God's eschatological ruler.

While most recent narrative critics of Mark recognize these basic narrative pieces, the way in which these critics understand the significance of these pieces within the Markan narrative varies. Some understand "Son of Man" to be an ambiguous form of self-reference for the Markan Jesus, one that is veiled enough so to avoid explicit messianic identity, but one that might carry implicit messianic significance when it is linked to Daniel 7:13-14.[20] Thus, while Jesus identifies

---

[20]A good example of such a position is Jack Dean Kingsbury, who concludes that "Son of Man" is a meaningful form of self-reference for Jesus but not a messianic or christological title within Mark; Kingsbury, *Christology of Mark's Gospel*, 157-76; Kingsbury, "The Christology of Mark and the Son of Man," in *Unity and Diversity in the Gospels and Paul: Essays in Honor of Frank J. Matera*, ed. Christopher W. Skinner and Kelly R. Iverson (Atlanta: Society of Biblical Literature, 2012), 55-70. For others who see "Son of Man" as an ambiguous or veiled form of self-reference (or christological title) see W. Schmithals, "Die Worte vom Leidenden Menschensohn," in *Theologia Crucis— Signum Crucis: Festschrift für Erich Dinkler zum 70 Geburtstag*, ed. C. Anderson and G. Klein

himself as "Son of Man" throughout the narrative, he is not using that descriptor to explicitly identify himself as God's Messiah. Such an understanding of Mark's use of "Son of Man" comports well with common understandings of the Markan "secrecy motif," in which it seems that Jesus seeks to keep his messianic identity a secret. If "Son of Man" was to be understood as an explicit messianic title, then many narrative explanations of Mark's secrecy motif would be in jeopardy.

Francis Moloney argues that "Son of Man" is a christological title in Mark, but its meaning and christological significance are only gradually revealed throughout Mark. According to Moloney, when the title is abruptly used for the first time in Mark 2:10, without explanation, it leaves the reader asking, "Who is this 'Son of Man'?"[21] It is only as the reader encounters the suffering Son of Man (e.g., Mk 8:31; 9:31; 10:33-34) and the references to the Danielic Son of Man (e.g., Mk 13:26; 14:62) that the reader understands the full significance of this christological title.[22]

Both of these means of assessing the significance of "Son of Man" in Mark seem to operate under the assumption that Mark's readers come to the text with little to no knowledge of this title.[23] Such an assumption is consistent with a strict narrative-critical reading, one that assumes nothing about the reader outside what the text implies. But our present interest is in the real first-century readers of Mark and how those readers would have understood Mark's narrative. It seems highly implausible that such readers came to the Gospel without any prior understanding of Jesus' identity as "Son of Man" or any notion of the messianic implications that the title carries when it is interpreted in light of Daniel 7:13-14. As noted above, scholars widely recognize that the historical Jesus used "Son of Man" as a means of self-identification, and as such this form of self-reference was

---

(Tübingen: J. C. B. Mohr, 1979), 432; Harry L. Chronis, "To Reveal and to Conceal: A Literary-Critical Perspective on 'the Son of Man' in Mark," *NTS* 51 (2005): 459-81; John G. Cook, *The Structure and Persuasive Power of Mark: A Linguistic Approach*, SBL Semeia Studies (Atlanta: Scholars Press, 1995), 320. In my initial work on Mark, I adopt a similar view regarding the meaning of "Son of Man"; see Winn, *Purpose of Mark's Gospel*, 106-7.

[21] Francis J. Moloney, *The Gospel of Mark* (Peabody, MA: Hendrickson, 2002), 62-63.

[22] In my previous work, I bring this reading of Mark's use of "Son of Man" together with the understanding of "Son of Man" as a veiled form of christological identification; Winn, *Purpose of Mark's Gospel*, 107.

[23] To be fair, Chronis argues that Mark's reader does indeed understand this title to be synonymous with "Son of God" and "Messiah," but that within the Markan narrative, the characters of the narrative world receive the title "Son of Man" as a veiled and cryptic form of identification. I would contend that Mark's intended readers were not making distinctions between their own understanding and that of Markan characters, and thus I find this distinction unhelpful for the purposes of this present project (Chronis, "To Reveal and to Conceal," 461-66).

likely deeply embedded in the Jesus tradition already known to Mark's readers. Regardless of the way in which the historical Jesus used "Son of Man" or the significance attributed to it (e.g., as a self-referential idiom, a prophetic identification, an apocalyptic messianic claim), the early church clearly connected Jesus' use of "Son of Man" with the figure described in Daniel 7:13-14. It is hard to imagine that such a connection was not established in the first decade of the Christian movement, as the church turned to its Scriptures to help it understand Jesus, his death, and resurrection.

Thus, as Mark was composed in the early 70s CE, it seems implausible to conclude that "Son of Man" did not already have rich christological significance in the early church, which an Evangelist could easily draw on without any need to explain such significance to readers. Mark's abrupt introduction to the title "Son of Man" in Mark 2:10, where no explanation of the title is given, is consistent with the conclusion that the Markan Evangelist anticipated that his readers fully understood "Son of Man" in terms of the divinely appointed ruler of Daniel 7. In fact, it seems the entire point of the verse is to make a bold statement about the divine prerogative that is shared with just such a figure. Who else but God's eschatological agent, an agent Mark has already identified as Jesus from the outset of the Gospel (Messiah in Mk 1:1 and Son of God possibly in Mk 1:1 and certainly in Mk 1:11), could have the power to forgive sins?[24] That Mark attributes to Jesus the power to forgive sins through his identity and role as "Son of Man," with no explanation offered to his readers as to the meaning of "Son of Man," strongly suggests they already possessed the necessary understanding of this identification for Jesus. In other words, for Mark's readers "Son of Man" was a title virtually synonymous with Messiah.

Such a conclusion is consistent with a number of examples in which "Son of Man" seems to be equated with the titles "Messiah" and "Son of God." For example, Mark follows Peter's declaration of Jesus' identity as the Messiah by saying, "Then he began to teach them that the Son of Man must undergo great suffering" (Mk 8:31). Here we have the Evangelist relaying indirect discourse of Jesus, and through it he identifies Jesus as "Son of Man." It seems quite clear that his use of "Son of Man" in Mark 8:31 is rightly equated with the "Christ" in Mark

---

[24]However, as some have suggested, and as I will suggest in this book's appendix, perhaps Mark is signaling that this "Son of Man" is none other than the God of Israel. For such a reading, see Timothy Geddert, "The Implied YHWH Christology of Mark: Mark's Challenge to the Reader to 'Connect the Dots,'" *Bulletin for Biblical Research* 25, no. 3 (2015): 329-31.

8:28, as narratively speaking Mark 8:31 is best understood as Jesus' clarification to Peter's messianic claim in Mark 8:28. Thus it seems that the Markan Evangelist understands these two titles as equivalent ways of referencing God's eschatological agent.[25]

There is a similar use of these titles in the transfiguration narrative. After God declares Jesus to be his son (Mk 9:7), Mark says, "As they were coming down the mountain, he ordered them to tell no one about what they had seen, until after the Son of Man had risen from the dead" (Mk 9:9). Here it seems that the Markan Evangelist perceives Jesus' identity as "Son of Man" as equivalent to his identity as God's Son (or "Son of God").

Finally, a third text in Mark links all three of these titles together, suggesting they are all to be understood as communicating Jesus' messianic identity. In Jesus' trial before the high priest, he is asked, "Are you the Messiah, the Son of the Blessed One?" (Mk 14:61). To this question Jesus replies,

> I am; and

> "you will see the Son of Man
>   seated at the right hand of the Power,"
> and "coming with the clouds of heaven." (Mk 14:62)

Here the Evangelist seems to equate both Messiah and divine sonship ("Son of Blessed One or God") with "Son of Man," as all three are referring to God's eschatological ruler.

That Mark can use "Messiah," "Son of God," and "Son of Man" to reference Jesus' messianic identity, with no explanation given to the reader, strongly suggests the reader already understood these titles as virtual synonyms. Thus, contra those who understand "Son of Man" as a veiled form of self-reference for Jesus and contra Moloney, who understands "Son of Man" to be a title that is gradually explained throughout the Markan narrative, I contend that "Son of Man" is a title that Mark's reader would have clearly understood from the outset as a reference to Jesus' messianic identity. Despite this perceived difference in the way the reader comes to the title "Son of Man" in Mark (as veiled messianic reference, gradual revelation, or full messianic title), all three assessments of the title see some level of unity with the other Markan christological titles, "Messiah"

---

[25]For a similar argument that Mark views "Messiah/Christ" and "Son of Man" as synonyms, see Collins, *Mark*, 69.

and "Son of God." Yet, one narrative assessment of the Markan "Son of Man" resists such unity.

Malbon has made much of the fact that only Jesus identifies himself as the Son of Man. She argues that this is a narrative device that contributes to an intentional juxtaposition of the christological perspective of Mark's narrator and that of the Markan Jesus. For Malbon, there is tension between the narrator's claim that Jesus is "Son of God" and Jesus' consistent claim (rebuttal?) that he is both the suffering and the powerful "Son of Man." Malbon's proposed reading makes good sense given her particular narrative reading strategy, one that identifies the narrator as a distinct character in the Markan narrative and presumes relatively little about the knowledge of the implied reader. But this reading makes little sense given the present reading strategy, one that seeks to read the Markan text from the perspective of a reconstructed historical community in post–70 CE Rome. In my estimation it seems highly unlikely that Mark's first-century Roman readers would have distinguished between the Markan author and narrator, and thus they would almost certainly have presumed a unity between the christological perspective of Mark's narrator and author and the Markan Jesus. In light of such an assumed unity, Mark's intended reader would likely have understood the narrator's description of Jesus and Jesus' description of himself as mutually interpreting rather than standing in tension. Such a conclusion is reinforced if one were to conclude that the intended reader came to the text with a prior understanding of "Son of Man" as a messianic title, one that is virtually synonymous with "Messiah"/Christ and "Son of God" (see the argument above).

But if the reader perceives these titles as relative synonyms (i.e., different ways of referencing Jesus' messianic identity) and thus understand them in terms of unity rather than tension, why does the Markan Jesus almost exclusively identify himself as "Son of Man" rather than Christ or "Son of God"? And why does no Markan character identify Jesus as "Son of Man"? I propose a simple explanation exists, one that need not attribute any narrative significance to this phenomenon in the Markan text. As I noted above, scholars widely accept that the earliest Christians remembered the historical Jesus as identifying himself as "Son of Man." While this memory was firmly planted in the Jesus traditions of the early church, it never led to the church's confessional use of the title "Son of Man." These two data points seem to suggest that the church protected the title "Son of Man" as a means by which Jesus referred to himself, a self-reference that was understood in light of Daniel 7:13-14. If this conclusion is accepted, then the fact that the title "Son of Man" only appears on the lips of Jesus in Mark can easily be explained in terms of the Evangelist inheriting, protecting, and perpetuating a tradition deeply embedded in the early church's remembrance of Jesus.

In light of this discussion I contend that "Son of Man" is an important christological title in Mark, one that, like both "Messiah" and "Son of God," conveys Jesus' identity as God's appointed eschatological agent and ruler. But unlike these two titles, "Son of Man" explicitly draws on the apocalyptic tradition of Daniel 7:13 and perhaps other apocalyptic traditions that employ Daniel 7:13 (e.g., Similitudes of Enoch). As such Mark understands Jesus to be a ruler to whom God has granted a universal reign, one in which all "peoples, nations, and languages should serve him" (Dan 7:14). Such an understanding of "Son of Man" was likely brought to the text by Mark's readers, who would seemingly have been familiar with traditions in which Jesus identifies himself as "Son of Man" and the interpretive traditions of the early church that understood that identity in light of Daniel 7:13-14. If such knowledge is granted to the reader, then Mark's readers understood "Son of Man" to be communicating Jesus' messianic identity from the Gospel's first use of the title in Mark 2:10. Thus there is no need to conclude that the title was in some way veiled to Mark's readers or that its meaning is gradually revealed. Such an understanding of "Son of Man" does create problems for many of the proposed interpretations of Mark's "secrecy motif," as Jesus' messianic claims through the use of the title "Son of Man" would violate this so-called secret. But this is an issue I will address in a later chapter.

SON OF DAVID

There has been much debate over the Markan Evangelist's estimation of the title "Son of David." The title is used three times in Mark. The first two occurrences come in the account of Jesus restoring the sight of Bartimaeus (Mk 10:46-52), when Bartimaeus twice identifies Jesus as "Son of David." In this story there is no suggestion that "Son of David" is an inappropriate title for Jesus. Jesus does not correct Bartimaeus or reject this identification in any way. On the face of the story, one would presume that the Markan Evangelist affirms Jesus' identity as "Son of David" and perceives it as simply one more way to refer to Jesus' messianic identity, as there is a clear connection between a descendant of David and the Messiah in much of Jewish and Christian messianic thought.

However, the picture becomes cloudier when Jesus himself teaches on this very title. In Mark 12:35 Jesus asks, "How can the scribes say that the Messiah is the Son of David?" He answers his own question by saying,

David himself, by the Holy Spirit, declared,

"The Lord said to my Lord,
 'Sit at my right hand,
        until I put your enemies under your feet.'"

David himself calls him Lord; so how can he be his son? (Mk 12:36-37)

This passage has been interpreted in a variety of ways: (1) as a means of rejecting any connection between Jesus' identity as Messiah and Davidic messianism (i.e., Jesus is not to be identified with "Son of David");[26] (2) as a means of showing that while "Son of David" is perhaps accurate in a biological and ancestral sense, it is an inadequate way of understanding Jesus' messianic identity (i.e., Jesus as Messiah is more than simply a "Son of David");[27] and (3) that Jesus is "Son of David" in some sense, but he is not the militaristic deliverer anticipated by many Jewish people.[28]

But all of these interpretive options stand in tension with the rest of Mark's narrative, in which it seems that Jesus is positively identified with David. I have already noted the straightforward identification of Jesus as "Son of David" in the Bartimaeus pericope. Additionally, in Mark 2:28 Jesus seems to identify himself with David when he defends his disciples for picking grain on the Sabbath. And in the account of Jesus' entry into Jerusalem, the people identify Jesus with the kingdom of their father David, an identification that the Gospel seems to affirm. There is no hint in any of these texts that linking Jesus' messianic identity with David is problematic. It also seems unlikely that early Christians reading Mark would have seen this title as problematic, given what seems to be a strong commitment in the early church to Jesus' connection to David (e.g., Rom 1:3; Mt 1; Lk 3:23-38).

---

[26]For example, see Paul J. Achtemeier, "'And He Followed Him': Miracles and Discipleship in Mark 10:46-52," *Semeia* 11 (1978): 126-30; Malbon, *Mark's Jesus*, 159-69.

[27]For example, see Ferdinand Hahn, *The Titles of Jesus in Christology: Their History in Early Christianity* (New York: World Publishing, 1969), 240-53; Joel Marcus, *Way of the Lord: Christological Exegesis of the Old Testament in the Gospel of Mark* (Louisville: Westminster John Knox, 1992), 151.

[28]For example, see Stephen P. Ahearne-Kroll, *The Psalms of Lament in Mark's Passion: Jesus' Davidic Suffering*, Society for New Testament Studies Monograph Series 142 (Cambridge: Cambridge University Press, 2007), 164-65; Collins, *Mark*, 582.

Another interpretive challenge the text presents is the response of the crowds to this statement of Jesus about the Messiah and the "Son of David." Mark claims that the crowd responds with delight to this teaching. But why would Jesus' juxtaposition of "Son of David" and Messiah, identities that are closely linked in both the Jewish and Christian movement, create such delight? Timothy Gray has offered a helpful way forward regarding the interpretation of this teaching of Jesus, one that makes sense of the people's delight.[29] Gray argues that Jesus presents the people with a riddle, one that must be understood in relation to the challenge from the chief priests, scribes, and elders regarding Jesus' authority to judge and condemn both themselves and the temple they serve (Mk 11:27–12:12). Most interpreters conclude that Jesus' question in Mark 12:37 is rhetorical and can only be answered negatively, that is, David could not call his own son "lord." But Gray argues that the question is not rhetorical at all and that Jesus is presenting a riddle that has a real answer, one that has significant implications for Jesus' authority over the temple and its leadership. The answer is found in both the implied historical setting of the psalm itself and in the historical remembrance of that setting found in 1 Kings. As David is the author of the psalm (from the perspective of Mark and his readers), and he is describing the enthronement of a king other than himself, the enthroned figure can be none other than Solomon. Thus David is saying, "The Lord [Yahweh] said to my lord [Solomon], 'Sit at my right hand . . .'." Jesus identifying Solomon as his lord fits with the historical remembrance of Solomon being enthroned as king in 1 Kings 1, where in order to secure the throne for Solomon, David establishes Solomon as king before his own death.

The answer to Jesus' riddle is not that the one David declares as his lord cannot be his son, but rather that he actually can be David's son when the story of Solomon's enthronement is envisioned. Thus Jesus is not drawing on Psalm 110 to deny or mitigate a connection between "Son of David" and the Messiah, but rather to understand the Messiah's identification as "Son of David" through a psalm that describes the enthronement of just such a son, Psalm 110. Gray notes that Psalm 110 declares the priestly identity and role that was granted to the Davidic king: "You are a priest forever according to the order of Melchizedek" (Ps 110:4). This connection between Davidic kings and priestly identity is also quite prevalent in the Deuteronomic history (e.g., 2 Sam 6:14, 18; 24:17; 1 Kings 8:14).

---

[29]For the following argument, see Timothy C. Gray, *The Temple in the Gospel of Mark: A Study in Its Narrative Role*, WUNT II/242 (Tübingen: Mohr Siebeck, 2008; repr., Grand Rapids: Baker, 2010), 79-90.

Thus, through his citation of the psalm, Jesus is both identifying himself with Solomon, the son of David who built the temple, and evoking the priestly authority and privilege of the sons of David. In this way Jesus responds to the challenges from the chief priests and scribes regarding his authority over the temple by establishing that very authority through his identity as the messianic "Son of David." Presumably it is this exposition of the prerogative of the Davidic Messiah over the temple, conveyed through a clever riddle, that delights Jesus' audience.

Gray's interpretation of this passage removes all doubt as to whether "Son of David" functions positively as a christological title in Mark. "Son of David" simply becomes another way in which the Markan narrative conveys Jesus' identity as God's Messiah, but it adds an additional dimension to that identity— namely, the priestly authority possessed by that Messiah.

LORD

There is debate among Markan interpreters as to whether "lord" (κύριος) is used as a christological title for the Markan Jesus. There is only one instance in Mark where Jesus is unambiguously identified as "lord." In this instance he is addressed by the Syro-Phoenician woman with the vocative (κύριε), a form of address that could simply be understood as a means of addressing a social superior, that is, something akin to "sir." With this sole example one would be hard pressed make a convincing case that Mark uses "lord" as a christological title. But the state of the question is complicated by a handful of examples in which the title "lord" might apply to Jesus but could also be understood to apply to God or even someone else (see Mk 11:3).

Perhaps the best starting point is the opening citation of Isaiah in Mark 1:3: "Prepare the way of the Lord, make his paths straight." In its original context this Isaianic text is referring to the God of Israel, and as such many interpreters have concluded that Mark's citation of the text should be understood in the same way. But others have argued that Mark is referring to Jesus, and that through a move of christological exegesis, has put Jesus in the place of Yahweh. It is indeed Jesus and not Yahweh for whom John the Baptist, clearly the voice calling in the wilderness, prepares the way. But it is also possible to read Mark's citation as referring to Yahweh, with Jesus being the eschatological agent of Yahweh and the one through whom Yahweh is symbolically present.[30] The ambiguity is difficult to resolve.

---

[30]As I will argue in the appendix, such ambiguity might be intentional.

Two other ambiguous cases exist. Following the healing of the Gerasene demoniac, Jesus tells the former demoniac, "Go home to your friends, and tell them how much the Lord has done for you, and what mercy he has shown you" (Mk 5:19). Jesus is the one who has freed the man from demon possession, and the following verse presents the man proclaiming what Jesus did for him: "And he went away and began to proclaim in the Decapolis how much Jesus had done for him" (Mk 5:20). Certainly one could interpret "the Lord" in Mark 5:19 as a reference to Jesus. But at the same time one could also conclude that Jesus tells the man to give credit for his freedom to God, through whose power Jesus exorcised the demons. Whether the man then disobeys Jesus by telling how much Jesus instead of God has done for him or whether telling what Jesus the agent of God has done is akin to telling what God has done is uncertain. Thus this reference could refer to Jesus or God.

Another ambiguous reference to "the Lord" comes in Mark 11:3, in the events preceding the triumphal entry. Jesus tells his disciples to tell anyone who questions their procuring of a colt, "The Lord needs it and will send it back here immediately." To be sure, it is Jesus who has need of the colt and will ride it, and thus "the Lord" could be a reference to Jesus. But "the Lord" could also be a reference to God, for whose purpose Jesus will be entering into the city. A third option also exists, as "the Lord" could be understood as the owner of the colt. The context allows for each possibility, and thus ambiguity remains.

It is noteworthy that there are eight instances in which "the Lord" (ὁ κύριος) clearly refers to Yahweh the God of Israel, and some may argue that such identification tips the scale in favor of "lord" as a reference to Yahweh in the ambiguous texts. While such a conclusion is plausible, it seems to deny the possibility that Mark could think about both Jesus and the God of Israel in terms of Yahweh, and that such thinking could lead to vacillation in his uses of the title "Lord." Such a debate lies beyond the scope of this book. However, due to the ambiguity that exists with Mark's identification of Jesus as "lord," it seems prudent to conclude that at the very least "lord" does not play a prominent role as an explicit christological title in Mark.

TITLES AND THE IDENTITY OF THE MARKAN JESUS

As discussed above, titles alone are not solely determinative of Mark's understanding of Jesus' identity, nor can they provide the totality of Mark's Christology, a Christology that is ultimately constructed through Mark's narrative. But christological titles are an important piece to Mark's Christology, and they do function to identify the Markan Jesus. Here I have considered the major christological titles in Mark, the knowledge of such titles that Mark's audience likely brought to the text, and evidence from the Markan text to help us best understand those titles. It is my contention that all of Mark's major christological titles (Messiah, Son of God, Son of Man, and Son of David) are largely synonymous and to a certain extent are interchangeable for the Markan evangelist and reader. Each title conveys Jesus' identity as God's final eschatological agent and ruler. Thus I conclude that these different christological titles do not reflect competing or contrasting under-standings of Jesus (e.g., Son of Man as the suffering Messiah versus Son of God as the powerful Messiah) but basically convey a singular identity.

Certain titles might convey or imply a particular nuance regarding Jesus' messianic identity. For example, "Son of Man" draws on the apocalyptic visions of Daniel 7:13 and thus depicts Jesus as a universal messianic ruler. As argued above, Mark seems to use "Son of David" to emphasize the priestly authority of Jesus' messianic identity. While keeping such nuances in view, I will read the christological titles of Mark's narrative as conveying Jesus' identity as God's es-chatological agent and messianic ruler. My analysis of Mark's narrative will then consider how the narrative presents Jesus as just such a Messiah.

CHRISTOLOGICAL TITLES AND FLAVIAN PROPAGANDA

There is little in the Markan titles for Jesus that necessitates understanding these titles as an attempt to respond to the propaganda of Vespasian. These titles can all be understood on their own apart from any Roman imperial context. With that said, two of the titles addressed here do fit particularly well with the pro-posed reconstruction of Mark's audience. Mark's claim that Jesus is Messiah does fit a situation in which Flavian propaganda has claimed that Vespasian was the true fulfillment of the messianic hope that Jews found in their Scriptures. And Mark's identification of Jesus as "Son of God" could certainly be understood within a Roman imperial milieu, one in which Roman emperors were often identified as "son of God." Whether Mark intends these titles to be read against such backgrounds cannot be determined by the titles themselves but can only be determined by the Markan narrative. To this narrative I now turn.

THREE

THE POWERFUL JESUS
OF MARK 1–8

H ERE MY ASSESSMENT OF Mark's narrative Christology begins. As noted in the introduction, the method of this project is both historical and narratival. By historical and narratival, I mean that I will offer a reading of the Markan narrative from a particular historical vantage point—the vantage point of post–70 CE Roman Christians living under the shadow of Flavian propaganda. Thus my approach to the Markan text will be twofold. I will first address the Markan narrative itself, noting its major features as well as its narrative progression and development. Due to the scope of this project, this treatment of Mark's narrative will be cursory in nature, often summarizing the narrative rather than offering the detailed analysis that one might find in a commentary or monograph that is focused on a single literary unit of Mark.[1] After this basic narrative analysis, I will consider the way in which this narrative and its various christological pieces might be read by Roman Christians living in the shadow of Flavian propaganda, with particular attention given to the way in which the

---

[1]It should be noted that while this study considers the entire narrative of Mark, it is not a strict "narrative-critical" reading of Mark, one that primarily derives meaning from the text through detailed analysis of characterization, plot, or narrative space and time. This study will pay attention to the development of Mark's narrative as it would be experienced by the Markan reader. It will certainly draw on insights from strict narrative-critical analysis at certain points, but it does not intended to produce such analysis.

narrative might address propagandistic challenges. This chapter will consider the first half of Mark's narrative, Mark 1–8.

THE MARKAN INCIPIT

It is widely recognized that Mark 1:1 functions as a title or incipit for the entire Gospel of Mark. Such titles were significant in ancient literature, as they often functioned as a programmatic statement for the reader, providing a lens through which the entire text should be read.[2] Thus paying close attention to Mark's incipit should offer the reader clues as to the function and purpose of the entire Gospel.

A number of brief preliminary exegetical comments can be made about Mark's incipit: "The beginning of the good news [gospel] of Jesus Christ, the Son of God." The reference to "beginning" (ἀρχή) could be a reference to the beginning of Jesus' earthly ministry, which will be described in Mark, or it could be a reference to the entirety of Jesus' ministry as outlined in Mark, that is, what is described in this text is only the beginning of God's work, not the entirety of it. "Gospel" (εὐαγγέλιον) generally refers to good news or glad tidings and is not here used in a technical sense to refer to genre, that is to say, Mark is not identifying this work as "a Gospel." Presumably this good news is about Jesus, who is identified as the Christ or God's Messiah.[3] Jesus' identity as the Christ is then further qualified by the title "Son of God," that is, Jesus is understood as Messiah in terms of divine sonship.

However, the title "Son of God" is textually uncertain, with the phrase being absent in one significant early manuscript (Codex Sinaiticus, ℵ*). Despite this omission, the reading "Son of God" is found in good and reliable early manuscripts (Codex Vaticanus, B; Codex Alexandrinus, A; Codex Bezae, D). Yet many scholars find it more likely that a scribe added the title than omitted it. It is possible, however, that the omission was accidental, as a scribe would have been looking at a list of six genitive words, with the sacred names abbreviated

---

[2]For the function of both incipits and prologues in ancient literature, see D. Earl, "Prologue-Form in Ancient Historiography," in *ANRW* 1:22, 843-56, and D. E. Smith, "Narrative Beginnings in Ancient Literature and Theory," *Semeia* 52 (1990): 1-9.

[3]Some interpreters have proposed that Jesus is the subject of the good news rather than the object, i.e., the proclaimer of the good news rather than the content of the good news. Such a conclusion does seem to work with the narrative, as Jesus will proclaim the kingdom of God and call people to believe in it as "good news" (Mk 1:15). At the same time, Jesus is the primary subject of Mark's Gospel, making it plausible that Jesus is better understood as the object of the good news. Both readings are plausible, and perhaps the reader is meant to understand Jesus in both ways.

and listed without spaces between them—ΙΥΧΥΥΥΘΥ.[4] This textual issue is impossible to resolve with any certainty, but there is adequate reason to accept "Son of God" as original to Mark's incipit, and I will cautiously move forward accepting the longer reading.

Thus Mark's incipit establishes Jesus' identity as God's Messiah (and plausibly Son of God) and clearly indicates that Mark has a strong christological interest. But such a conclusion is rather generic and gives the reader little insight into how Mark might understand these titles or to what ends these titles are used in Mark. To glean more from Mark's incipit, attention must be given to the possible backgrounds against which the language of the incipit could be read. Many interpreters have argued that the language of Mark's incipit finds meaning against the background of Isaiah's Servant Song, in which "the one who proclaims good news" (εὐαγγελιζόμενος, a participle from the same root as the noun εὐαγγελίον, "good news") is prominent (e.g., Is 40:9 [2x]; 41:27 [Masoretic Text]; 52:7 [2x]; 60:6; 61:1). The "one who proclaims good news" announces God's victory over the enemies of Israel (Is 41:27) and the reestablishment of God's righteous reign over Israel (Is 40:9-10; 52:7). That the incipit is followed by a citation from Isaiah's Servant Song (Is 40:3) serves to strengthen the connection between Mark's incipit and "the one who proclaims good news" in Isaiah. Such a conclusion is also supported by the first words spoken by the Markan Jesus, who enters Galilee saying, "The time is fulfilled, and the kingdom of God has come near; repent, and believe in the good news" (Mk 1:15). Thus through the incipit Mark is intentionally identifying Jesus as the one who both proclaims and establishes the Isaianic good news.

But other interpreters have noted that the language of the Markan incipit strongly echoes the language of the Roman imperial world. Εὐαγγέλιον was a word regularly associated with Roman emperors. It was often used to describe their birth, political ascension, and military victories. Josephus writes that on receiving the news of Vespasian's rise to power, "every city kept festivals for the good news [εὐαγγέλια] and offered sacrifices on his behalf."[5] He also writes, "On reaching Alexandria, Vespasian was greeted by the good news [εὐαγγέλια] from Rome and by embassies of congratulation from every quarter of the world, now

---

[4]For discussion see Bruce M. Metzger, *A Textual Commentary on the Greek New Testament*, 2nd ed. (New York: UBS, 2002), 62.

[5]Josephus, *J.W.* 4, trans. H. St. J. Thackeray, LCL, vol. 3 (Cambridge, MA: Harvard University Press, 1928).

his own."[6] But perhaps most significant is the Priene Calendar Inscription, written in honor of the emperor Augustus:

> Since Providence, which has ordered all things and is deeply interested in our life, has set in most perfect order by giving us Augustus, whom she filled with virtue that he might benefit humankind, sending him as a savior, both for us and for our descendants, that he might end war and arrange all things, and since he, Caesar, by his appearance (excelled even our anticipations), surpassing all previous benefactors, and not even leaving to posterity any hope of surpassing what he has done, and since the birthday of the god [θεοῦ] Augustus was the *beginning* [ἦρξεν] of the good tidings [εὐαγγελίων] for the world that came by reason of him.[7]

Here we see a striking similarity with the Markan incipit, as both refer to the "beginning of the good tidings [*gospel*]." And while in this inscription Augustus is identified as a god, he and his successors were often given the title "son of God" (see discussion above in chapter two), a title present in the Markan incipit. If one were to remove "Jesus Christ" from the Markan incipit and replace it with "Caesar Augustus," the resulting text would be quite similar to Roman imperial inscriptions found throughout the empire. Undeniably the first century Greco-Roman reader would have recognized the presence of Roman imperial language in Mark's incipit. To such a reader it would have appeared that Mark intentionally replaced Caesar with Jesus and thus attributed to Jesus the honor that was regularly reserved for the emperor alone.

The similarities that Mark's incipit shares with both the language of Isaiah and the language of the Roman imperial world have led many interpreters to argue for one background over against the other.[8] While such a choice might seem the only way forward, both Craig Evans and I have argued for a third possibility—namely, that the Evangelist has intentionally brought together the language of both the Jewish and the Roman world.[9] The intentional merging of such language would be perfectly suited to address a crisis created by Flavian

---

[6]Josephus, *J. W.* 4.11.5, translated in ibid.

[7]For this English translation see Craig A. Evans, "Mark's Incipit and the Priene Calendar Inscription: From Jewish Gospel to Greco-Roman Gospel," *Journal of Greco-Roman Christianity and Judaism* (2000): 69 (see Greek text on page 68). For the entire Greek inscription see W. Dittenberger, ed., *Orientis Graecae Inscriptiones Selectae* (Leipizig: S. Hirzel, 1903–1905; repr., Hildesheim: Olms, 1960), 2:48-60.

[8]See Adam Winn, *The Purpose of Mark's Gospel: An Early Christian Response to Roman Imperial Propaganda*, WUNT II/245 (Tübingen: Mohr Siebeck, 2008), 97-98.

[9]See Evans, "Mark's Incipit," 77; Winn, *Purpose of Mark's Gospel*, 98-99.

propaganda, propaganda in which Vespasian had already merged Jewish messianic hope with Roman imperial realities. Mark's merging of Isaianic language (clearly understood messianically) and the language of the Roman imperial world could easily and naturally have been understood as an intentionally mirroring of and response to Vespasian's merging of these same two realities. Thus, from the outset of Mark's Gospel, he proclaims the "good news" of Jesus contra Vespasian, that Jesus is the true Messiah and fulfillment of Jewish Scriptures contra Vespasian, and that Jesus is true "Son of God" contra Vespasian. Thus I propose that through an incipit tailor made to address the crisis facing the Markan community, the Evangelist sets the agenda for the entire Gospel and provides the reader with the proper lens for reading the entire narrative.

JOHN THE BAPTIST AND JESUS

After the Markan incipit, the reader is introduced to John the Baptist, a figure established as a powerful prophet of God and one who plays a preparatory role for God's salvific work. Mark styles John after the powerful prophet Elijah, as he is dressed in a similar fashion (2 Kings 1:8). John's role is relatively minor in Mark's Gospel. Though he does not use Jesus' name, he declares that Jesus will be even greater than himself and that Jesus will baptize people with the Holy Spirit. At the baptism of Jesus the wilderness prophet fades into the background (though he reappears in Mk 6) while God declares Jesus to be his beloved son, and Jesus is anointed with the Spirit of God. Jesus is then driven into the wilderness for forty days, where he is presumably victorious over the testing of Satan and the threat of wild beasts, and is subsequently attended to by angels.

In these opening verses of Mark's narrative Jesus is presented as an impressive and powerful figure. He is greater than the powerful prophet John and will have the ability to wield the very Spirit of God. Jesus' baptism reaffirms the claim of Mark's incipit that Jesus is the "Son of God." Mark's echo of Psalm 2:7, a royal coronation psalm, presents Jesus' baptism as just such a coronation. The latter half of the divine saying, "the Beloved; with you I am well pleased," echoes Isaiah 42:1, which describes God's servant assigned to an eschatological task.[10] Thus at his baptism Jesus begins his reign as God's appointed eschatological ruler. As

---

[10]See Joel Marcus, *Mark 1–8: A New Translation with Introduction and Commentary*, AB 27 (New York: Doubleday, 2000), 166; M. E. Boring, *Mark*, NTL (Minneapolis: Fortress, 2006), 45-46.

God's ruler, Jesus is victorious over both spiritual and physical opposition, and he regains his strength from the aid of divine agents. It is this powerful figure who will enter Galilee and dominate the first half of Mark's Gospel.

THE GALILEAN MINISTRY

In Mark 1:15 Jesus enters Galilee proclaiming the "good news" of the coming kingdom of God. With Jesus' recent appointment as God's ruler, the reader might rightfully conclude that Jesus should be understood as the ruler of this kingdom, though he is ruling on behalf of God himself. The narrative that follows this proclamation of the kingdom of God is dominated by the powerful actions of Jesus, including healings, exorcisms, power over nature, and the power to multiply food. Interspersed with these powerful actions are accounts of people's reactions to Jesus, both positive and negative, and Jesus' teaching on the nature of the kingdom of God. Throughout this portion of the narrative there are persistent questions about Jesus' identity, with some perceiving it clearly and others failing to do so.

As I noted in the introductory chapter, most narrative assessments of Mark have tended to give narrative priority to the various responses to Jesus throughout the Galilean ministry, with the powerful deeds of Jesus often treated as mere vehicles for addressing discipleship and proper responses to Jesus. As such the miracles of Jesus often play a minor role in narrative assessments of Mark's Christology. Such an approach to understanding the Jesus of Mark's Galilean ministry seems tragically misguided, as Jesus' deeds of power seem to dominate the narrative space of the first eight chapters of Mark's Gospel. That Mark devotes such space to Jesus' great deeds of power suggests that those deeds of power are intended to communicate important aspects of Jesus' identity. To be sure, people's responses to Jesus' deeds of power are important for the Markan narrative, but are they truly primary over the powerful deeds of Jesus? I propose that the powerful deeds of Jesus are primary for Mark's presentation of Jesus and that the reactions to these deeds often function both to illustrate the significance of the deeds themselves and to identify the proper response to such deeds. Often the reader is pushed to make an assessment about what the deeds mean for Jesus' identity, as questions about his identity often accompany his deeds of power.

To illustrate, I offer a narrative overview of a section of Mark's Galilean ministry, Mark 1:21–3:35. This section of Markan text begins with Jesus exorcising a demon through a verbal command. This episode illustrates for the reader an important part of Jesus' identity as God's Messiah and Son—that he possesses extreme power, including power over the supernatural realm that opposes God. The response of those present for the exorcism, "What is this? A new teaching—with authority! He commands even the unclean spirits, and they obey him" (Mk 1:27), both magnifies the significance of Jesus' power and raises the question of its nature and origin, both of which the reader already knows are related to Jesus' identity as God's Messiah. This pericope is followed by Jesus healing Peter's mother-in-law, another sign of the scope of Jesus' messianic power (Mk 1:29-31). These powerful deeds performed by Jesus presumably lead to a high level of recognition and popularity, as the entire city brings their sick and demon possessed to Jesus, all of whom he heals (Mk 1:32-34). Again the extreme power of Jesus' messianic identity is on display for Mark's readers. Jesus then leaves Capernaum and takes his powerful messianic ministry to other villages. In one of these villages, Jesus encounters a leper, whom he heals, and as a result Jesus' popularity grows even greater.

This series of miracles culminates in Jesus' healing of a paralytic (Mk 2:1-12). In this pericope Jesus' popularity has reached such a height that those who wish to see him cannot even make it to the front door, and thus they have to resort to creating a hole in the roof. While the previous miracles in this series have primarily focused on Jesus' power alone, this episode also addresses Jesus' identity and the origin of the power he possesses. Instead of healing the paralytic, Jesus tells him that his sins have been forgiven. This declaration elicits a negative internal reaction among the scribes, who attribute blasphemy to Jesus and ask who can forgive sins but God (Mk 2:7). These thoughts allow the Markan Jesus to address both the scope of his power and his identity. Jesus asks, "Which is easier, to say to the paralytic, 'Your sins are forgiven,' or to say, 'Stand up and take your mat and walk'?" (Mk 2:9). While the answer to the question could be (and has been!) debated, the point seems to be that both tasks are extremely difficult—and the Markan Jesus will demonstrate his ability to accomplish both. Jesus then says, "But so that you may know that the Son of Man has authority on earth to forgive sins . . . I say to you, stand up, take your mat and go to your home" (Mk 2:10-11).

This statement of Jesus accomplishes two things. First, through healing the paralytic, Jesus demonstrates that his power extends beyond healing to forgiving sins as well. Second, Jesus links his power, presumably the power both to heal and to forgive sins, to his identity as the Son of Man. Here Jesus not only answers the scribes' questions in the present pericope but also answers the question of those who witnessed his first exorcism (Mk 1:27). Here Jesus identifies himself as the Son of Man for the first time, and as I argued previously, the context of this first self-identification precludes interpreting "Son of Man" in a generic way, that is, myself or one like me. The intention of Jesus' statement seems to be an explanation of the scope of the Son of Man's power on earth, power that presumably, to the surprise of Jesus' audience, includes the power to forgive sins. This statement by Jesus presumes that his audience knows what "Son of Man" he is talking about, otherwise his explanation of the scope of the Son of Man's power becomes unintelligible. Jesus' statement makes perfect sense as a statement about the scope of the divine power and authority granted to the eschatological "Son of Man" in Daniel (Dan 7:13-14), a figure that Mark presupposes both the characters in his narrative and his readers are familiar with. Thus I contend that the Markan Jesus is identifying himself as God's Messiah in this passage. Literarily, the passage functions as a culmination of the series of miraculous deeds that illustrate Jesus' messianic power, but it also expands that power to include the forgiveness of sins and grounds that power in Jesus' identity as the eschatological and Danielic Son of Man.

While each of the pericopes in this block of Mark involves microlevel responses to Jesus' power (questioning the nature of his power [Mk 1:27], service to Jesus [Mk 1:31], increased popularity of Jesus [Mk 1:32-33], and skepticism and accusations of blasphemy [Mk 2:7]), I contend that Mark 2:13-28, which includes a series of three pericopes, functions as a macrolevel response to this series of miracles, one that includes contrasting responses from individuals and groups as well as further teaching from Jesus on the nature of his identity. The first pericope (Mk 2:13-17) includes two contrasting responses. The first response is that of Levi the tax collector, who correctly responds to Jesus by leaving behind his livelihood and following Jesus. But this positive response becomes the opportunity for a negative response, as the scribes and Pharisees question Jesus' choice to eat with tax collectors and sinners. Jesus responds by communicating that the scope of his messianic ministry involves the restoration of sinners. It seems likely that this statement of Jesus should be understood within the context of Jesus as the Son of Man who on earth possesses the divine prerogative to forgive sins.

The second pericope (Mk 2:18-22) includes another negative response to Jesus, one from the disciples of John and the disciples of Pharisees, who question why Jesus and his disciples do not fast. To this negative response Jesus replies with a series of short parables that illustrate his messianic significance. The implications of the bridegroom parable seem quite clear. Just as fasting would be inappropriate at a wedding, so also is it inappropriate when God's messianic agent is present. Thus Jesus' messianic identity and presence are so significant that they demand a cessation of fasting.

A similar negative response follows in the third pericope (Mk 2:23-28), as the scribes and Pharisees accuse Jesus' disciples of breaking the Sabbath. In response Jesus criticizes what he perceives to be an overly strict interpretation of the Sabbath, but he also identifies himself as one whose significance supersedes that of the Sabbath, declaring that as Son of Man he is "lord even of the sabbath." Again, the scope of Jesus' messianic identity and power is expanded to include lordship over the Sabbath.

This pattern of providing signs that explain and illustrate Jesus' messianic power and identity, followed by examples of responses and interpretations of Jesus' identity, continues throughout the Galilean ministry. The miracles of Mark 3:1-12 are followed by response and interpretation in Mark 3:13-35. The miracles of Mark 4:35–5:43 are followed by response and interpretation in Mark 6:1-29. The miracles of Mark 6:30-56 are followed by the response of Mark 7:1-23.[11] Again, even within the miracle episodes themselves, microlevel responses to Jesus are provided (Mk 3:6; 4:41; 5:20). And the macrolevel responses often include both positive and negative examples of response to Jesus. The religious leaders of Israel consistently respond negatively, while the response of the populace is often mixed. Mark's presentation of Jesus' disciples is also mixed. At times they are presented as responding correctly, by leaving what they have to follow Jesus, by accepting positions as "apostles," and by exercising the power that Jesus has entrusted to them. But often they show a lack of understanding and faith, for which they are criticized (Mk 4:13, 38-40; 5:31; 6:37, 51-52; 7:17-18).

---

[11]I must be clear that I am not arguing that such a division of the Markan text necessarily represents the narrative structure of Mark. There are other themes that are woven through this material and play a significant role in Mark's narrative flow (e.g., interaction with Gentiles versus Jews, foreshadowing of Jesus' death, public versus private healings, and sea crossings). Here I am simply illustrating that Mark seems to consistently juxtapose powerful deeds of Jesus with responses to Jesus, and such is a narrative creation of the Markan Evangelist.

This pattern of juxtaposing Jesus' deeds of power and with people's responses culminates in Mark 7:24–8:21. Mark 7:24–8:9 records three miracles: the exorcism of the Syro-Phoenician woman's daughter, the healing of a deaf-mute man, and the feeding of the four thousand. This series of miracle episodes is then followed by a scene in which Jesus instructs his disciples about proper response to his identity. While the scene is immediately juxtaposed with the miracles of Mark 7:24–8:9, it seems to function as a culminating statement about responses to Jesus' identity throughout the entirety of Mark's Galilean ministry. This response episode begins with Jesus encountering Pharisees who ask Jesus for a sign, a request that Jesus denies (Mk 8:11-13). The reader perceives the irony of this request by the Pharisees, as Jesus has provided countless signs demonstrating his identity from the beginning of the Galilean ministry, none of which have been accepted by the Pharisees. The question itself then highlights the lack of faith and proper response illustrated by the Pharisees. This interaction with them is followed by Jesus and his disciples crossing the sea (Mk 8:14-21), for which we are told the disciples have forgotten to bring along enough bread, that is, only one loaf (Mk 8:14). While in the boat, Jesus warns his disciples to "beware of the yeast of the Pharisees and the yeast of Herod" (Mk 8:15). While there has been a great deal of debate over what the "yeast of the Pharisees and the yeast of Herod" refers to, within the narrative a clear answer seems present—namely, a lack of faith in and opposition toward Jesus, God's Messiah. From the beginning of the narrative the Pharisees have opposed Jesus and refused to recognize him as God's Messiah—they have even conspired to kill him (Mk 3:6). And in the little we are told about Herod in Mark's Gospel, we know that he has failed to understand Jesus' true identity, and he has executed John the Baptist, God's messianic prophet. Seemingly both the Pharisees and Herod lack the proper recognition of and faith in Jesus, realities that best explain the "yeast" Jesus attributes to them.

But the Markan disciples are vexed with confusion that has regularly characterized them throughout the Galilean ministry. They fail to understand Jesus' reference to the yeast of the Pharisees and Herod and wonder whether Jesus is upset that they have not brought enough bread. This confusion brings a harsh rebuke from Jesus, who says, "Why are you talking about having no bread? Do you still not perceive or understand? Are your hearts hardened? Do you have eyes, and fail to see? Do you have ears, and fail to hear?" (Mk 8:17-18). Here the Markan Jesus echoes his earlier words about outsiders who have not received the secrets of the kingdom (Mk 4:12), implying that the failing of the twelve to understand might identify them as outsiders rather than insiders. He then reminds them of the two feeding miracles and the number of loaves left over. It seems this reminder highlights the double nature of the disciples' lack of understanding. Not only do they not understand what Jesus means by the yeast of the Pharisees and Sadducees, but this particular misunderstanding (concern over a lack of bread) reflects that they do not truly understand or have proper faith in Jesus' power and identity. As his miracles of twice multiplying loaves have illustrated, lack of bread should be of little concern for the messianic Son of Man. The pericope ends with significant doubt about the disciples' status as insiders, as Jesus asks, "Do you not yet understand?" (Mk 8:21), a question that implies that the Twelve might have already fallen victim to the yeast of the Pharisees and Herod.

The Galilean ministry ends with a final healing, one in which Jesus cures a blind man. That a healing in which sight is restored follows immediately after a pericope in which Jesus' disciples fail to demonstrate proper understanding of him is certainly intentional on the part of the Markan Evangelist. Many interpreters have noted that this blind man represents the disciples, who are victims of spiritual blindness.[12] As we will see, this pericope not only closes out the Galilean ministry, but it is a hinge passage that also functions to introduce the next literary unit in the Gospel. But as a conclusion to the Galilean ministry this pericope brilliantly brings together the two motifs juxtaposed throughout this literary unit. Here Jesus' physical healing of a blind man parallels the impending spiritual healing of the Twelve, who to this point in the narrative have failed to consistently respond properly to the miraculous deeds that illustrate Jesus' true identity.

In this brief narrative analysis I have sought to demonstrate that the miraculous deeds of Jesus, deeds that dominate the Galilean ministry, play a primary rather than secondary role in Mark's presentation of Jesus. These deeds establish Jesus as a Messiah of extreme power, who can cure disease, raise the dead, exorcise and command supernatural demons, calm the winds and the waves, walk on water, multiply food, and give sight to the blind. The sheer amount of narrative attention given to these miracles demonstrates that they play a major rather than minor role in Mark's characterization of Jesus as God's Messiah and Son. For the reader these deeds both verify and explain the declaration of the Markan incipit.

---

[12]For example, see Francis J. Moloney, *The Gospel of Mark* (Peabody, MA: Hendrickson, 2002), 163; Boring, *Mark*, 233; et al.

But at the same time these powerful deeds are inextricably linked to various responses to Jesus, responses that are also prominent throughout the Galilean ministry. However, these responses cannot and should not be given narrative priority over Jesus' deeds of power. In fact these responses should be seen as predicated on correctly or incorrectly understanding the significance of these powerful deeds for properly establishing Jesus' identity. Some characters, such as the scribes and the Pharisees, witness Jesus' great deeds but fail to accept him as God's Messiah, attribute his powerful deeds to the work of Satan (Mk 3:22), and conspire to kill him (Mk 3:6). Some characters, particularly minor characters such as the woman with the issue of blood (Mk 5:25-34), the Syro-Phoenician woman (Mk 7:24-30), and Bartimaeus (Mk 8:22-26), respond favorably to Jesus' powerful deeds, rightly concluding from them that Jesus is God's Messiah, and as a result trust in Jesus to heal them. But characters such as the Markan disciples are more ambivalent, at times demonstrating faithful response to Jesus' powerful deeds (e.g., leaving everything to follow him and successfully casting out demons through the power he grants them) yet also at times failing to understand the significance of his powerful deeds and the implication of them deeds for proper recognition of Jesus' identity. The conclusion of the Galilean ministry suggests that such blindness exhibited by the Markan disciples puts them in close company with the scribes and the Pharisees who willfully oppose Jesus.

I would agree with the many Markan interpreters who perceive these various responses to Jesus as playing a heuristic role for Mark's readers.[13] The scribes and Pharisees function as negative examples that are not to be emulated, while the minor characters demonstrate models of faithful discipleship worthy of imitation.[14] But what is to be made of the Markan disciples? Many have concluded that the disciples are the characters in whom Mark's readers will best see themselves. Their current stance toward Jesus is one of ambivalence, marked by a certain degree of faithfulness but also marked by a lack of properly understanding and

---

[13]For example, see J. R. Donahue, *The Theology and Setting of Discipleship in the Gospel of Mark*, 1983 Père Marquette Theology Lecture (Milwaukee: Marquette University Press, 1983); Robert Meye, *Jesus and the Twelve: Discipleship and Revelation in Mark's Gospel* (Grand Rapids: Eerdmans, 1968); E. Best, *Disciples and Discipleship* (Edinburgh: T&T Clark, 1986); R. C. Tannehill, "The Disciples in Mark: The Function of a Narrative Role," in *The Interpretation of Mark's Gospel*, ed. Mark Telford, Issues in Religion and Theology 7 (Philadelphia: Fortress, 1985), 134-57; Elizabeth Struthers Malbon, *In the Company of Jesus: Characters in Mark's Gospel* (Louisville: Westminster John Knox, 2000).

[14]See Elizabeth Struthers Malbon, "The Major Importance of the Minor Characters in Mark," in *The New Literary Criticism and the New Testament*, ed. Elizabeth Struthers Malbon et al., JSNTSup 109 (Sheffield, UK: Sheffield Academic, 1994).

responding to Jesus' true identity as God's Messiah. Thus, through Mark's presentation of these various characters, readers are challenged to abandon their current ambivalence and to fully embrace the faith displayed by the minor characters in Mark's Gospel. But at the same time readers are warned that such ambivalence is little different from willful opposition, and that failure to change may result in the same judgment as that awaiting the scribes, Pharisees, and Herod.

In the literary analysis above I argue that the powerful deeds of Jesus need to be recognized as primary ways in which Mark conveys Jesus' christological identity and significance. I also argue that the various responses to Jesus' deeds of power function heuristically for Mark's readers and address their own situation as disciples of Jesus. Now I will consider these two narrative strands of Mark's Galilean ministry in light of the proposed historical situation of Mark's audience—namely, Roman Christians living under the shadow of Flavian propaganda. I will first consider how the various powerful deeds of Jesus might take on added significance and meaning when read in light of this propaganda. I will then consider how the various responses of Markan characters to the Markan Jesus specifically address the situation facing Mark's readers.

THE POWERFUL DEEDS OF JESUS AND FLAVIAN PROPAGANDA

In the Galilean ministry the Markan Jesus is presented as a powerful healer, a powerful exorcist, one who has power over nature, and one who offers supernatural provision of food. Aside from presenting Jesus as a figure of great power and one who is the bearer of God's kingdom, what other significances might these powerful deeds of Jesus convey to Roman readers living under the shadow of Flavian propaganda? Here I will consider each category and illustrate ways in which the pericopes within them find significance in light of Flavian propaganda.[15]

Powerful healer. Perhaps more than any other trait, the Galilean ministry emphasizes Jesus as a powerful healer. The Galilean ministry records seven specific healings performed by Jesus (Mk 1:29-34, 40-45; 2:1-12; 3:1-6; 5:21-43; 7:31-37; 8:22-26). At three different points the narrative describes scenes in which the masses bring their sick to Jesus and he heals them (Mk 1:32-34; 3:9-10; 6:53-56). These healings by Jesus are both diverse and impressive, including the healing of the deaf, paralyzed, blind, deformed, and diseased. Yet perhaps most

---

[15]The discussion below is an updated reworking of material first published in my *Purpose of Mark's Gospel*, 180-86.

impressive of all is Jesus' ability to raise the dead. While this résumé of healings would certainly have impressed the ancient reader and communicated the presence of divine power in the ministry of Jesus, these healings take on new significance when considered in light of Flavian propaganda. As noted previously, supernatural healings played a significant role in the propaganda of Vespasian. When Vespasian was in Alexandria, he was credited with performing two healings, restoring the sight of a blind man and restoring a man's disfigured hand.[16] It is noteworthy that the Markan Jesus performs these same miracles in the Galilean ministry. But even more significant is that both the Markan Jesus and Vespasian restore a man's sight through the use of spittle! While many interpreters have noted this similarity, few have drawn any intentional significance from this seemingly striking parallel.[17]

If Mark is writing to Roman Christians living under the shadow of Flavian propaganda, propaganda that includes the emperor Vespasian restoring the sight of the blind with spittle, Mark's inclusion of a story in which Jesus also heals in the same manner is surely of particular significance. It seems implausible that Mark's readers would have missed this striking parallel to the propaganda that was currently circulating throughout the city of Rome. The presence within Mark's narrative of two healing miracles that directly parallel the miracles of Vespasian suggests intentionality on the part of the Evangelist. I contend that the motif of Jesus as a powerful healer functions to counter the parallel claims of healings that are found in Flavian propaganda. The Markan Jesus not only matches the powerful miracles of Vespasian by healing the blind and restoring a disfigured hand, but he also greatly exceeds them by healing the deaf, the paralyzed, the diseased, and even the dead! In this way Mark demonstrates that Jesus is superior to Vespasian and further evinces the claims made in the incipit that Jesus rather than Caesar is the true Messiah and ruler of the world.

Powerful exorcist. Not only is Jesus presented as a powerful healer in Mark's Galilean ministry, but he is also presented as a powerful exorcist. The Galilean ministry records three specific episodes in which Jesus exorcizes a demon or demons (Mk 1:23-28; 5:1-20; 7:24-30), and there are four places where Jesus' general activity as an exorcist is described (Mk 1:32-34, 39; 3:11-12, 20-30).

---

[16]For these stories see Tacitus, *Hist.* 4.81.1-3; Suetonius, *Vesp.* 7.2; Cassius Dio, *Roman History* 66.8.1.
[17]For interpreters who have drawn such significance, see Brian Incigneri, *The Gospel to the Romans: The Setting and Rhetoric of Mark's Gospel*, Biblical Interpretation Series 65 (Leiden: Brill, 2003), 170-71; Eric Eve, "Spit in Your Eye: The Blind Man of Bethsaida and the Blind Man of Alexandria," *NTS* 51, no. 1 (2008): 1-17.

"Demons" or supernatural spirits and beings were recognized by virtually everyone in the Greco-Roman world. Such beings were perceived to hold great power, power often connected with the concept of fate. It was widely believed that such beings intervened in human affairs and that they had the power to control and even torment people.[18] In light of these perceptions of "demonic" powers, Jesus' ability to control and expel them would have communicated to Mark's readers Jesus' tremendous supernatural power. While exorcisms and exorcists were known in the ancient Mediterranean world, the relative scarcity of such figures in literature outside the New Testament indicates that they were rare. The manner in which Jesus exorcises demons—by audible command alone—sets him apart from even the known exorcists of ancient literature, who regularly had to rely on incantations and magic formulas to achieve success.[19] As such Mark's portrayal of Jesus as an exorcist establishes Jesus as one with unmatched power over the supernatural realm.

While there are no traditions in which Roman emperors are associated with exorcisms or power over demonic forces, one particular exorcism account in the Mark's Galilean ministry has been recognized to have strong parallels to the Roman imperial order. In Mark 5:1-20 Jesus encounters a demoniac in the region of the Gerasa.[20] In Jesus' dialogue with the demoniac, Jesus requests the name of the demon that possesses the man, to which he receives the reply, "My name is Legion; for we are many" (Mk 5:9). The name of the demons is significant, as it finds its primary definition within the Roman imperial order. A legion was the largest Roman military unit, consisting of five to six thousand soldiers. Though each legion had its own general, the Roman emperor was the ultimate commander of these legions, and through these legions the emperor both expanded and controlled the empire.

While some might suggest that this reference to "Legion" is innocuous and merely a colloquial way of saying "many," there are many details in the pericope

---

[18]For discussion on demons in the ancient world, see Werner Foerster, "δαίμων, δαιμόνιον," *TDNT* 2:120; J. Z. Smith, "Towards Interpreting Demonic Powers in Hellenistic and Roman Antiquity," *ANRW* 2.16.1, 425-39; D. G. Reese, "Demons: New Testament," *ABD* 2:140-42; G. H. Twelftree, "Demon, Devil, Satan," in *Dictionary of Jesus and the Gospels*, ed. Joel B. Green, Scot McKnight, and I. Howard Marshall, 1st ed. (Downers, Grove, IL: InterVarsity Press, 1992), 163-72.

[19]For example, see Tobit 8:3 and Josephus, *Antiquities* 8.45-49.

[20]The name Gerasa is textually uncertain but is the preferred reading of most Markan commentators; see Adela Yarbro Collins, *Mark: A Commentary*, Hermeneia (Minneapolis: Fortress, 2007), 263-64; Moloney, *Gospel of Mark*, 101; Boring, *Mark*, 148-49. For discussion of the relevant evidence, see Metzger, *Textual Commentary*, 72.

that suggest an intentional reference to Roman military power.[21] The word ἀγέλη, a word often used to describe military forces, is used to describe the herd of pigs.[22] Similarly, the word ὁρμάω, a word commonly used to describe the charge of soldiers, is used to describe the pigs rushing over cliffs and into the sea (e.g., see Josh 6:5; Judg 20:37; 2 Macc 9:2; 12:22). It is noteworthy that the demons do not request to remain in the man, but they request not to be driven out of the "territory." Such a request evokes the image of military units occupying a particular region. The prominent role played by pigs in this pericope also finds a striking parallel with Roman military power, as the tenth Roman legion, the legion stationed in Palestine, carried the image of a boar on its shields and banners. It was in fact this tenth legion that, in response to the Jewish revolt, destroyed the city of Gerasa and its surrounding villages. From these numerous parallels to Roman military power, the reader is invited to interpret Jesus' dramatic exorcism as a symbolic exorcism and defeat of Roman military power.[23] Through the name "Legion," Mark intertwines the identity of supernatural demonic forces with those of Roman power (a move that the author of Revelation also makes), and thus the Markan Jesus defeats both.

I argue elsewhere that through this pericope Mark presents Jesus commanding and defeating powerful legions, and in doing so seeks to counter the power of Vespasian that largely rests on his control over Rome's legions.[24] While such a conclusion may still be true, I wonder whether it falls short of recognizing the full import of the pericope's claims. As noted above, it was under the banner of a boar that the tenth legion of Rome destroyed the city of Gerasa during the Jewish Revolt. The general in command of these legions was Vespasian himself, whom Nero put in charge to put down the revolt. Thus Mark is not simply presenting Jesus as commanding and defeating powerful legions, but he has created a reversal or perhaps even an avenging of Vespasian's victory in the region of Gerasa. Through this pericope Mark is not simply countering Vespasian's command of

---

[21]For example, see W. L. Lane, *The Gospel of Mark*, New International Commentary on the New Testament (Grand Rapids: Eerdmans, 1974), 183-84; R. T. France, *The Gospel of Mark*, NIGTC (Grand Rapids: Eerdmans, 2002), 229.

[22]See Boring, *Mark*, 151.

[23]For others who interpret this pericope in light of Roman power, see Richard Horsley, *Hearing the Whole Story: The Politics of Plot in Mark's Gospel* (Louisville: Westminster John Knox, 2001), 140-41; Ched Myers, *Binding the Strong Man: A Political Reading of Mark's Story of Jesus* (Maryknoll, NY: Orbis Books, 1992), 190-92; Marcus, *Mark*, 251-52.

[24]See Winn, *Purpose of Mark's Gospel*, 183-84.

powerful legions with Jesus' similar activity, but he is presenting a reversal of Vespasian's military success, or put another way, Jesus' military victory over Vespasian. Understood in this way this Markan pericope would have been a powerful statement to Christians living under the shadow of Flavian propaganda.

Power over nature. On two occasions Mark presents Jesus as possessing power over the natural world. In Mark 4:35-41 Jesus calms a raging sea storm with a simple audible command. In Mark 6:45-52 Jesus walks on the waters of the Sea of Galilee in the middle of raging storm, and when he gets into the boat with the Twelve, the winds cease. Interpreters have proposed a wide variety of significances and backgrounds for these two pericopes (e.g., an adaptation of the Jonah narrative, Jesus as one acting like Yahweh, or a creative imitation of a Homeric episode), all of which might produce meaningful readings. But in light of my proposed reconstruction of Mark's historical setting, another strong contender emerges.

Calming sea storms and bringing peace to the seas was a common motif in propaganda of ancient rulers. Second Maccabees 9:8 describes Antiochus IV as one who believed he had the power to "command the waves of the sea." This motif shows up prominently in descriptions of Augustus, who himself claimed to bring peace to the seas by ridding them of pirates, making them safe for Roman travel.[25] Philo's description of this achievement is significant: "This is the Caesar who calmed the torrential storms on every side. . . . This is he who cleared the sea of pirate ships and filled it with merchant vessels."[26] Roman inscriptions praise Augustus as "overseer of every land and sea," a phrase that was also attributed to the emperor by the Augustan poets.[27] Augustus's successors also sought to associate themselves with such power.[28] In light of this motif Jesus' control of the winds and waves take on a political and polemical dimension. I contend that through these stories Mark not only places Jesus in the company of the greater rulers of the world but also demonstrates Jesus' superiority to them. While Augustus might bring metaphorical peace to the seas and calm the storms, Jesus is literally able to do both. Such stories would have functioned as powerful responses to Flavian propaganda and would have further demonstrated Jesus' superiority to Vespasian.

---

[25]*Res Gestae divi Augusti* 4.25.

[26]Philo, *On the Embassy to Gaius* 145-46, trans. F. H. Colson, LCL, vol. 10 (Cambridge, MA: Harvard University Press, 1962).

[27]See Peter Bolt, *Jesus' Defeat of Death: Persuading Mark's Early Readers* (Cambridge: Cambridge University Press, 2003), 132-33.

[28]See ibid., 133.

Supernatural provision of food. Mark's Galilean ministry includes Jesus' miraculous feeding of both five thousand and four thousand people with a disproportionately small amount of food. These two feeding miracles have, with good reason, been understood in terms of a variety of traditions, including the Eucharist, God's provision of manna, and Elisha's multiplication of loaves (2 Kings 4:42-44), among others. But few have considered the way in which these miracles might be understood in a Roman imperial context. In many ways the Roman emperor was regarded as patron to the citizens of Rome and client to none, save the gods, with many emperors bearing the title "Father of His Country." As such, good emperors acted as generous benefactors to the people, with such benefaction taking on greater significance during times of need. According to his *Res Gestae*, Augustus frequently gave generous gifts of money (up to four hundred sesterces) to the Roman plebeians, a group that never numbered lower than 250,000. In times of need among the people, Augustus claims to have given out generous gifts of grain to meet the need of hunger in the city.[29] As mentioned previously, when Vespasian finally secured the Principate, only a ten-day supply of grain remained in the city, a need that Vespasian met by sending grain from Alexandria (a city that was legally regarded as the personal property of the emperor).[30] And when Vespasian finally entered Rome, he gave out three hundred sesterces apiece to the plebeian population.[31]

Such generous benefaction from Roman emperors, particularly the distribution of grain to those in need, offers an intriguing background for the significance of Jesus' actions in the Markan feeding narratives. Here Jesus' actions of providing bread to people in need emulate the generous benefaction of Roman emperors who did the same thing for their own people. But the Markan Jesus not only emulates these emperors, he surpasses them. While emperors such as Augustus and Vespasian were able to use their existing abundance to address scarcity, Jesus is able to create abundance from scarcity in order to meet the needs of his people—a superior feat by any measure! The Markan reader living in the shadow of Flavian propaganda would have been unlikely to miss the similarity between

---

[29]*Res Gestae divi Augusti* 15.1-4; 18.1.

[30]See P. Garnsey, *Famine and Food Supply in the Graeco-Roman World: Responses to Risk and Crisis* (Cambridge: Cambridge University Press, 1988), 218-27; cf. Barbara Levick, *Vespasian* (New York: Routledge, 1999), 124-25. Levick also notes that the Roman plebs gave formal thanks to Vespasian in response to his gift of grain; *Vespasian*, 124n2; cf. CIL 6, 3747; see also McCrum and Woodhead, *Select Documents*, 141n468.

[31]Levick, *Vespasian*, 125.

Jesus' distribution of food and that of the new reigning emperor, particularly in light of challenges to such propaganda that precede these feeding pericopes.

RESPONSES TO THE MARKAN JESUS AND FLAVIAN PROPAGANDA

As I argued in the assessment of Mark's narrative, the various responses of different characters to Jesus likely function heuristically for Mark's readers. The disciples offer for these readers both positive and negative examples of discipleship for the purpose of shaping the readers themselves into better disciples of Jesus. Such an understanding of these responses fits quite well with readers who were living under the shadow of Flavian propaganda. As argued before, this propaganda likely led some Gentile believers, particularly recent converts, to waver in their Christian faith. Family and friends might have pointed to recent political developments such as the destruction of the Jewish temple, questioning how a commitment to such a god was still tenable, particularly when the Flavian alternative was so impressive. Such wavering Christians would have identified quite well with Mark's ambivalent disciples, who express initial faith but later demonstrate startling blindness in the face of all that they have seen Jesus do. Like the disciples in Mark, these wavering disciples had committed themselves to the crucified Jesus and had no doubt heard the traditions of his great and powerful deeds. Perhaps they had even witnessed the power of the risen Jesus in various ways through their own engagement with the Christian community. But despite such experiences, like the disciples in Mark, they were now exhibiting blindness and faithlessness. Thus, through its depiction of ambivalent disciples, Mark offers his readers a mirror in which they can see themselves and their current failings. He also offers them examples of faithful discipleship that they should follow (e.g., minor characters), along with examples of those who are enemies of the faith (e.g., the Pharisees and Herod). With regard to the latter, Mark seeks to show his readers that their ambivalence puts them in the same danger as those who openly and willfully oppose Jesus.

CONCLUSION

Here I have offered my first attempt to assemble the christological pieces of Mark's Gospel, first considering the narratival pieces in the first half of the Gospel and then considering the way in which the pieces of Mark's reconstructed historical setting might fit with these narratival pieces. In my evaluation of the former set of pieces, I contend that the miracles and powerful deeds of Jesus must be recognized as significant to the Markan narrative in and of themselves and not simply as foils for addressing particular responses to Jesus, though I do not deny such a secondary narrative function. Regarding the latter pieces, I have illustrated the particular significance of the Markan Jesus' miracles and powerful deeds when they are read from the perspective of a particular historical location— namely, that of a Roman church facing the challenging propaganda of the new Flavian dynasty. Through the presentation of this powerful Jesus, Mark deftly crafts a powerful résumé for Jesus to counter the powerful resume of Vespasian and to demonstrate that Jesus is in all ways superior to this new Roman emperor.

In the Galilean ministry Mark presents Jesus as the true Christ and true Son of God contra the propagandistic claims of Vespasian. Jesus' power is thus central to Mark's understanding of Jesus' identity and should not be separated from it (contra narrative readings such as that of Moloney). As demonstrated by previous narrative studies of Mark and my discussion above, the powerful deeds of Jesus are regularly followed by responses from various characters in the story (e.g., the disciples, Pharisees, scribes, or minor characters). These responses function heuristically for Mark's readers and were carefully crafted to challenge disciples whose faith is wavering in the face of Flavian propaganda. Through these responses the Evangelist seeks to jolt his readers, cure them from their blindness, and lead them to see the powerful Jesus as God's Son and Messiah.

FOUR

THE SUFFERING JESUS
OF MARK 8:22–10:52

MARK 8:22–10:52, which I will refer to as Mark's central section, is widely recognized as a distinct literary unit in Mark and is the focus of the present chapter. In the last chapter I offered a narrative analysis of the Markan text and then considered that text from the vantage point of Roman Christians living under the shadow of Flavian propaganda. I follow a similar pattern here. I first offer a brief narrative analysis of Mark's central section and then consider the same narrative in light of my reconstruction of Mark's historical setting.

MARK'S NARRATIVE "HINGE" BETWEEN THE GALILEAN MINISTRY AND THE CENTRAL SECTION

This literary unit begins with what I identified previously as a narrative hinge, Mark 8:22–9:1, that functions to link Mark's central section to the Galilean narrative that precedes it.[1] Jesus' healing of a blind man (Mk 8:22-26) and Peter's confession at Caesarea Philippi (Mk 8:27–9:1) function both as the culmination of the Galilean ministry and as the introduction to Mark's central section. Central to this hinge is the theme of sight. The final miracle of the Galilean ministry is

---

[1]For a similar assessment, see Francis J. Moloney, *The Gospel of Mark* (Peabody, MA: Hendrickson, 2002), 163; Adela Yarbro Collins, *Mark: A Commentary*, Hermeneia (Minneapolis: Fortress, 2007), 391; et al.

Jesus' healing of a blind man, a miracle that finds a thematic connection to the previous pericope, in which the blindness of Jesus' disciples (i.e., the failure to recognize Jesus' identity), comes to a climactic head (Mk 8:14-21; see discussion above in chapter three). Both the motif of blind disciples and Jesus' healing of a blind man have a strong narrative connection to Peter's confession at Caesarea Philippi. In one sense Peter's confession is the culmination of Mark's motif of blind disciples, as finally at Caesarea Philippi the disciples correctly identify Jesus as the Messiah for the first time—in other words, they see! But as many narrative critics have demonstrated, Peter's sight (and presumably that of all Jesus' disciples) parallels the sight of the blind man who was healed in the preceding pericope.[2] Like the initial healing of the blind man, a healing that is only partial, so Peter's recognition of Jesus' identity is only partial. More is needed for Peter to see Jesus' identity clearly. Like the blind man, Peter and the disciples will need another work of Jesus to fully restore their vision and to see Jesus' identity completely. This second work of Jesus is the focus of Mark's central section.

Before considering this second work of Jesus, a work that will bring true recognition of his identity, attention needs to be given to the partial sight expressed by Peter and the way in which Mark's reader is meant to understand Peter's confession. Some interpreters have argued that Peter's confession of Jesus as the Messiah is in some way erroneous or incorrect and that the confession simply represents a continuation of a "blind disciples" motif.[3] Such a position seems untenable given a number of features within Mark's Gospel.

First, the confession matches that of the narrator in the Gospel's incipit and thus would be recognized as both accurate and trustworthy by the reader. Second, given the widely recognized conclusion that Peter's confession intentionally parallels the healing of the blind man that immediately precedes it, the reader is led to conclude that, like the blind man who sees partially, Peter also *sees* partially. While one can conclude from this parallel that Peter's confession is in some way partial or incomplete, one would be violating the parallel by concluding that Peter's confession does not represent some sort of "seeing," even if that seeing is incomplete. Finally, there is nothing in the Markan text to suggest that Peter's confession is in any way wrong

---

[2]See for example Moloney, *Gospel of Mark*, 166-67; M. E. Boring, *Mark*, NTL (Minneapolis: Fortress, 2006), 231-32; Sharyn Dowd, *Reading Mark: A Literary and Theological Commentary on the Second Gospel* (Macon, GA: Smyth & Helwys, 2000), 84; Morna Hooker, *The Gospel According to St. Mark*, Black's New Testament Commentaries 2 (Peabody, MA: Hendrickson, 1991), 197-203.
[3]For example, see Richard Horsley, *Hearing the Whole Story: The Politics of Plot in Mark's Gospel* (Louisville: Westminster John Knox, 2001), 250-51.

(i.e., a misidentification or erroneous identification). While Jesus instructs his disciples not to tell anyone that he is the Messiah, such an instruction should not be understood as a denial of the confession itself. However one might interpret such an instruction, there is no basis for which to interpret it as a rejection of the confession. In fact it might be better read as a tacit acceptance of the confession, as Jesus' request implies that there is something to be told.

But if Peter's identification of Jesus is accurate, in what way is it incomplete or partial? The nature of Peter's lingering blindness is quickly revealed in the exchange between Peter and Jesus regarding Jesus' first passion prediction. Peter's rebuke of Jesus for the passion prediction and Jesus' subsequent identification of Peter with Satan make it quite clear to the reader that what Peter does not see clearly is Jesus' messianic mandate to suffer and die, a mandate that is inseparable from his identity.

Thus, beginning with this "hinge" passage, Mark introduces the reader to the primary purpose of his central section: that Jesus' suffering and death are a significant part of Jesus' messianic identity. Mark's central section repeatedly emphasizes the connection between Jesus' messianic ministry and identity and Jesus' suffering and death (Mk 9:9-10, 30-32; 10:32-34, 35-45). But closely related to this emphasis on Jesus' suffering and death is an emphasis on the implication of Jesus' suffering for his disciples. Like their master, Jesus' disciples must embrace suffering and death in order to truly follow him (Mk 8:34-38; 10:35-40). The humility, dispossession, sacrifice, and service that characterize Jesus' suffering and death must be embraced by his disciples (Mk 9:33-37, 42-50; 10:1-12, 13-16, 17-31, 41-45). Thus it seems for the Markan narrative that truly "seeing" Jesus requires that he be seen in light of these realities. Yet while the disciples are finally able to recognize Jesus as Messiah after the Galilean ministry, they consistently fail to see Jesus fully throughout Mark's central section, as they are confused by his passion predictions and persistently pursue greatness and authority over humility and service.

The Evangelist deftly bookends this central section with stories in which Jesus heals a blind man. As discussed above, the first story recounts a two-stage healing, one in which the man's vision is partially restored before being completely restored. Through this story the Evangelist prefigures Peter's confession of Jesus as the Messiah, a confession that represents a partial healing of Peter's (and the disciples') blindness but not a complete healing. The central section that follows shows the reader what is necessary for seeing Jesus fully, mainly his suffering and death and the costly discipleship it demands. The central section concludes with a second account of Jesus healing a blind man, though in this second episode the blind man is healed instantly rather than in two stages. While the first healing story prefigures disciples who do not fully see, the second likely prefigures disciples who fully see. Those disciples in Mark's community who hear and embrace the message of Mark's central section are like the second blind man, whose sight is completely restored. Unlike the disciples of Mark who continue to see only in part, these disciples see in whole.

COMMON CHRISTOLOGICAL INTERPRETATIONS OF MARK'S CENTRAL SECTION

Mark's central section is generally given great weight in the assessment of Mark's Christology. As noted in the introductory chapter, redaction critics often saw this passage as presenting an intentional corrective to the "Christology" of power that dominated the first half of Mark's Gospel. While narrative critics have rejected such a "corrective" reading of this section, the vast majority still attribute greater christological significance to Mark's central section than they do Mark's Galilean ministry. It is frequently argued that the central section shifts its presentation of Jesus away from power and toward suffering and death, and that such a shift is indicative of Mark's christological perspective (i.e., suffering and death is primary over power and glory in Mark's narrative Christology). Often related to such a perspective is a particular interpretation of Mark's "sight and blindness" motif. Truly *seeing* Jesus involves seeing him in terms of his suffering and death, while blindness is associated with seeing Jesus in terms of power and glory—the Markan Jesus is Messiah primarily in terms of the former rather than the latter. Thus the reader must avoid the mistake of Peter, which is often understood as perceiving Jesus as Messiah in terms of popular messianic ideas, most of which would be characterized by power and glory.[4]

While I strongly affirm much of the narrative analysis that has been provided by recent interpreters of Mark (analysis reflected above), I object to many of the christological conclusions that are often drawn from that analysis. While Mark's central section certainly represents a major shift in Mark's Gospel, I reject the conclusion that the shift is one toward suffering and death *and away* from power and glory. A shift toward suffering and death is quite clear, as this section not only

---

[4]For example, see Moloney, *Gospel of Mark*, 166; R. T. France, *The Gospel of Mark*, NIGTC (Grand Rapids: Eerdmans, 2002), 330-31; John R. Donahue and Daniel J. Harrington, *The Gospel of Mark*, Sacra Pagina 2 (Collegeville, MN: Liturgical Press, 2002), 262-66; Collins, *Mark*, 402.

includes the first explicit mention of Jesus' death but also is structured around three passion predictions. But a move *toward* suffering and death does not necessarily imply a move *away* from power and glory. The Markan narrative itself resists such a conclusion. First, the Evangelist devotes the first eight chapters of the Gospel to presenting a powerful Jesus, a Jesus who is able to heal the sick, exorcise legions of demons, raise the dead, calm storms, walk on water, and create massive amounts of food. As argued in the previous chapter, these activities of Jesus, activities that communicate overwhelming power, play a vital role in Mark's Christology. To deny such a conclusion would minimize virtually half of the Markan narrative.

Second, after Jesus' first passion prediction, the powerful Jesus is not eclipsed by the suffering Jesus, but rather they coexist throughout the rest of the narrative. Based on the way some interpreters speak of the second half of Mark's Gospel, one might conclude that the Jesus of power has simply vanished, only to be replaced by a Jesus characterized by suffering.[5] Surely there is a greater emphasis on Jesus' suffering in the second half of the Gospel than there is in the first half, but the powerful Jesus is still quite present. Perhaps most telling is the transfiguration narrative that immediately follows Jesus' first passion prediction (Mk 9:2-8). Here Jesus' glorious identity is revealed, he is elevated above Israel's greatest prophets, and he receives a divine declaration of sonship. Such a presentation of Jesus is consistent with the powerful Jesus that dominates the first half of Mark's Gospel. The placement of this pericope immediately after the first passion prediction might suggest a narratival attempt to keep the reader from concluding that Jesus' suffering mitigates or conflicts with his identity as God's powerful son. In addition to the transfiguration, numerous examples of a powerful and glorious Jesus can be found, including Jesus' exorcism of a powerful demon, his triumphal entry into Jerusalem, his symbolic judgment of Jerusalem, his destruction of a fig tree, his thwarting of Jewish religious authorities, and his prophetic power. Even the way in which Mark introduces Jesus' death into the narrative, via a prediction from Jesus himself, would have been understood in the first-century Mediterranean world as a sign of significant power.[6]

---

[5]For example, see Moloney, *Gospel of Mark*, 182, "Subsequent to the wonder of the transfiguration, Jesus has led the thoughts of Peter, James, and John back to the message which has begun . . . and will continue to dominate 8:31–15:47: there can be no glory without the cross."

[6]Philo, *On the Life of Moses* 2.51 §§291-290; Suetonius, *Domitianus* 15.3; Iamblichus, *De vita pythagorica* 136. See David Aune, *Prophecy in Early Christianity and the Ancient Mediterranean World* (Grand Rapids: Eerdmans, 1983), 178; A. B. Kolenkow, "Miracle and Prophecy," *ANRW* 2:23.2, 1470-1506, esp. 1494.

Thus, while many narrative critics are correct to emphasize the christological import of the suffering Jesus who is introduced in Mark's central section, any attempt to mitigate or marginalize the christological import of the powerful Jesus in favor of the suffering Jesus is in my estimation misguided and does not recognize the totality of the christological content of Mark's narrative. Any narrative assessment of Mark's Christology must affirm both poles of Mark's presentation of Jesus. As noted in the introduction, some narrative critics have successfully affirmed both aspects of Mark's Christology, yet those who do so ultimately propose an irreconcilable tension between the two.[7] They affirm that the Markan Jesus is at the same time both a suffering and a powerful Messiah but make no effort to resolve the tension. To be sure, holding these two apparently paradoxical christological poles in tension with each other is to be preferred to privileging one over the other. But finding a unity between the two, something few interpreters have attempted, would, in my estimation, be preferable to unresolvable tension.

At this point of perceived paradoxical tension within the Markan narrative, one's interpretive methodology becomes significant. If one approaches the text through the methods of narrative criticism, that is, without significant concern for the original setting of the Gospel, then there is little recourse for resolving this narrative tension when the text itself provides no perceivable way forward. But if one attempts to read Mark's narrative in light of a reconstructed historical setting, such a reconstruction might provide the necessary piece(s) of the puzzle to resolve what appears to be unresolvable narrative tension. Thus the method I have employed to this point in reading Mark might prove fruitful in resolving the narrative tension between these two apparently disparate pieces of Markan Christology.

What follows is an attempt to read Mark's central section in light of my reconstructed historical setting for Mark. Mark 10:42-45 is widely regarded as both the narrative and christological climax of Mark's central section, and in many ways it summarizes and epitomizes the literary unit's primary message.[8] In light of this literary function, I will begin by analyzing this particular text from the vantage point of Christians living in the shadow of Flavian propaganda,

---

[7]Elizabeth Struthers Malbon, *Mark's Jesus: Characterization as Narrative Christology* (Waco, TX: Baylor University Press, 2009), 210; Boring, *Mark*, 258, among others noted. See discussion in the introduction.

[8]For such a conclusion, see Boring, *Mark*, 297-98; Moloney, *Gospel of Mark*, 203-8; Collins, *Mark*, 498; et al.

and then work backward from this analysis to an assessment of the narrative function of the entire central section. But before I offer analysis of this significant Markan text, I must devote significant attention to the political ideology of Mark's Roman readers, as such an ideology sheds light on the function and purpose of Mark 10:42-45.

MARK 10:42-45: CONSIDERING A POLITICAL CONTEXT[9]

Despite the vast amount of scholarship devoted to Mark 10:42-45 in the past century, virtually no attention has been given to the way in which the Roman imperial world might inform one's reading of this text.[10] This omission is quite striking given that this passage opens with a contrast between Jesus and Roman rulers (Mk 10:42). Given the proposed setting for Mark's Gospel—specifically, Roman Christians living in the shadow of Flavian propaganda—I want to consider this climatic Markan text in light of the unique political ideology that existed in Rome, an ideology that would have been familiar to Mark's readers.

Roman political ideology and the evaluation of Roman rulers. Both a commitment to self-rule and a rejection of monarchial tyranny were deeply engrained in the Romans' memory of their own political history. Roman historians report that even the earliest Roman kings were elected by the Roman people; these kings listened to and honored the Senate, and they shared judicial and religious power. However, in response to the tyranny of King Lucius Tarquin Superbus, the Roman people revolted and subsequently established the Roman Republic.[11] With the Republic, the ideals of self-rule were formalized, and a system was established to protect the people from tyrannical rulers. Even under republican government, great power occasionally fell into the hands of a single individual, but the Roman commitment to self-rule consistently inhibited

---

[9]Much of the following material was first published in Adam Winn, "Tyrant or Servant: Roman Political Ideology and Mark 10:42-45," *JSNT* 36, no. 4 (2014): 325-52; it is used with the permission of the publisher.

[10]Both Adela Yarbro Collins (*Mark*, 499) and Dowd (*Reading Mark*, 112-13) give brief consideration to the notion of "servant kings" in Hellenistic philosophy, but neither addresses the possible significance of such a notion for reading Mk 10:42-45. David Seeley ("Rulership and Service in Mark 10:41-45," *Novum Testamentum* 35 [1993]: 234-50) analyzes Mk 10:41-45 in light of the Hellenistic concept of the ideal king as servant; however, he gives no attention to a distinctly Roman perspective.

[11]For Roman accounts of their earliest history, see Livy, *History of Rome*, book 1. For secondary literature on Rome's earliest history, see Klaus Bringmann, *A History of the Roman Republic* (Cambridge: Polity, 2007), 1-56.

monarchial ambitions. The example of a figure such as Cincinnatus—who, though holding absolute political power, handed it over to the Roman Senate— loomed large in the Roman estimation of political virtue.[12]

However, with the dynasts of the late republican period, a precedent was set that ended true "republican rule." The accomplishments of Julius Caesar made it quite clear that Rome and its empire could and would be controlled by a single figure. Figures such as Julius Caesar and Octavian, who achieved complete control in Rome, found themselves in a difficult position. In all ways they were autocrats who had absolute power at their fingertips, but their power was over a people in whom republican virtues and ideals were deeply ingrained. Julius Caesar emphasized the former and neglected the latter, a decision that was likely responsible for his assassination.[13]

Perhaps learning from his adoptive father's mistake, Octavian cleverly balanced these conflicting realities by employing a strategy of *recusatio*. This strategy involved resisting or protesting all realities that might convey one's possession of absolute political power, but it did not involve the surrender of any true power.[14] The strategy was broad in scope, thoroughly pervading both the private and public life of Augustus. For the most part *recusatio* was embraced by Augustus's successors, though a few boldly rejected it. This strategy is seen in the histories produced by Suetonius and Cassius Dio, with additional evidence of its employment in the writings of Seneca, Philo, and Tacitus. In their evaluations of Rome's emperors, these authors regularly consider the employment of *recusatio* in six distinct areas: (1) attitudes and actions related to public offices and titles, (2) attitudes and actions related to public honors, (3) attitudes and actions toward the Roman Senate and *populus* (people), (4) attitudes and actions toward *lex* (law) and *libertas* (liberty), (5) attitudes and actions toward public appearance and private residence, and (6) actions and identity as benefactors. Emperors who consistently practiced *recusatio* in these areas generally receive favorable evaluations, while emperors who did

---

[12]See Livy, *History of Rome* 3.26-29.

[13]See Suetonius, *Divus Julius* 76.1; Cassius Dio, *Roman History* 44.4-6. For discussion, see R. A. G. Carson, "Caesar and the Monarchy," *Greece & Rome* 4, no. 1 (1957): 53, and V. Ehrenberg, "Caesar's Final Aims," *Classical Philology* 68 (1964): 149-61.

[14]For discussion on the strategy of *recusatio*, see J. Béranger, "Le Refus du Pouvoir," *Museum Helveticum* 5 (1948): 178-96; A. Wallace-Hadrill, "Civilis Princeps: Between Citizen and King," *JRS* 72 (1982): 32-48; A. Yakobson and H. M. Cotton, "Caligula's *Recusatio Imperii*," *Historia: Zeitschrift für Alte Geschichte* 34, no. 4 (1985): 497-503.

not always receive negative evaluations. Thus it seems that the employment of *recusatio*, particularly in these six areas, forms a distinct motif or trope in Roman literary assessments of its own emperors. Here I will review the ways that Roman emperors employed *recusatio* in these six distinct areas, and from that analysis the expectations of the Roman people for their rulers will emerge.

Attitudes and actions related to public offices and titles. In the ancient Roman world political power was closely associated with public offices and titles. Certain titles and offices had a long and respected place in Roman republican government, while others were perceived as antithetical to such a government. Thus it is noteworthy that, beginning with Augustus, there was a consistent effort made by Roman emperors to resist and/or reject public offices and titles that would have been offensive to Roman republican sensibilities. For example, Augustus rejected efforts to make him dictator for life and a permanent consul.[15] He also rejected the title "Lord" and long resisted the title "Father of His Country."[16] Such an attitude toward public offices and honorific titles was adopted by Augustus's successors Tiberius, Claudius, and Vespasian.[17] Roman emperors who did not follow this Augustan pattern but instead accepted and/or demanded titles that violated republican sensibilities were remembered as tyrants.[18]

Actions and attitudes related to public honors. Monarchial ambition and identity could also be communicated through particular public honors. Honors such as public worship, temples, priests, and statues were closely associated with the Eastern kings of Persia, Greece, and Egypt, making them offensive to Roman sensibilities. It is therefore noteworthy that Augustus rejected all such honors, refusing temples and statues in his honor.[19] According to Augustus himself, he

---

[15]Suetonius, *Aug.* 52.2; cf. Tacitus, *Ann.* 1.9; *Res Gestae divi Augusti* 5.3.

[16]Suetonius, *Aug.* 53.1; cf. Philo, *On the Embassy to Gaius* 23.254; Suetonius, *Aug.* 52.1; *Res Gestae divi Augusti* 5.1.

[17]For Tiberius, see Suetonius, *Tib.* 24.1; 26.2; Cassius Dio, *Roman History* 57.2.1; 57.8.1. For Claudius, see Suetonius, *Claud.* 12.1; Cassius Dio, *Roman History*, 60.3.2. For Vespasian, see Suetonius, *Vesp.* 12.

[18]Julius Caesar accepted the title and office of dictator for life, and his assassination was perceived to be motivated by fears that he intended to replace the republic with a monarchy (Suetonius, *Divus Julius* 76.1; Cassius Dio, *Roman History* 44.4-6). Caligula claimed, in reference to himself, "Let there be one Lord and King," and in essence he replaced the principate with a monarchy (Suetonius, *Cal.* 22.1-3). Domitian demanded that he should be addressed, in both writing and speech, as "Our Lord and our God" (Suetonius, *Domitianus* 13.2).

[19]Suetonius, *Aug.* 52.1; Cassius Dio, *Roman History* 52.35. Tacitus seems to contradict Suetonius's testimony here, claiming that "he had left small room for the worship of heaven, when he claimed to be himself adored in temples and in the image of godhead by flamens and by priests!" (*Ann.* 1.10). Because Tacitus's testimony is so inconsistent with that of all other historians on this point, many have rejected Tacitus's claims as inaccurate, perhaps reflecting the historian's bias against

declined all but three triumphs that were voted to him by the Senate.[20] Cassius
Dio's words regarding Augustus's attitude toward public honors are noteworthy:

> As regards your subjects, then, you should so conduct yourself, in my opinion. So far
> as you yourself are concerned, permit no exceptional or prodigal distinction to be
> given you, through word or deed, either by the senate or by anyone else. For whereas
> the honor which you confer upon others lends glory to them, yet nothing can be
> given to you that is greater than what you already possess, and, besides, no little
> suspicion of insincerity would attach to its giving. No subject, you see, is ever sup-
> posed to vote any such distinction to his ruler of his free will, and since all such
> honors as a ruler receives he must receive from himself, he not only wins no com-
> mendation for the honor but becomes a laughing-stock besides. You must therefore
> depend upon your good deeds to provide for you any additional splendor. And you
> should never permit gold or silver images of yourself to be made, for they are not only
> costly but also invite destruction and last only a brief time; but rather by your bene-
> factions fashion other images in the hearts of your people, images which will never
> tarnish or perish. Neither should you ever permit the raising of a temple to you.[21]

Augustus's successors Tiberius and Claudius demonstrated fidelity to Roman
political ideology by embracing this practice of rejecting excessive honors,[22] while
emperors such as Gaius and Domitian showed no such restraint, a failure that
helped shape their remembrance as tyrants in Roman history.[23]

Actions and attitudes toward the Senate and the Roman populus. The Roman
Senate was the most conspicuous institution of the Roman Republic, and as

---

the Augustan Principate (for example, see F. R. D. Goodyear, *The Annals of Tacitus: Books 1-6*
[Cambridge: Cambridge University Press, 1972], 2:166). However, Ittai Gradel has argued that
Tacitus is referring to Augustus's desire (and perhaps instruction) to be deified posthumously by
the Roman senate (*Emperor Worship and Roman Religion*, Oxford Classical Monographs [Oxford:
Oxford University Press, 2002], 276-77). For the refusal of statues, see Suetonius, *Aug.* 52.1; *Res
Gestae divi Augusti* 24.2; cf. Cassius Dio, *Roman History* 52.35.

[20] *Res Gestae divi Augusti* 4.1.

[21] Cassius Dio, *Roman History* 52.35, trans. Earnest Cary, LCL, vol. 7 (Cambridge, MA: Harvard
University Press, 1924).

[22] Tiberius and Claudius refused the voting of temples or flamens and priests in their honor (Suetonius, *Tib.* 26.1; *Claud.* 12.1; Cassius Dio, *Roman History* 57.9.1; 60.5.4). Tiberius regularly refused to
have statues made in his honor, and those that were made could not be placed among the statues
of the gods (Suetonius, *Tib.* 26.1; Cassius Dio, *Roman History* 57.9.1). For similar examples see
Suetonius, *Tib.* 26.2; Cassius Dio, *Roman History* 57.8.1; 60.5.4. Also see Ittai Gradel's analysis that
Vespasian ended the practice of worshiping the emperor's "genius" (*Emperor Worship*, 189-90).

[23] Gaius Caligula sought to be worshiped as a god and established temples and priests to facilitate
such worship (Suetonius, *Cal.* 22.1-3). Domitian erected numerous honorific statues and arches
for himself throughout the city, the number of which brought censure from the people (Suetonius, *Domitianus* 13).

such it symbolized the Roman value of self-rule more than any other political entity. An emperor's actions and attitudes toward the Senate were a barometer for measuring his commitment to Roman political ideology and his own political aspirations. By honoring and respecting the Senate, the emperor sent a clear message that he respected Roman political values and that he viewed himself not as a monarch but as the "first among equals." Conversely, emperors who disrespected or threatened the Senate demonstrated a rejection of cherished political values and betrayed monarchial ambitions.

As part of his strategy of *recusatio*, Augustus adopted the former approach in his relationship with the Senate, and this attitude of respect set a precedent for those who succeeded him. In his *Res Gestae* Augustus claims that when all power rested with him, he handed that power over to the Senate and restored the Roman Republic.[24] When meeting the Senate, Augustus refused to let the senators stand to honor him. Additionally, he addressed them all by name— behavior that communicated a high level of respect.[25] Tiberius, Claudius, and Vespasian all exhibited such respect for the Senate.[26]

Not all emperors followed this precedent set by Augustus. Caligula regularly dishonored the Senate, both openly insulting and threatening it.[27] Nero frequently disrespected the Senate and in fact strongly hinted that he intended to remove the ruling body completely.[28] Such actions are censured by Roman historians and contribute to the remembrance of these rulers as tyrants.

Lest one conclude that the strategy of *recusatio* was simply employed to appease the senatorial class, it is important to note that Roman emperors also

---

[24]*Res Gestae divi Augusti* 34. For discussion of this action by Augustus, see G. E. F. Chilver, "Augustus and the Roman Constitution 1939-1950," *Historia* 1 (1950): 408-35; E. T. Salmon, "The Evolution of Augustus' Principate," *Historia* 5 (1956): 456-78; W. K. Lacey, *Augustus and the Principate: The Evolution of the System* (Leeds, UK: Francis Cairns, 1996), 77-99; M. D. H. Clark, *Augustus, First Roman Emperor: Power, Propaganda and the Politics of Survival* (Exeter, UK: Bristol Phoenix, 2010), 91-95.

[25]Suetonius, *Aug.* 53.

[26]Tiberius described himself as a servant of the Senate, addressed the senators as "lords and masters" (while refusing the title to be applied to himself), and maintained the dignity and power of the senate by regularly bringing before it public and private matters (Suetonius, *Tib.* 27-31; Cassius Dio, *Roman History* 53.7.2; for discussion see B. Levick, *Tiberius the Politician*, rev. ed. [New York: Routledge, 1999], 82-91). Claudius likewise showed great respect to the Senate and even expanded its provincial powers (Tacitus, *Ann.* 12.5-7; Suetonius, *Claud.* 12, 25; for discussion see B. Levick, *Claudius* [New Haven, CT: Yale University Press, 1990], 93-103). Vespasian also regularly honored the Senate and recognized its governing authority by consulting it on all matters (Cassius Dio, *Roman History* 65.10.4-6).

[27]Suetonius, *Cal.* 26, 45, 48-49; Cassius Dio, *Roman History* 59.16.1, 25.5; cf. Cassius Dio, *Roman History* 59.26.3.

[28]Suetonius, *Nero* 37.

sought to recognize the authority and voice of the Roman *populus*—a significant Republican voice in its own right. Augustus regularly presented himself before the *comitia* (various groupings of the Roman *populus* that participated in electing magistrates) and engaged in the traditional act of canvassing, which involved humbly kneeling before the assembled people.[29] After the *comitia* lost their electoral power in 15 CE, public games and circuses replaced them as the official assembly of the people.[30] At such assemblies the emperor had the opportunity to hear the voice of the people and their various requests.[31] The emperor's response to the people was an opportunity to honor Roman political values by recognizing the people who theoretically shared governance. Listening and showing deference to the people was expected and thus practiced.[32]

In his praise of the emperor Trajan, Pliny the Younger describes the emperor's interaction with the people at the circus: "Requests were granted, unspoken wishes were anticipated, and he did not hesitate to press us urgently to make fresh demands; yet still there was something new to surpass our dreams. How freely too the spectators could express their enthusiasm and show their preferences without fear!"[33] Contrast this with Josephus's account of Gaius responding to the requests of the *populus*:

> At this time occurred chariot races. This is a kind of spectator sport to which the Romans are fanatically devoted. They gather enthusiastically in the circus and there the assembled throngs make requests of the emperors according to their own pleasure. . . . So in this case they desperately entreated Gaius to cut down imposts and grant some relief from the burden of taxes. But he had no patience with them, and when they shouted louder and louder, he dispatched agents among them in all directions with orders to arrest any who shouted, to bring them forward at once and to put them to death.[34]

Josephus goes on to link these actions of Gaius with the emperor's assassination only a few weeks later.

---

[29]Suetonius, *Aug.* 56. For discussion, see Wallace-Hadrill, "Civilis Princeps," 38. Such canvassing with the *comitia* was also practiced by Vitellius and Trajan (ibid.).

[30]See A. Cameron, *Circus Factions: Blues and Greens at Rome and Byzantium* (New York: Oxford University Press, 1976); Wallace-Hadrill, "Civilis Princeps," 38. Cicero indicates that the amphitheater (*spectacula*), where games and the circuses were held, was an arena for expressing popular opinion prior to the establishment of the principate (*Pro Sestio* 106, 115).

[31]See Suetonius, *Aug.* 68; *Tib.* 45; *Galba* 13.

[32]Cf. Suetonius, *Aug.* 34.2; *Claud.* 21.5; Tacitus, *Ann.* 2.77-78.

[33]Pliny the Younger, *Panegyricus* 33.2-3, trans. Betty Radice, LCL, vol. 2 (Cambridge, MA: Harvard University Press, 1969).

[34]Josephus, *Jewish Antiquities* 19.24, trans. Louis H. Feldman, LCL, vol. 8 (Cambridge, MA: Harvard University Press, 1965).

The *princeps'* display of such deference to the Roman people further demonstrates that *recusatio* was not simply a strategy designed to appease the Senate. Certain behaviors violated the virtue of *dignitas* and were thus offensive to the senatorial class.[35] But as Wallace-Hadrill notes, "Only an emperor could regard self-degradation as magnificent."[36] By showing respect to Rome's traditional republican institutions, the emperor created further separation between the outward appearance of autocratic power and his possession of such power.

Actions and attitudes toward lex *and* libertas. Under the Republic, all *libertas* ("freedom") enjoyed by the Roman people was guaranteed by Roman *lex* ("law") that was set forth by the Senate and the people. Though not a reality publicized by Augustus, under the Principate he became the guarantor of Roman *libertas* and the ultimate source of Roman *lex*. Such power could be closely linked with a monarchial identity, and the abuse of such power would be quickly linked to tyranny. As such Augustus was careful in the way he approached both realities. Regarding *libertas*, Augustus presented himself as *Libertatis Populi Romani Vindex*, "Champion of the Liberty of the Roman People."[37] Far from being a tyrant who denied liberty, he presented himself as a defender of traditional liberty. Such an identity expresses itself in Augustus's attitude toward freedom of speech. Though frequently harassed, rebuffed, and even interrupted by senators, Augustus never punished or rebuked anyone for "speaking freely or even insolently."[38] Such attitudes toward the liberty of the people were embraced by Tiberius, Claudius, and Vespasian.[39]

Regarding *lex*, Augustus worked hard to present himself as a citizen living under the law rather than as an emperor over the law. He gave no special legal privilege to family members or friends, he was a willing witness who allowed himself to be questioned in court, and he was careful to avoid behavior that would have prejudiced legal decisions.[40] By and large Tiberius followed Augustus's

---

[35]For the senatorial attitude toward canvassing the *comitia*, see Cicero, *Pro Plancio* 12, 49.

[36]Wallace-Hadrill, "Civilis Princeps," 38.

[37]This inscription can be found on Augustan coins in 27–28 BCE (M. Hammond, "*Res Olim Dissociabiles: Principatus ac Libertas*: Liberty Under the Early Roman Empire," *Harvard Studies in Classical Philology* 67 [1963]: 94-95). See also the opening line of Augustus's *Res Gestae: per quem publicam a domination factionis oppressam in libertatem vindicavi* ("and with it, I championed into liberty a state dominated by factions").

[38]Suetonius, *Aug.* 54 LCL; cf. Suetonius, *Aug.* 55-56.

[39]For Tiberius see Suetonius, *Tib.* 28. For Claudius see Hammond, "*Res Olim Dissociabiles*," 98n29. For Vespasian see ibid., 101n49.

[40]Suetonius, *Aug.* 56.

example in presenting himself as one under Roman law.[41] It seems that Claudius also followed this example.[42] Pliny's praise of Trajan indicates that this emperor also presented himself as a Roman citizen living under the authority of Roman law: "A man three times consul acted as he did at his first election: a prince showed himself no different from a commoner, an emperor no different from one of his subjects: this is surely beyond all praise."[43]

Such attempts by these emperors to present themselves as citizens who were subject to Roman law stand in stark contrast to the behavior of Caligula and Nero, both of whom boldly presented themselves as *supra leges* ("above law"). Collectively their behavior included unjust executions, taking the wives of married men, voiding legal wills, confiscating property, fraud, extortion, and blackmail.[44] Such violations of Roman law and liberty greatly contributed to both Caligula and Nero being identified as tyrants. However, by promoting the liberty of the Roman people and publicly submitting to Roman law, good emperors reinforced their identity as Rome's first citizens and created greater distance between themselves and the appearance of absolute power.

Attitudes and actions related to public appearance and private residence. Extravagant dress, spectacular entourages, and luxurious private dwellings were closely associated with the kings of Greece, Persia, and Egypt. Therefore avoiding the appearance of a monarch required the emperor to distance himself from monarchial extravagances. Augustus's behavior is telling in this regard. He dressed modestly, only wearing ordinary clothes made by the women in his household.[45] In the city he moved about on foot, without a formal entourage, and

---

[41]Suetonius, *Tib.* 31. There is some debate over Tiberius's attitude toward the law. While he seems to have followed Augustus's precedent of presenting himself as one under the authority of Roman law, he is also censured for his use of *maiestas*, a law associated with damaging the "majesty" of Rome. Tiberius seems to have used this law as a political weapon against his opponents (for a discussion of this debate see Levick, *Tiberius the Politician*, 180-200).

[42]His marriage to Agrippina is an interesting case. Given that she was Claudius's niece, the marriage—in legal terms—was incestuous. However, at Claudius's request (via Vitellius), the Senate altered the law to allow the marriage (Tacitus, *Ann.* 12.5-7; Suetonius, *Claud.* 26.3). While one could argue that Claudius used his power to supersede the law, his request to the Senate speaks to his concern to at least *appear* as one under the law. Such a concern is further affirmed by Tacitus. He tells us that when Claudius was asked whether the will of the people and the Senate might dissuade him from pursuing the marriage, the emperor acknowledged that "he was a citizen among citizens, and incompetent to resist their united will" (Tacitus, *Ann.* 12.5, trans. in John Jackson, LCL [Cambridge, MA: Harvard University Press, 1937]).

[43]Pliny the Younger, *Panegyricus*, translated in Radice.

[44]Suetonius, *Cal.* 23-26, 38; *Nero* 32-35.

[45]Suetonius, *Aug.* 78.

to avoid public ceremonies he would frequently enter and leave cities and towns at night.[46] His house, in which he lived for forty years, was unpretentious, with modest furnishings, and according to Suetonius it was barely suitable for a private citizen.[47] Little is said in the ancient sources about the dress and domicile of Tiberius, but it appears that he followed the modest practices of Augustus and avoided the extravagances of Eastern kings. Regarding Vespasian, Suetonius tells us that he embraced his humble origins and demonstrated great indifference to "pomp and outward show."[48] The modesty of such emperors stands in stark contrast to the extravagances of Caligula and Nero, extravagances that imitate those associated with Eastern monarchs.[49] Here is yet another sphere of the emperor's life in which he had the opportunity to distance himself from the appearance of absolute power. Those who used the opportunity to embrace modesty further established themselves as good emperors, while those who embraced extravagance only further confirmed their identity as monarchial tyrants.

Actions and identity as benefactor. Less directly linked to the imperial strategy of *recusatio* but no less related to Roman political ideology was the emperor's role as benefactor. As Rome's first citizen, the emperor was a patron to all and a client to none, save the gods. His generous benefaction to the Roman *populus* was expected, and his success as emperor was often evaluated in terms of the quantity and quality of that benefaction. In this regard Augustus set the bar quite high. In his *Res Gestae* Augustus provides a catalog of his remarkable acts of benefaction.[50] These acts included enormous gifts of money and food to the Roman state, improvements to the city's infrastructure, the beautification of the city and its buildings, and the construction of numerous temples and public buildings—gifts that supposedly total 2.4 billion sesterces.[51]

While no successor surpassed or even met this level of benefaction, many of Augustus's successors followed his example of generosity.[52] This generosity contrasts sharply with the wasteful spending of both Caligula and Nero. Suetonius

---

[46]Suetonius, *Aug.* 53.

[47]Suetonius, *Aug.* 77.

[48]Suetonius, *Vesp.* 12, trans. J. C. Rolfe, LCL, vol. 2 (Cambridge, MA: Harvard University Press, 1914).

[49]Suetonius, *Cal.* 22, 37, 52; *Nero* 30.

[50]Many of these acts of benefaction are also remembered by Suetonius (*Aug.* 29-30, 41) and Cassius Dio (*Roman History* 53.2; 55.10, 26).

[51]*Res Gestae divi Augusti* 15-20.

[52]Cf. Suetonius, *Claud.* 18-20; *Vesp.* 8-9.

reports that, in less than a year, Caligula wasted an enormous fortune on personal luxuries, including twenty-seven million gold pieces amassed by the
frugal Tiberius during his reign.[53] Like Caligula, Nero spent massive amounts
of money on extravagance and luxury, both for himself and his friends.[54] To
continue such spending habits, both emperors resorted to corrupt and de-
structive means of securing additional resources, including coercion to be
named in wills, confiscation of property, looting of temples, and heavy taxation.[55]
Such selfish spending had consequences for the empire, and at the time of Nero's
death the empire was at the brink of financial ruin.

Roman political ideology and the evaluation of Roman rulers: A summary.
Through this analysis of the use of both *recusatio* and generous benefaction by
the Roman emperors, two important points emerge. First, it must be concluded
that the imperial strategy of *recusatio* thoroughly pervaded the lives of Rome's
emperors, and as a result it cannot be regarded as simple and superficial lip
service to waning republican traditions and sentiment.[56] Regardless of what one
concludes about such emperors' motives, it cannot be denied that most emperors took seriously the need to present themselves as Rome's prince and first
citizen. In fact it is quite clear that Roman emperors went to great lengths to
distance themselves from the appearance of a monarch. Exceptions such as
Caligula and Nero only serve to magnify the significant efforts of those emperors who resisted monarchial identity.

Second, the imperial actions and attitudes addressed above surely reflect the
expectations and desires of the Roman *populus*. They demonstrate that the
Roman people expected good rulers to present themselves as private citizens
rather than monarchs, as servants to the state rather than masters of the state,
and as benefactors rather than tyrants. Such expectations are seen in Seneca's
De beneficiis. In seeking to explain why God allowed the tyrannical rule of Caligula, Seneca argues that this divine benefit was granted not on Caligula's behalf
but on behalf of his noble ancestors—ancestors who included Rome's first two
emperors, whom he describes in the following way:

---

[53]Suetonius, *Cal.* 37.
[54]Suetonius, *Nero* 30-31.
[55]Suetonius, *Cal.* 38-41; *Nero* 32.
[56]See Wallace-Hadrill, "Civilis Princeps," 32-48; cf. A. Alfödi, *Die monarchische Repräsentation im römischen Kaiserreiche* (Darmstadt: Wissenschaftliche Buchgesellschaft, 1970); F. Millar, "Trium-virate and Principate," *JRS* 63 (1973): 50-67.

It [the divine benefit of ruling] was accorded to his father Germanicus, to his grandfather [Tiberius], and to his great-grandfather [Augustus] and to others before them, men who were no less glorious, even if they passed their lives as private citizens on a footing equal with others. . . . God says: "Let these men be kings because their forefathers have not been, because they have regarded justice and unselfishness as their highest authority, because, instead of sacrificing the state to themselves, they have sacrificed themselves to the state. Let these others reign, because someone of their grandsires before them was a good man who displayed a soul superior to Fortune, who in times of civil strife preferred to be conquered than to conquer, because in this way he could serve the interest of the state. . . . How can these critics know that hero of old, who persistently fled from the glory that followed him . . . who never separated his own interest from that of the state?"[57]

Here Seneca describes the virtues of ideal Roman rulers, who exercised their authority as humble citizens rather than kings and who sacrificed their own interests for those of the state.

A Roman reading of Mark 10:42-45. In light of this analysis of Roman political ideology, Mark 10:42-45 takes on new meaning. A point often neglected by Markan interpreters is that the instructions in these verses are for those who *already* possess positions of power. It is quite clear that Jesus is speaking to the Twelve in this passage (see Mk 10:41), that is, to those who held unique positions of power in his ministry (e.g., Mk 3:13-15; 4:11; 6:6-13). Presumably Markan readers knew that the Twelve held such authority. Thus I contend that the verses are answering the question, "How should those in authority exercise their power?" As demonstrated above, answers to such a question already existed in the Roman world, and it is therefore highly relevant to consider the way in which Jesus' answer might be related to such existing answers, particularly the answers offered by Rome's political ideology.

For the sake of analysis, I will divide Mark 10:42-45 into three sections: (1) negative instruction, or "what those in power ought not do"; (2) positive instruction, or "what those in power ought to do"; and (3) the basis for instruction, or the example of Jesus.

Negative instruction (Mk 10:42). "So Jesus called them and said to them, 'You know that among the Gentiles those whom they recognize as their rulers lord it over them, and their great ones are tyrants over them.'" Jesus begins his instruction

---

[57]Seneca, *Ben.* 4.31.2-3; 4.32.2, 4, trans. John Basore, LCL, vol. 3 (Cambridge, MA: Harvard University Press, 1935).

by using Gentile authorities (presumably Roman rulers and officials) as a negative example: the Twelve must not exercise their authority in the manner of Gentile rulers. The characterization of these authorities and their manner of ruling is of particular importance.[58] Mark uses two verbs to describe how these Gentile authorities exercised their power, κατακυριεύω and κατεξουσιάζω.[59] Both are compound verbs created by combining the simple verbs κυριεύω and ἐξουσιάζω (which carry the general idea of exercising authority or power) with the preposition κατά (a preposition that often carries the directional notion of going "down from/upon" or the hostile notion of "against").

There is debate among Markan interpreters as to whether these two compound verbs are synonymous with κυριεύω and ἐξουσιάζω, expressing the general sense of power and authority, or whether they are intensified forms of these verbs, expressing domineering authority or tyrannical use of power.[60] Aside from its use here in Mark and in the Matthean parallel, κατακυριεύω appears at two different points in the New Testament (Acts 19:16; 1 Pet 5:3). In Acts 19:16 the verb is used to describe a demoniac violently overpowering and abusing the sons of Sceva who had attempted an exorcism. In 1 Peter 5:3 those who hold the office of elder are told not to act as κατακυριεύοντες but instead to be "examples to the flock." The author of 1 Peter is not instructing the elders of the church to refrain from exercising authority (the conclusion one would have to make if κατακυριεύω were

---

[58]Interpreters seem to be divided as to whether Mark's description of Gentile authorities as οἱ δοκοῦντες ἄρχειν τῶν ἐθνῶν should be taken as a pejorative, "those who seem to rule," i.e., indicating that such rulers only appear to rule but in reality are subject to God's sovereignty. While such a reading is possible, the description could be translated as "those who are recognized as rulers." Adela Yarbro Collins provides an example in which this phrase is used in the latter sense, without a deprecating connotation (Euripides, *Hecuba* 294-295; see Collins, *Mark*, 499). While this evidence demonstrates that the phrase need not be read negatively, it does not mean that such a reading was not intended by the Evangelist—the negative tone of the entire sentence might support the pejorative reading. Ultimately we can only be certain that Mark is describing those who held positions of authority (genuine or not) over Gentiles.

[59]I will not speculate as to whether these words were the choice of the Evangelist or simply received by him in his source material. The present work is ultimately the work of the Evangelist, and it is only the final form of the work we are considering here.

[60]For those who argue that these verbs communicate the general exercise of authority, see Boring, *Mark*, 302; K. W. Clark, "The Meaning of (Kata)Kyrieyein," in *The Gentile Bias and Other Essays*, ed. K. W. Clark (Leiden: Brill, 1980), 208-9; A. M. Kaminouchi, *"But It Is Not So Among You": Echoes of Power in Mark 10.32-45*, JSNT Sup 249 (New York: T&T Clark, 2003), 126-27. For those who argue that these verbs communicate abusive authority, see France, *Mark*, 418-19; W. Grundmann, *Das Evangelium nach Markus*, 6th ed., Theologischer Handkommentar zum Neuen Testament 2 (Berlin: Evangelische Verlagsanstalt, 1973), 219; W. L. Lane, *The Gospel of Mark*, New International Commentary on the New Testament (Grand Rapids: Eerdmans, 1974), 383.

simply a synonym for κυριεύω). Rather, the author is addressing the manner in which they exercise their authority: they are not to act in a domineering way or flaunt their positions of authority. In both instances it seems that κατακυριεύω has a negative connotation, and particularly in 1 Peter it implies a domineering use of authority. Κατακυριεύω also appears sixteen times in the LXX and generally communicates complete dominance or power over something (e.g., Gen 1:28; 9:1; Num 21:24; 1 Macc 15:30; Ps 9:2; 18:14; Jer 3:14). However, it does not seem to possess the negative connotation that we encounter in the New Testament.[61]

It is thus clear that κατακυριεύω is not simply a synonym for κυριεύω. The addition of the preposition intensifies the word by emphasizing full dominance over someone or something. In certain instances, the word even carries the negative connotation of domineering or lording one's authority over others. Regardless of the specific nuance of κατακυριεύω in Mark's Gospel, the word would have had a particularly negative connotation for readers influenced by Roman political ideology. Both exercising complete authority and lording one's authority over others were incompatible with Roman expectations for their rulers. It is noteworthy that κατακυριεύω is closely related to the noun κύριος, a title that Augustus strongly resisted. Thus it seems that a ruler who exercised κατακυριεύω might not be favorable to Roman readers.

Unfortunately, κατεξουσιάζω is essentially a *hapax legomenon*, as it only appears in Mark 10:42 and its Matthean parallel. Its use in Greco-Roman literature is also extremely rare. The majority of Markan commentators conclude that it communicates the abusive use of power or tyranny, and perhaps the best piece of evidence for such a conclusion is a synonym for ἐξουσιάζω, the word δυναστεύω, "I hold power or exercise authority."[62] This verb does not appear anywhere in the New Testament, but a compound form of this verb (καταδυναστεύω) seemingly conveys the oppressive and tyrannical use of power, both in the New Testament (Jas 2:6; Acts 10:38) and the LXX (e.g., Ex 1:13; 1 Sam 12:4; 2 Macc 1:28). If the addition of κατά changes the meaning of the verb δυναστεύω from "holding or exercising power" to "oppressing" or "tyrannizing," it seems plausible that adding the same preposition to ἐξουσιάζω might result in a similar change in meaning.

---

[61]Clark, "Meaning of (Kata)Kyrieyein," 202–11; Robert Gundry, *Mark: A Commentary on His Apology for the Cross* (Grand Rapids: Eerdmans, 1993), 579.

[62]France, *Mark*, 418–19; Grundmann, *Das Evangelium nach Markus*, 219; Lane, *The Gospel of Mark*, 383; Moloney, *Gospel of Mark*, 207; et al.; see also Frederick W. Danker, Walter Bauer, William F. Arndt, and F. Wilbur Gingrich, *Greek-English Lexicon of the New Testament and Other Early Christian Literature*, 3rd ed. (Chicago, University of Chicago Press, 2000), 531.

It must be noted that Mark makes frequent use of ἐξουσία—the noun form
of ἐξουσιάζω—and he could have easily used either the verb or the noun if he
were simply describing the general use of authority. But it seems Mark is intentionally contrasting the way in which Jesus uses his authority (ἐξουσία) with the
way in which Roman rulers use theirs (κατεξουσιάζω). Again, it seems that
κατεξουσιάζω is not simply a synonym for ἐξουσιάζω but that it conveys the
oppressive or tyrannical use of power. Thus, like κατακυριεύω, κατεξουσιάζω
would have conflicted with the political ideals of Roman readers.

It seems quite certain that Roman readers would have understood this critique of their own rulers in the context of their own political ideals—ideals that
thoroughly rejected the tyrannical abuse and ostentatious demonstrations of
power. The Markan Jesus' rejection of domineering and tyrannical rule would
have been favorably received by Mark's Roman audience, which saw in Jesus'
teaching their own deeply held political convictions.

While Jesus' rejection of tyrannical authority was probably heard with singular agreement by Roman readers, his critique of Roman rulers would likely
have been heard in diverse ways. Some of Mark's readers would have heard the
Evangelist making a sharp contrast between Jesus and Roman emperors, whom
they believed were using *recusatio* to mask tyrannical ambition. Note, for example, Tacitus's sharp critique of Augustus's reign: "On the other side it was
argued that 'filial duty and the critical position of the state had been used merely
as a cloak: come to facts, and it was from the lust of dominion that he excited
the veterans by his bounties, levied an army while yet a stripling and a subject,
seduced the legions of a consul, and affected a leaning to the Pompeian side.'"[63]
For readers who shared such sentiments, Mark presents Jesus as a ruler promoting their ideals over and against past and present rulers who are tyrants in
sheep's clothing, rulers who include Augustus, Tiberius, and Vespasian. However,
for many readers, emperors such as Augustus would have been highly esteemed,
and any association between these rulers and tyranny would have been regarded
as unlikely. Such readers would have recognized in Mark 10:42 a contrast not so
much between Jesus and all Roman rulers but between good rulers and bad

---

[63]Tacitus, *Ann.* 1.10, translated in Jackson. It should be noted that Tacitus was not inherently opposed to the Principate but simply felt that both the Julio-Claudian and Flavian families fell short
of meeting Roman political ideals. Tacitus's favorable evaluation of the Emperor Nerva supports
this conclusion (*Agricola* 3.1). John Percival ("Tacitus and the Principate," *Greek & Rome* 27 [1980]:
119-33) makes a convincing case that Tacitus was not opposed to the idea of the Principate.

ones. That is, Jesus is instructing his disciples not to imitate the behavior of tyrants such as Caligula and Nero.

Positive instruction (Mk 10:43-44). "But it is not so among you; but whoever wishes to become great among you must be your servant, and whoever wishes to be first among you must be slave of all." The negative instruction of Mark 10:42 is immediately followed by positive instruction in Mark 10:43-44. In contrast to the tyranny and ostentation of Gentile rulers, Jesus' disciples are instructed to rule as humble servants: anyone who desires to be "great" (μέγας) must become a "servant" (διάκονος; Mk 10:43). While many interpreters understand Jesus to be introducing a radically new behavior, I propose that such an instruction would actually have resonated with the political ideals of Mark's Roman readers. As I have demonstrated above, according to Roman political ideology, those who desired to be great among the Romans only assured true greatness through humble service to the Roman state.

Similarly, in Mark 10:44 Jesus instructs that all who desire to be "first" (πρῶτος) must become the "slave" (δοῦλος) of all. The language of this statement is of particular importance. The common title of the Roman emperor was *princeps* ("first citizen"), which was derived from the *Princeps Senatus* ("first or primary member of the Senate"). As already noted, ideal Roman emperors distanced themselves from appearing as a monarch and instead presented themselves as the "first" or "preeminent" Roman citizen, that is, as *princeps*. While the common Greek translation for *princeps* is ἡγεμών, which generally refers to one who leads, rules, or governs, it seems to lack the ideological significance of the title *princeps*, or one who is first among equals. However, the word πρῶτος, when compared to ἡγεμών, better captures the ideological significance of *princeps*: to be preeminent among a group of people or things. For Mark's Roman readers the notion of "desiring to be first" when placed in the context of a political critique would likely have been understood in terms of the Roman *princeps*, or the one who was first or preeminent among all other Romans.

However, Mark's combination of "first" (πρῶτος) with "slave" (δοῦλος) would have been jarring to Roman readers because such an association was foreign to the language and scope of Roman political ideals. Romans would never have conceived of their ruler or *princeps* in such lowly terms—to serve is one thing, but to be a "slave" (δοῦλος) is quite another. Some might protest that Mark's use of δοῦλος undercuts any conclusion that the Evangelist is alluding to Roman political ideals in Mark 10:43-44, arguing that the dissonance between the two roles is simply too great. But such a protest is unnecessary and neglects the clear allusions to these ideals that, as I have previously argued, would have been detected by Mark's Roman readers. Instead Mark's use of δοῦλος can be understood as hyperbolic language (a literary device used elsewhere in this same unit; see Mk 9:42-45; 10:25), used to stretch the boundaries of the readers' political ideology. Thus, while Roman political ideals call rulers to serve the state, Jesus calls his disciples to even greater service and humility in their capacity as δοῦλος. While Mark may be using Roman political ideals to contextualize Jesus' teaching on the use of authority and power, he may also be radicalizing these ideals by pushing them to an extreme.

The basis for instruction (Mk 10:45). "For the Son of Man came not to be served but to serve, and to give his life as a ransom for many." To this point Mark 10:42-44 has specifically addressed the behavior of Jesus' disciples, instructing them on how they should exercise their positions of power. Mark 10:45, however, grounds this instruction in the behavior of Jesus and the manner in which he exercises his role as God's messianic ruler. The disciples' positions of power are to be characterized by humble service precisely because this is how Jesus' rule is described.[64] Jesus famously claims that he has not come "to be served but to serve, and to give his life as a ransom for many" (διακονηθῆναι ἀλλὰ διακονῆσαι καὶ δοῦναι τὴν ψυχὴν αὐτοῦ λύτρον ἀντὶ πολλῶν).

The language of the Markan Jesus in Mark 10:45 is strikingly similar to that of Seneca in *De beneficiis* 4.32.2 (see quotation above under "Roman political ideology and the evaluation of Roman rulers: A summary"). Seneca describes Augustus and emperors like him by saying, "Instead of sacrificing the state to themselves, they have sacrificed themselves to the state" (*quia non rem publicam sibi, sed se rei publicae dicaverunt*), and they "preferred to be conquered than to conquer because in this way [they] could serve the interest of the state" (*quoniam ita expediebat rei publicae, vinci quam vincere maluit*). Mark's phrase "came not to be served but to serve" and Seneca's "preferred to be conquered rather than to conquer" are structurally similar, as are the meanings of the two phrases. By "conquer" Seneca does not have military victory in mind but political superiority and domination. The ideal ruler chooses not to dominate his people (conquer

---

[64]See Craig A. Evans, *Mark 8:27–16:20*, WBC 34B (Nashville: Thomas Nelson, 2001), 125; Moloney, *Gospel of Mark*, 207-8; Boring, *Mark*, 302.

them) but to serve them (be conquered by them). Thus we see that both Seneca and Jesus are promoting the ideal of a ruler who serves rather than is served.

Perhaps of even greater significance is the similarity between the ideal emperor's willingness to "sacrifice [himself] to the state" and Jesus' willingness to "give his life as a ransom for many," that is, sacrifice himself for the subjects of his kingdom. Seneca is obviously speaking figuratively here, referring to the emperor sacrificing his own power, glory, and wealth for the good of the Roman state. There was no precedent or even expectation for the emperor to sacrifice his own life for that of the state. But again, Mark may be radicalizing Roman political ideals by taking them to their extreme but logical conclusion: a ruler who sacrifices his own power, glory, and wealth for his people is good, but a ruler who would sacrifice his very life for his people is even better.

Considering possible objections. *The shame crucifixion.* In response to my exegesis of Mark 10:45, some might note that Jesus' sacrifice involves shameful crucifixion, a manner of execution about which Cicero says the following: "But the executioner, the veiling of heads, and the very word 'cross' let them all be far removed from not only the bodies of Roman citizens but even from their thoughts, their eyes, and their ears."[65] In light of this Roman attitude toward crucifixion, is it plausible that any Roman could bring their political ideology together with the supreme shame of crucifixion? Can the above reading of Mark 10:45 overcome such a hurdle? If Mark's reader were Cicero, Seneca, Augustus, or even a common plebeian, the answer to these questions would most certainly be no. For the average Roman reader, crucifixion and cherished political ideals would make uncomfortable bedfellows, to say the least.

However, most Markan interpreters conclude that Mark is writing for Christians rather than non-Christians.[66] If this conclusion is accurate, then the objection noted above quickly disappears. If Mark is writing for Roman *Christians,* they have presumably already accepted the shame of the cross to some degree and are willing to reconcile it with the messianic identity of Jesus (as challenging as such a reconciliation may be). For Roman Christians, crucifixion would not have had the same shameful sting that it had for most Romans, and bringing together crucifixion and political ideology would have been an amenable move for Mark's readers. In fact, placing the crucifixion within the context of Roman

---

[65]Cicero, *Pro Rabirio Perduellionis Reo* 16, trans. N. H. Watts, LCL (Cambridge, MA: Harvard University Press, 1931).

[66]See Moloney, *Gospel of Mark*; Boring, *Mark*; Collins, *Mark*; contra Gundry, *Mark: A Commentary.*

political ideology might actually have helped make the crucifixion more palatable for Roman Christians, for whom the sting of crucifixion had not yet fully disappeared. Thus, while Mark's linking of Roman political ideology to Jesus' crucifixion may have stretched his readers somewhat, such a stretch is not impossible given their established Christian identity and commitments. Mark's creative connection may actually address any lingering cognitive dissonance that the gospel of "Christ crucified" had created for them.

The absence of Roman imperial language? Some readers may object to reading this text against the background of Roman political ideology on the basis that these four Markan verses lack any explicit use of Roman imperial language. However, the absence of such language is mitigated by a number of factors. As we have demonstrated previously, the Markan text has already sent clear signals to the reader that the Gospel should be read as a response to Roman imperial power and the claims of the Roman emperor, signals that include Roman imperial language (e.g., Mk 1:1; 5:1-20). Thus the Markan reader is keenly attuned to reading the entire Gospel in light of such a response. The text in question further draws the reader's attention to the Gospel's response to Rome when it specifically critiques "the rulers of the Gentiles," that is, Roman rulers! And while the text does not contain explicit Roman imperial language, it does share strong conceptual similarities with Roman political ideology. It thus seems probable that a Roman reader, aware of Mark's critique of Roman imperial power, would have perceived the strong conceptual similarities between Mark 10:42-45 and their own political ideology and would have read the text in light of such an ideology.

Isn't Mark's Jesus a king? Much of the analysis above has been based on a particular Roman political ideology, an ideology that rejects kings and tyrants. Some Markan interpreters might object to my argument based on their belief that Jesus is presented as a king in Mark's Gospel. It might be argued that if Mark portrays Jesus as a king, then the claim that Mark 10:42-45 reflects Roman political ideology is undermined. Why would Mark draw on such ideology only to undermine it by presenting Jesus as a king?

But while royal imagery is frequently attributed to Jesus in Mark's Gospel, the title βασιλεύς, "king," is surprisingly not. Elizabeth Struthers Malbon has noted that Jesus is only identified as βασιλεύς by those who are clearly his opponents (i.e., by Pilate [Mk 15:2, 9, 12], Pilate's inscription above the cross [Mk 15:26], the

Roman soldiers [Mk 15:18], and the chief priests and scribes [Mk 15:32]), characters who are certainly untrustworthy to the reader.[67] She argues further that
all referenced "kings" in Mark are portrayed in a negative light, including Herod
Antipas (Mk 6:14, 22, 25, 26, 27) and those whom Jesus' disciples will stand
before (Mk 13:9).[68] Not even God is identified as a king in Mark's Gospel. The
apparent unimportance (or perhaps negative connotation) of this title in Mark
is all the more striking when Mark is compared to Matthew. The title is much
more frequent in Matthew's Gospel and is frequently used in a positive way. In
four different non-Markan parallels, Jesus is identified, either by himself or by
the narrator, as a king (Mt 2:2; 21:5; 25:34; 25:40).[69] Matthew even indirectly
identifies God as a king in the parable of the wedding feast (Mt 22:2-14). Why
is Mark willing to attribute royal imagery to Jesus but, unlike Matthew, apparently reluctant to identify Jesus as βασιλεύς?

The vast majority of interpreters see no reluctance on the Evangelist's part to
identify Jesus as king. Most point to the kingly identifications made by Pilate,
the Roman soldiers, and the chief priests and scribes, and conclude that while
these identifications are clearly derisive, they are steeped in irony and are thus
ultimately true. However, in light of the evidence noted above, the astute reader
knows that no trustworthy voice in the story (e.g., Jesus, the narrator/author,
God, the disciples, or any of the insightful minor characters) has identified Jesus
as βασιλεύς. Therefore it might be more accurate to interpret the derisive identifications of Jesus as king not only as derisive but also as wrong! Thus for the
author and audience, identifying Jesus as βασιλεύς is just one more false charge
among many others (e.g., general false charges [Mk 14:56]; the charge of destroying the temple [Mk 14:58]; the charge of blasphemy [Mk 14:64]; and general
accusations before Pilate [Mk 15:3]). Malbon suggests that this "antikingship"
element of Mark is similar to the "antimonarchial" strand of tradition that can
be found in the Hebrew Bible, particular in the David stories—an apt comparison indeed.[70] But in light of Mark's Roman audience, this "antiking" motif

---

[67]Malbon, *Mark's Jesus*, 119-20. Note that contra the present argument, Malbon concludes that
neither the title βασιλεύς nor royal imagery is viewed favorably in Mark's Gospel. For Malbon
"reign" and "ruling" in Mark belong to God and not to Jesus. Instead Jesus is God's ambassador
who announces God's reign.

[68]Ibid., 119-20.

[69]This number could actually be five, if the reference to the "great king" in Mt 5:35 is understood
as a reference to God's Messiah—a conclusion that seems highly likely.

[70]Malbon, *Mark's Jesus*, 121.

might be best explained in light of Roman disdain for kings and tyrants. The Markan Evangelist does not identify Jesus as a king because Roman readers would have abhorred such a title.

A ROMAN READING OF MARK'S CENTRAL SECTION

This proposed reading of Mark 10:42-45 has significant ramifications for both the way in which one understands the narrative within Mark's central section and the way in which that central section functions in the entirety of Mark's narrative. This reading illuminates the motif of blindness that is prominent within the central section. The oft-proposed notion that the disciples' blindness is the recognition of Jesus as a powerful Messiah *instead* of a suffering and dying Messiah is misguided. Based on the first half of Mark's Gospel, there is nothing wrong with concluding that Jesus is a powerful Messiah. Such vision is not wrong, but it is incomplete or partial. It fails to see the humility, service, and sacrifice that are inseparable from such power. This blindness is evinced both through the disciples' failure to understand Jesus' passion predictions and through their own selfish desires—motifs that make up a large portion of Mark's central section. Like the tyrants of Rome, the Markan disciples seek power over others as well as their own prestige and greatness—attitudes and ambitions that Jesus repeatedly rejects throughout the central section. As those appointed with authority from Jesus, the disciples must exercise that authority in the way Jesus himself will exercise it—as a humble servant who is willing to give up his life for his people. It is not accidental that immediately after Jesus' climactic teaching in Mark 10:42-45, teaching that is paradigmatic for the entire central section, Jesus heals a blind man in a single attempt. Through this narrative structure the Gospel signals to the reader that those who understand Jesus' teaching in Mark 10:42-45 see Jesus clearly and completely.

Not only does Mark's central section function to help the reader see Jesus fully, but it also functions as a narrative bridge in Mark's Gospel, one that joins the Galilean ministry with Jesus' passion in Jerusalem. Often Mark's central section is perceived as standing in unity with Jesus' passion and in tension with Jesus' Galilean ministry, with the result that the latter's narrative significance is minimized. But my proposed reading of the central section resists such perceptions and allows both the Galilean ministry and the passion narrative to play prominent roles in Mark's narrative. The two convey equally significant information about God's Messiah and Son, Jesus.

Closely related to this function as a narrative bridge is the central section's function as a christological bridge. My proposed reading eliminates the long-perceived tension between the power elements of Mark's Christology and the suffering and death elements. Through the use of Roman political ideology, Mark is able to bring these two realities into a meaningful and tension-free union. The cross does not contradict or stand in tension with the tremendous power of Jesus, power that evinces Jesus' identity as God's appointed ruler. Instead the cross is presented as the ideal way in which a ruler would and should exercise divinely granted authority. Thus Mark's central section, culminating in Mark 10:42-45, provides the crucial bridge between the two poles of Mark's Christology, the powerful Jesus and the suffering Jesus, which have long vexed Markan interpreters.

How then does Mark's central section address the crisis of Flavian propaganda that faces Mark's readers? As argued in chapter three, Mark uses the Galilean ministry to create a counter-résumé to that of Vespasian. At numerous points the Evangelist demonstrates Jesus' superiority over Vespasian in order to support the claim of the Markan incipit—namely, that Jesus is God's Messiah, Son, and appointed ruler over the world, not Vespasian. But as impressive as the Markan Jesus is within the Galilean ministry, the Galilean ministry does not address the largest challenge the Evangelist faces in establishing Jesus' superiority to Vespasian—Jesus' crucifixion by Roman authorities. In order to offer a satisfactory response to Flavian propaganda, it is necessary to address this shameful event, and Mark's central section offers just such a response.

As argued above, the Markan disciples parallel Mark's Roman audience. After reading and hearing about the Galilean ministry, Mark's audience, like Peter and the Markan disciples, should clearly see that Jesus is God's true messianic ruler and that he is greater than all competitors. But the partial blindness that plagued Peter and Jesus' disciples presumably plagues Mark's audience as well, as it fails to understand Jesus' death and suffering. Like Peter and the Markan disciples (and many of Mark's modern interpreters!), the audience perceives Jesus' suffering and death to stand in conflict with Jesus' identity as God's powerful messianic ruler.

Through the central section the Evangelist challenges this misguided conclusion. It is significant that Mark introduces Jesus' death through Jesus' own prediction of it, a prediction that would have demonstrated to the ancient reader Jesus' divine power. Such a move functions to eliminate the perceived tension between suffering and power. The transfiguration functions in a similar way, as on the heels of Jesus' first passion prediction his heavenly identity and divine sonship are powerfully confirmed. Again the tension between suffering and power is mitigated. Finally, Jesus' exorcism of a powerful demon shows the reader that the Jesus who will suffer and die still wields extreme power, and that these two aspects of his identity are not in conflict.

But when Jesus again foretells his suffering and death, his disciples fail to understand its significance and the way in which such a fate could coexist with Jesus' powerful identity, failure that likely parallels the same challenge within Mark's intended audience. This confusion is manifest in the disciples' desire for their own greatness and their resistance to humility, sacrifice, and service, realities inseparable from Jesus' future suffering and death and thus inseparable from his followers.

Finally, a third passion prediction is given, and for a third time Jesus' disciples fail to understand its significance and its relationship to Jesus' identity as God's powerful Messiah, failure that is manifest in the request of James and John for places of power and privilege—again failure that parallels those within Mark's audience. This failure and confusion is addressed for the final time in the climactic teaching of Mark 10:42-45. Through the use of the audience's own political ideology, the Evangelist bridges the gap for the reader between Jesus' great power and future suffering. Jesus' suffering and death are contextualized as acts of generous benefaction and humble service for his people, acts that Mark's Roman audience would have expected from their own rulers. Mark cleverly follows this climactic text—a text through which Mark's readers should finally see the connection between Jesus' power and suffering—with the healing of Bartimaeus, a healing that happens in one step rather than two, unlike the first healing of a blind man. The reader who sees Jesus' death within the context of Roman political ideology has, like Bartimaeus, been cured of blindness and sees Jesus clearly and completely.

But the central section does not only function to overcome the challenge of Jesus' shameful death by bridging the gap between power and suffering. At the same time it takes Jesus' death and transforms it into another way in which Jesus is superior to Vespasian. While Vespasian sought to present himself as a second Augustus in terms of benefaction and service to Rome, one who embodied Rome's cherished political ideology, Mark presents Jesus as vastly superior in such an embodiment. Jesus is a greater benefactor and greater servant as he willingly sacrifices his life for the sake of his people. Thus in Mark's central section Jesus further out-Caesars Caesar.

Again the narratival pieces of Mark have been merged with the pieces of Mark's reconstructed setting. Through the merging of these two sets of pieces, a long-perceived christological and narrative tension in Mark has been alleviated, and the resulting reading provides a plausible way in which the Gospel might have addressed the needs of first-century Christians.

FIVE

A ROMAN READING OF MARK'S
SO-CALLED SECRECY MOTIF

U NTIL THIS POINT I HAVE NOT accounted for the christological
significance of the so-called Markan secrecy motif. As noted in the
introduction, the motif of secrecy has often been closely associated with
Mark's Christology. For redaction critics the motif played a pivotal role in the
Evangelist's attempt to correct a Christology of "power and glory." For
Kingsbury it is the primary motif by which Mark's christological titles must
be understood, with Kingsbury's ultimate conclusion being that Jesus' identity
as the Son of God, not Messiah, is kept a secret until the crucifixion. For
many narrative critics it functions as a literary device to point the reader
toward properly recognizing Jesus as the Messiah primarily (only?) in terms
of suffering and death. These readings certainly differ in numerous ways, but
all seem to link this secrecy motif to understanding Jesus' messianic identity
in terms of suffering and death.

While such readings of Mark's secrecy motif have played a significant role in
understanding Mark's Christology over the past century, following the recent
work of David F. Watson, I propose a radical departure from the status quo. In
his recent monograph, *Honor Among Christians: The Cultural Key to the Messianic Secret*, Watson has taken a decisive step forward in the interpretation of

Mark's secrecy motif, a step I have built on.[1] While Watson rightfully reads the text in light of the first-century honor-shame value system, I believe his reading only partially resolves the conundrum of Mark's secrecy motif. In this chapter I seek to complement Watson's work by adding a political dimension to his insights. In particular Jesus' actions will again be viewed through the lens of Roman political ideology, and I will compare them to the actions of Roman emperors. The results will be combined with Watson's insights on the Markan secrecy motif in an attempt to explain the motif's significance for Mark's Christology.

DAVID F. WATSON: SECRECY OR HONOR?

In Watson's recently published monograph, *Honor Among Christians*, he applies the tools of social-scientific criticism both to the meaning of secrecy in the ancient Mediterranean world and to the Markan pericopes that are so often associated with secrecy in modern scholarship. Regarding the former, Watson argues that the language and function of secrecy are virtually absent in Mark's Gospel. Words closely associated with secrecy (particularly in religious texts), such as κρύπτω, ἀποκρύπτω, λανθάνω, ἄρρητος, and μυστήριον, are virtually absent in Mark's Gospel.[2] In fact Watson demonstrates that in the whole of Mark's Gospel the language of secrecy only occurs four times, three of which come in two verses of Mark 4. Watson demonstrates that secrecy functioned in three primary ways in the ancient world: to protect from danger, preserve community boundaries, and to defend an individual's or group's reputation. According to Watson, none of these prominent functions of secrecy are prominent in Mark's Gospel. Ultimately Watson concludes that what is often described as a "secrecy" motif in Mark is misleading and that Mark's intended readers would not have understood the pericopes that form such a motif in terms of secrecy.

But if Mark's readers would not have understood these pericopes in terms of secrecy, how would they have understood them? Watson proposes that these pericopes must be understood in light of the honor-shame value system

---

[1]David F. Watson, *Honor Among Christians: The Cultural Key to the Messianic Secret* (Minneapolis: Fortress, 2010); Adam Winn, "Resisting Honor: The Markan Secrecy Motif and Roman Imperial Ideology," *JBL* 133, no. 3 (2014): 583-601. The majority of this chapter comes from this *JBL* article and is used with the permission of the publisher.

[2]Κρύπτω (1x, Mk 4:22), ἀποκρύπτω (1x, Mk 4:22), λανθάνω (1x, Mk 7:24), ἄρρητος (no occurrences), and μυστήριον (1x, Mk 4:11).

that dominated the ancient Mediterranean world.[3] He first considers pericopes in which Jesus performs a healing and commands the recipient not to
report or speak of the healing (Mk 1:40-45; 5:21-24, 35-43; 7:31-37; 8:22-26).
Watson demonstrates that in these healing pericopes the dynamics of a
client-patron relationship are present. Mark's readers would have recognized
Jesus as the patron and the sick person as the client. Once Jesus has healed
the sick person, the client is obligated to reciprocate by showing Jesus, the
patron, honor—honor that would involve public praise of the patron. Watson
argues that Jesus' actions of silencing the healed person would not have been
understood as an attempt to keep the actions a secret but as resistance to
"achieved" honor.[4]

Similarly, Watson argues that when demons declare Jesus to be "the Holy
One of God" (Mk 1:24) or "Son of God," the value system of honor and shame
is again at work. These are honorific titles being given to Jesus, and their
proclamation by demons would have led to the spread of Jesus' honor. Watson
also suggests that the giving of these titles might be a way of demons drawing
Jesus into an obligation to reciprocate. Again, Jesus' actions would not have
been understood as attempts to keep his identity secret but as resistance to
"ascribed" honor.[5]

Watson argues that Jesus' resistance to honor is only half of the story. Jesus
is not rejecting the honor-shame system in toto—a system too deeply ingrained
in ancient Mediterranean culture—but rather he is offering a new vision of what
is honorable and shameful. While Jesus resists the commonplace markers of
honor and shame (e.g., acts of power, benefaction, and honorific titles), he also
establishes new markers (e.g., service, self-sacrifice, suffering, and crucifixion).
Jesus establishes these new markers through his passion predictions (Mk 8:31;
9:31; 10:33) and teaching on discipleship (Mk 8:34-38; 9:33-36; 10:13-16, 29-31,
35-45). For Watson the Markan Jesus ultimately inverts standard conventions

---

[3]Both Bruce Malina and John Pilch have argued that Jesus' action of silencing those he healed
should be understood in terms of honor and shame; see Malina, *The New Testament World: Insights from Cultural Anthropology*, 3rd ed. (Louisville: Westminster John Knox, 2001), 125, and
Pilch, "Secrecy in the Gospel of Mark," *Professional Approaches for Christian Educators* 21 (1992):
150-53. Both argue that such silencing functions as a defense against envy, envy that would ultimately result in the removal of honor. Malina understands Jesus to be "concealing" or "hiding"
honor rather than publicly rejecting it. Later we will consider whether rejecting public honor
was used as a strategy in the ancient world for defense against envy.
[4]Watson, *Honor Among Christians*, 37-56.
[5]Ibid., 56-62.

by claiming that the least, the suffering, and the servants should be honored, while the great and the powerful should be ashamed.[6]

Such an explanation of Jesus' resistance to honor runs into trouble, however, when one considers the numerous places in Mark where Jesus embraces rather than resists public honor. Watson actually addresses Markan pericopes in which the Evangelist puts Jesus' honor on display and in which Jesus publicly embraces honor according to standard Mediterranean convention. In fact Watson notes eighteen examples where Jesus' honor is on display before others, and he either does not resist/reject honor or actually embraces the honor he is due.[7] Unlike many interpreters, Watson rejects efforts to remove or mitigate the honor from these pericopes and claims that they are in fact as they appear, clear examples of Jesus playing by the standard conventions of honor and shame.[8]

Watson's explanation for these conflicting motifs is that each is used by the Evangelist to advance different themes, themes that would have been recognized by Mark's readers. He argues that such inconsistent material was quite common in ancient literature, and as such Mark's readers would have been untroubled by these conflicting motifs standing beside each other.[9] But such a conclusion is unsatisfactory and seems to undermine Watson's explanation for the Markan Jesus' resistance to honor—namely, that Mark is seeking to invert or subvert conventional markers of honor and shame. It may be true that ancient readers were more comfortable with inconsistent literary motifs than modern readers, but would or could they have concluded that Jesus is inverting or subverting the conventions of honor and shame when he frequently participates in such conventions throughout Mark's Gospel? Such a conclusion seems improbable. Ultimately the pericopes in which the Markan Jesus displays and embraces public honor undermine Watson's conclusion that the Evangelist is seeking to invert or subvert the honor and shame conventions of the Mediterranean world.

While Watson takes a decisive step forward in identifying Jesus' commands for silence as resistance to honor, he fails to explain adequately the purpose or significance of such resistance in Mark's Gospel. My purpose is to build off Watson's decisive step and provide an explanation for the Markan Jesus' frequent efforts to resist

---

[6]Ibid., 63-85.

[7]See ibid., 89 (Mk 1:21-28, 29-31, 32-34; 2:1-12, 28; 3:1-6, 7-12; 4:35-41; 5:1-20, 24-34; 6:30-44, 45-52, 53-56; 7:24-30; 8:1-9; 9:14-28, 38-41; 10:46-52). These examples do not include the triumphal entry in Mk 11:10, a clear example of Jesus receiving public honor.

[8]For Watson's discussion of these pericopes, see *Honor Among Christians*, 87-114.

[9]Ibid., 115-37.

honor, an explanation that is not in conflict with the numerous pericopes in which Jesus publicly accepts honor. I seek to find an existing paradigm in the Greco-Roman world in which resistance to honor would have been both normative and expected, and would have been easily recognized by the first readers of Mark's Gospel.

THE DESIRE FOR HONOR IN THE GRECO-ROMAN WORLD

Before we consider possible paradigms for understanding the behavior of the Markan Jesus, I will briefly consider the pride of place given to honor in the ancient Mediterranean world. Existing primary sources make it quite clear that honor was one of the greatest and most prized virtues.[10] In Thucydides's *History of the Peloponnesian War*, Pericles is reported to say, "For the love of honour alone is untouched by age, and when one comes to the ineffectual period of life it is not 'gain' as some say, that gives the greater satisfaction, but honour."[11] In Xenophon the poet Simonides states:

> For indeed it seems to me, Hiero, that in this man differs from other animals—I mean, in this craving for honour. In meat and drink and sleep and sex all creatures alike seem to take pleasure; but love of honour is rooted neither in the brute beasts nor in every human being. But they in whom is implanted a passion for honour and praise, these are they who differ most from the beasts of the field, these are accounted men and not mere human beings.[12]

Aristotle emphasizes honor as the greatest external good:

> Now the greatest external good we should assume to be the thing which we offer as a tribute to the gods, and which is most coveted by men of high station, and is the prize awarded for the noblest deeds; and such a thing is honour, for honour is clearly the greatest of external goods. Therefore the great-souled man is he who has the right disposition with regard to honours and disgraces. And even without argument it is evident that honour is the object with which the great-souled are concerned, since it is honour above all else which great men claim and deserve.[13]

---

[10]For an excellent discussion on honor and shame in the primary literature, see Mark Finney, *Honour and Conflict in the Ancient World: 1 Corinthians in Its Greco-Roman Social Setting*, LNTS 460 (London: T&T Clark, 2012). For this source I am greatly indebted.

[11]Thucydides, *History of the Peloponnesian War* 2.44.4, trans. C. F. Smith, LCL, vol. 1 (Cambridge, MA: Harvard University Press, 1919).

[12]Xenophon, *Hiero* 7.3, trans. C. E. Marchant and G. W. Bowersock, LCL (Cambridge, MA: Harvard University Press, 1925).

[13]Aristotle, *Nicomachean Ethics* 4.3.10, trans. H. Rackham, LCL (Cambridge, MA: Harvard University Press, 1926).

Roman writers confirm the high opinion of honor found within the Greek world. Cicero writes, "Nature has made us, as I have said before—it must often be repeated—enthusiastic seekers after honour, and once we have caught, as it were, some glimpse of its radiance, there is nothing we are not prepared to bear and go through in order to secure it."[14]

In light of this testimony and the prominent place it gives honor in the ancient Mediterranean world, it is all the more striking for Jesus to reject the honor he deserved. Certainly Mark's readers would have been struck by such behavior and would have sought a plausible explanation. I now turn my attention to paradigms that might give just such an explanation for Jesus' odd behavior.

REJECTING HONOR: POSSIBLE PARADIGMS

We will consider three possible paradigms that might explain Jesus' rejection of public honor: (1) Cynic philosophy and praxis, (2) envy avoidance strategies, and (3) Roman political ideology.

Cynic philosophy and praxis. Such love of honor certainly characterized the great majority in the Mediterranean world, but it did not characterize all. The Cynics are perhaps the most noteworthy example of the minority who did not embrace the virtue of φιλοτιμία, "the love of honor."[15] Cynics rejected material possessions, physical comfort, and societal convention. Such things were replaced with material poverty, ascetic practices, and shameful public behavior.[16] But while Cynics are accurately described as people who resisted public honor, there are many reasons to reject Cynic philosophy and praxis as a paradigm for understanding the behavior of the Markan Jesus. While the Markan Jesus does share some features with Cynics (e.g., itinerant, without a home, few material possessions, taught in bold aphorisms), many features of the Markan Jesus are radically inconsistent with Cynic practice (e.g., calling disciples and regularly participating in social feasts and meals). Mark also makes no explicit effort to

---

[14]Cicero, *Tusculanae disputationes* 2.24.58, trans. John E. King, LCL (Cambridge, MA: Harvard University Press, 1927). See also Cicero, *Pro Archia* 28-29; *De finibus* 5.22.64; *De officiis* 1.18.61.

[15]Here we are primarily referring to "hard" Cynicism as opposed to "soft" Cynicism. "Soft" Cynics were more likely to participate in societal and political institutions. On Cynics and the difference between hard and soft Cynics, see John R. Morgan, "Cynics," in *Oxford Classical Dictionary*, ed. Simon Hornblower and Antony Spawforth, 3rd ed. (Oxford: Oxford University Press, 2003), 418-19. On hard Cynics, see Diogenes Laertius, *Lives of Imminent Philosophers* 6.

[16]For more discussion of Cynics, see Everett Ferguson, *Backgrounds of Early Christianity*, 3rd ed. (Grand Rapids: Eerdmans, 2003), 348-53; Morgan, "Cynics," 418-19.

link Jesus to the Cynics through his appearance or actions. Jesus is not described as wearing ragged or dirty garments, the attire of a Cynic, nor is Jesus presented as begging or partaking in shameful public activity. In fact Jesus' instructions to his disciples not to take a bag on their mission may be an intentional attempt on the part of the Markan Evangelist to distinguish Jesus and his disciples from Cynics, who customarily carried a beggar's bag.

Perhaps more important is the difference between the Markan episodes in which Jesus resists honor and such resistance by the Cynics. Jesus' resistance to honor is situation specific and sporadic, differing from the philosophical and categorical rejection of honor exhibited by Cynics. In other words, Cynics largely avoided behavior or a reputation that would have merited honor, whereas Jesus rejects honor that his behavior and reputation merit. For these reasons it seems unlikely that Mark's readers would have recognized Cynic philosophy and praxis as a paradigm for understanding Jesus' occasional resistance to public honor.

Envy avoidance strategies. While honor was deeply desired in the ancient Mediterranean world, acquiring it was a double-edged sword. Honor was perceived as a limited good, meaning that one person's acquisition of honor meant another's loss.[17] The perception that honor was limited naturally led to the increase of envy (φθόνος), an emotion widely regarded as a dangerous and volatile vice that could result in hatred, harm, and potentially the loss of honor.[18] Thus the virtue of φιλοτιμία, "love of honor," required a balancing act, one in which a person must find a way of obtaining and securing honor without incurring the dangerous envy of others.[19]

---

[17]This perception is clearly seen in the primary literature. Iamblicus states, "People do not find it pleasant to give honor to someone else, for they suppose that they themselves are being deprived of something" (*Anonymous Iamblichus*, in Hermann Diels, *Die Fragmente der Vorsokratiker, Griechisch und Deutsch*, 5th ed., ed. W. Kranz [Berlin: Weidmann, 1934–1937], 2:400). And Plutarch states, "And whereas men attack other kinds of eminence and themselves lay claim to good character, good birth, and honour, as though they were depriving themselves of so much of these as they grant to others" (Plutarch, *An seni respublica gerenda sit* 7, trans. Harold N. Fowler, LCL, vol. 10 [Cambridge, MA: Harvard University Press, 1936]). For secondary literature on honor as a limited good, see Jerome H. Neyrey and Richard L. Rohrbaugh, "'He Must Increase, I Must Decrease' (John 3:30): A Cultural and Social Interpretation," *CBQ* 63 (2001): 468-69, and Malina, *New Testament World*, 81-107.

[18]See Cicero, *De oratore* 2.209-210. Also note that envy and hatred are not the same, though the former is often closely related to the latter; see Plutarch, *Inv. Od.*

[19]According to Plutarch, the moderate person is able to enjoy honors and prosperity without exciting the envy of others; *De liberis educandis* 10.

Some interpreters have argued that Jesus' commands for silence in Mark could be understood as a means of preventing or curbing envy, a possibility we will consider here.[20] Greek and Roman authors provide a number of ways that one can avoid or mitigate the dangers of envy. These means include (1) using one's honors in order to benefit others rather than for purposes of self-interest or vainglory, (2) adopting an attitude of humility toward one's honors, (3) downplaying or undervaluing one's honors, (4) demonstrating a life of great virtue, (5) giving praise and honor to others, (6) giving credit for honor and prosperity to divine fortune, and (7) practicing self-deprecation.[21] Relevant to our purposes is the absence of any instruction that one should reject bestowed honors as a means of avoiding envy.[22] No such instructions can be found. Therefore, while some of Jesus' behaviors in Mark might be interpreted in terms of avoiding envy (e.g., his avoidance of crowds [Mk 4:36; 7:24], giving credit to God [Mk 5:19; 9:29], and questioning the descriptor *good* [Mk 10:18]), his rejection of deserved honors does not seem best understood in such terms.

Roman political ideology. The previous discussion on Roman political ideology again becomes significant, as it provides one of the only spheres in the ancient world in which public honor was refused. As discussed above, the Roman political strategy of *recusatio*, employed by Roman emperors, involved the regular refusal of public honors. Here the evidence related to Augustus is repeated, with additional examples from other Roman emperors also provided. Augustus strenuously refused to be addressed as "Lord" and once issued an edict that sharply censured a crowd that had innocently applied the title to him.[23] When the Senate and people conferred to Augustus the position of dictator, he refused the position

---

[20]See Malina, *New Testament World*, 125, and Pilch, "Secrecy in the Gospel of Mark," 150-53.

[21]On these strategies for avoiding and/or minimizing envy, see Cicero, *De oratore* 2.209-211, and Plutarch, *Inv. Od.* 6; *De Laude* 4, 6, 9, 11, 12.

[22]Malina's assessment of Jesus' commands for silence—namely, that Jesus is concealing his actions to avoid envy—is largely dependent on envy-avoidance behaviors outlined in George Foster's article "The Anatomy of Envy: A Study of Symbolic Behavior," *Current Anthropology* 13 (1972): 165-202. Foster lists four types of behavior used for avoiding or mitigating envy: concealment, denial, symbolic sharing (Malina uses the term "conciliatory bribe"), and true sharing. Clearly these four categories overlap with the behaviors I have noted above, and Foster's work is indeed helpful for analyzing envy and responses to envy in the New Testament. But the rejection of honor does not seem to fit into the categories provided by Foster. Because Malina understands Jesus' behavior as concealing honor rather than rejecting honor, he finds support in Foster's work. But if Jesus' actions are understood as rejecting honor, Foster's work does not prove as useful for understanding this behavior.

[23]Suetonius, *Aug.* 53.1; cf. Philo, *On the Embassy to Gaius* 23.254.

and begged the people not to insist on it.[24] Augustus repeatedly refused attempts by the people and the Senate to honor him with the title "Father of His Country" and only accepted after great persistence.[25] Likewise he rejected the attempts of the Senate and the people to honor him with a lifelong consulship.[26] He emphatically refused attempts to build or dedicate, within the city, temples in his honor.[27] He also melted down all silver statutes in the city of Rome that had been erected in his honor.[28] Augustus himself notes that he only participated in three triumphs and that he declined all other triumphs voted to him by the Senate.[29]

Like Augustus, Tiberius also frequently resisted public honor. While Tiberius immediately succeeded Augustus by taking up imperial authority, he refused the formal title for a significant period of time, accepting it only after the Senate expressed great frustration at his reluctance.[30] He also refused to take the title "Augustus" for himself.[31] Like Augustus, Tiberius refused the voting of temples, flamens, or priests in his honor.[32] He refused the honorific titles "Imperator" and "Father of His Country," and he refused efforts to name the month of September after him.[33] He regularly refused to have statues made in his honor within the city, and any statue he allowed could not be set among the statues of the gods.[34] He also refused the honor of the civic crown being placed at his door, an honor granted to Augustus identifying him as savior of the Roman citizenry.[35]

The resistance to public honor is again seen in the careers of Claudius and Vespasian, though fewer specific examples are found in our sources. By all accounts Claudius refused excessive honors and acclamations.[36] According to Suetonius, he even refused the title "Imperator."[37] Cassius Dio claims that Claudius initially refused the title of "Father of His Country," though he eventually accepted

---

[24]Suetonius, *Aug.* 52.2; cf. Tacitus, *Ann.* 1.9.

[25]Suetonius, *Aug.* 52.1; *Res Gestae divi Augusti* 5.1.

[26]*Res Gestae divi Augusti* 5.3.

[27]Suetonius, *Aug.* 52.1; Cassius Dio, *Roman History* 52.35.

[28]Suetonius, *Aug.* 52.1; *Res Gestae divi Augusti* 24.2; cf. Cassius Dio, *Roman History* 52.35.

[29]*Res Gestae divi Augusti* 4.1.

[30]Suetonius, *Tib.* 24.1; Cassius Dio, *Roman History* 57.2.1. Suetonius views Tiberius's actions as hypocritical and a sign of false modesty. It seems that Tiberius was trying to follow the example of the reluctant ruler set by Augustus but that he was not as adept at the strategy as his predecessor.

[31]Cassius Dio, *Roman History* 57.2.1; 57.8.1.

[32]Suetonius, *Tib.* 26.1; Cassius Dio, *Roman History* 57.9.1.

[33]Suetonius, *Tib.* 26.2; Cassius Dio, *Roman History* 57.8.1.

[34]Suetonius, *Tib.* 26.1; Cassius Dio, *Roman History* 57.9.1.

[35]Suetonius, *Tib.* 26.2.

[36]Suetonius, *Claud.* 12.1; Cassius Dio, *Roman History* 60.5.4.

[37]Suetonius, *Claud.* 12.1.

it. He also did not allow himself to be worshiped as a god or to be offered any sacrifice. With few exceptions, he rejected honorific statues that were voted to him.[38] Suetonius also claims that Vespasian was reluctant to accept his tribunican powers as well as the title "Father of His Country."[39] It seems that Vespasian ended the practice of Romans worshiping the "genius" of the living emperor, a practice instituted by Gaius Caligula.[40]

Again I must stress that such imperial acts of resisting public honor should not be understood as examples of true humility but rather in terms of Roman political ideology. Honors such as monarchial or divine titles, direct worship, temples, priesthoods, and excessive triumphs were, in the minds of Romans, all associated with tyrannical kings of the East, and as such Augustus and many of his successors rejected such honors. It must be noted that Roman emperors did indeed receive and embrace great public honors, but these honors were distinctly Roman honors, that is, honors that were largely grounded in Roman tradition and consistent with Roman political sensibilities. Yet even such Roman honors were not to be enjoyed in excess, lest one Roman be elevated too highly above his peers. As argued above, the successful Roman emperor who took seriously (at least publicly) Roman political ideology and his identity as *princeps* or "first citizen" would have avoided the appearance of being a monarch and thus would resist any public honor that would be associated with such a figure. Ultimately resisting these excessive honors led to greater honor for the Roman emperor in the eyes of the Roman citizenry.

POLITICAL IDEOLOGY OF *RECUSATIO* AND THE MARKAN JESUS

It seems that the Roman political strategy of *recusatio* offers one of the only meaningful paradigms for understanding Jesus' rejection of public honor, and it is a paradigm that fits quite well with both my proposed reconstruction of Mark's setting and the reading that grows from it. As demonstrated previously, Mark presents Jesus as a world ruler. When such an identity is paired with frequent resistance to honor, it seems highly probably that Roman readers would

---

[38]Cassius Dio, *Roman History* 60.3.2; 60.5.4.

[39]Suetonius, *Vesp.* 12. Vespasian's tribunican powers were reckoned from July 1 of AD 69. It is possible that Suetonius is referring to his official use of these powers rather than their official reckoning. For this solution, see Barbara Levick, *Vespasian* (London: Routledge, 1999), 67.

[40]For this conclusion, see Ittai Gradel, *Emperor Worship and Roman Religion*, Oxford Classical Monographs (Oxford: Oxford University Press, 2002), 189-90.

have interpreted Jesus' resistance to public honor in light of similar resistance practiced by their own emperors. The case becomes stronger when placed alongside the evidence that suggests Mark is responding to Flavian propaganda.

Thus I propose that, through co-opting the imperial motif of resisting public honor, Mark offers a contextualization of Jesus' identity as world ruler that would have resonated with Roman readers. Unlike recent Roman rulers such as Caligula and Nero, Jesus embodies what was truly good and virtuous from Roman political ideology—the rejection of tyrannical behavior—rejection that is symbolized by resistance to public honor. If, as has been argued elsewhere, Mark is a response to the propaganda of Vespasian, Jesus' resistance to public honor may be an attempt to counter similar behavior exhibited by the new Flavian emperor. In essence the Markan Jesus beats the Roman emperors at their own game by easily embodying the ideology they must work so hard to appease. In other words, through resisting public honor, the Markan Jesus again out-Caesars the new Caesar, Vespasian.

AN ADVANTAGEOUS SOLUTION

The lack of consistency is a notorious problem for interpretations of Mark's secrecy motif. While Jesus at times silences those who proclaim his identity, he does not always do so (Mk 5:7; 10:47-48). And while Jesus commands some recipients of healings to be silent, he does not command all (e.g., Mk 2:1-12; 3:1-6; 5:24-34; see Mk 5:19, in which Jesus orders the former demoniac to proclaim what has been done for him). Such inconsistencies forced Wrede to conclude that the "messianic secret" was not the creation of the Evangelist but simply the remnants of earlier efforts within the Jesus tradition to explain why Jesus was not recognized as the Messiah. Later solutions that attributed the secrecy motif to the Evangelist have difficulty explaining the inconsistent application of the motif. If the motif serves to advance a theology of the cross in which Jesus cannot be truly identified as Son of God or Messiah before his crucifixion, then why is the secret broken before Jesus' crucifixion (Mk 5:7; 10:47-48; 14:62)?[41] If the motif is an apologetic device to explain why Jesus'

---

[41]For those who support this reading of the Markan secrecy motif, see Jack Dean Kingsbury, *The Christology of Mark's Gospel* (Philadelphia: Fortress, 1983); Francis J. Moloney, *The Gospel of Mark* (Peabody, MA: Hendrickson, 2002), 59-60; M. E. Boring, *Mark*, NTL (Minneapolis: Fortress, 2006), 270; et al. Among current Markan interpreters this is the most widespread interpretation of the Markan secrecy motif.

contemporaries did not recognize him as the Messiah, how are the proclamations of Jesus' messianic identity in Mark accounted for (Mk 5:7; 10:47-48)?[42] If
the secrecy motif serves to highlight Jesus' identity through the intentional and
frequent breaking of the secret, why is the secret not broken at certain points
(Mk 1:25, 34; 3:12; 8:30; 9:9)?[43] If the secrecy motif is not about secrecy at all but
rather an attempt to invert societal understandings of honor and shame, then
why are traditional understandings of honor and shame affirmed throughout
Mark's Gospel? The inconsistency of the Markan secrecy motif is a sandbar on
which numerous explanations of the motif have run aground. But this problem
of the motif's inconsistency poses no problems for my proposed solution.

While resisting public honor was an expression of Roman political ideology,
absolute resistance to public honor was not. Roman emperors were both allowed and expected to receive public honor to a point. Resistance to public
honor was a means by which the emperor drew a line between appropriate and
excessive honor, a way in which the emperor could outwardly affirm his identity
as first citizen and his commitment to Roman political ideology. Thus that Jesus
receives public honor at numerous points throughout Mark is not problematic
for our proposed solution. As God's appointed ruler, Jesus is both allowed and
expected to accept honor. But his occasional resistance to honor demonstrates
his consistency with Roman political ideology and thus contributes to Mark's
response to Roman imperial claims.

CONCLUSION

Since the work of Wrede, the so-called Markan secrecy motif has been understood
to play a significant role in Mark's Christology. Here, following the lead of David
Watson, I have reassessed the meaning and significance of this important christological piece of Mark, concluding that these pieces are best understood in light of
resisting honor rather than concealment of identity. This assessment of the motif
finds added significance when merged with the pieces of Mark's reconstructed
historical setting. Again, such a merging of pieces produces a coherent reading of
Mark, one that would have spoken powerful to first-century Roman Christians.

---

[42]For those who propose an apologetic reading, see Martin Dibelius, *From Tradition to Gospel*, trans.
Bertram Lee Woolf (London: James Clarke, 1971), 230-31, and T. A. Burkill, *Mysterious Revelation:
An Examination of the Philosophy of St. Mark's Gospel* (Ithaca, NY: Cornell University Press, 1963).

[43]For such a solution, see Hans Jürgen Ebeling, *Das Messiasgeheimnis und die Botschaft des Marcus-
Evangelisten* (Berlin: A. Töpelmann, 1939), esp. 167-70.

SIX

JESUS AND THE TEMPLE

T O THIS POINT I have sought to bring together the various pieces of Mark's Christology into a coherent whole by reading Mark's narrative from the vantage point of Roman Christians living in the shadow of Flavian propaganda. I have argued that the pieces of Mark's narrative that present a powerful Jesus and those pieces that present a suffering Jesus are of equal importance in the Markan narrative Christology, and that those pieces find narrative and theological cohesion in the Roman political ideology of Mark's Roman readers. Inseparable from the unity of these pieces are the pieces that interpreters have long understood in terms of secrecy, but which I have argued are best understood as the actions of an ideal ruler resisting public honor. Together these pieces form a narrative that is carefully crafted to respond to Flavian propaganda and ultimately function to address the various crises that such propaganda created for the Roman church.

But to this point my analysis has only brought us through Mark 1–10 and has yet to consider the remaining six chapters of the Gospel. Can the rest of Mark be reasonably understood in terms of my proposed reading of the first ten chapters? While space does not permit an exhaustive analysis of these final six chapters, the next two chapters of this book will consider the way in which two

Much of this chapter is a revised version of my essay "'No Stone Left upon Another': Considering Mark's Anti-Temple Motif in Both Narrative and History," in *Christian Origins and the Formation of the Early Church*, ed. Stanley E. Porter and Andrew W. Pitts, Early Christianity in Its Hellenistic Context Series 4 (Leiden: Brill, forthcoming).

significant portions of the remaining chapters in Mark fit quite well with my previous analysis and further contribute to the Gospel's response to Flavian propaganda. This chapter will examine Jesus' activity in relationship to the temple (Mk 11:1–13:2), while the following chapter will examine the narrative of Jesus' crucifixion, covering portions of Mark 15.

THE TEMPLE IN MARK 11:1–13:2: NARRATIVE CONSIDERATIONS

After being completely absent in the first ten chapters of Mark's Gospel, the temple and its leadership burst on the scene in Mark 11 with remarkable narrative force. As briefly noted in chapter one above, it is widely recognized that these two chapters form a distinct literary unit in Mark, one that is dominated by an antitemple motif. As in previous chapters, I will begin with an assessment of the Markan narrative itself and then consider the way in which that narrative addresses the situation of Mark's Roman readers.

The triumphal entry (Mk 11:1-11). The opening passage of this literary section only mentions the temple explicitly at the end, but it is the final destination of the described procession, and thus it is presupposed throughout the entire pericope. As Jesus enters the city, the present crowds receive him favorably, placing cloaks and branches before him and identifying him as the long-awaited Messiah who will bring about God's salvation (Ὡσαννά) through the establishment of David's kingdom.[1] The crowd's citation of Psalm 118:26 (LXX), εὐλογημένος ὁ ἐρχόμενος ἐν ὀνόματι κυρίου (blessed is the one who comes in the name of the Lord), is noteworthy, as this psalm is a famous Jewish pilgrimage hymn. Thus the crowd's citation of this psalm provides the setting of the event—namely, both they and Jesus are making a pilgrimage to the temple.[2] Yet, the present pilgrimage is unprecedented, as this pilgrimage includes the long-awaited Messiah as a participant. Presumably the crowds anticipate that

---

[1]Francis Moloney argues that the people's acclamation and desire for the kingdom of David is misguided and stands in contrast with the Gospel's clear teaching that Jesus will bring about the kingdom of God (*The Gospel of Mark* [Peabody, MA: Hendrickson, 2002], 219-20); see also Timothy C. Gray, *The Temple in the Gospel of Mark: A Study in Its Narrative Role*, WUNT II/242 (Tübingen: Mohr Siebeck, 2008; repr., Grand Rapids: Baker, 2010), 21-22, and R. T. France, *The Gospel of Mark*, NIGTC (Grand Rapids: Eerdmans, 2002), 434. However, such a conclusion seems unnecessary, as the kingdom of David could certainly be synonymous with the kingdom of God in a Second Temple Jewish context, i.e., it is a descendant of David who will (re)establish God's kingdom. The everlasting kingdom that God promises to David's descendants in 2 Sam 7:16 would not have been understood as a kingdom other than God's own kingdom.

[2]See Gray, *Temple in the Gospel of Mark*, 20-23.

this pilgrimage will end differently from all that have preceded it—specifically, that it will culminate in the establishment of David's messianic kingdom.

When the triumphal entry is understood in this way, Jesus' (and presumably the crowd's) arrival at the temple becomes tremendously significant, as Mark's description of these events builds anticipation for the impending reception of Jesus at the temple. But when Jesus enters the temple with the Twelve, he looks around and then leaves because of the late hour. That Jesus receives no welcome at the temple is striking, and it starkly contrasts with the reception Jesus received from the pilgrims who welcomed him into the city. Here Mark has created an anticlimax where the reader anticipated a climax. The temple authorities, unlike the pilgrims, fail to recognize or receive God's Messiah and apparently have no interest in the salvation he brings. Through this sharp contrast between the pilgrims and the temple authorities, the Markan Evangelist has crafted a pericope that communicates the failure of Israel's leadership. This first critique is only implicit, but as the narrative moves forward, it will quickly be followed by an explicit critique.

While this pericope certainly has its eye on the temple and its failures, it also presents Jesus as God's messianic agent and ruler. In no way does Jesus resist being identified as one who will bring about God's salvation and the kingdom of David. While riding on a donkey might convey humility, this pericope depicts Jesus as a popular and powerful figure, one whose identity should be recognized by the Jewish temple authorities.

A fruitless fig tree and a fruitless temple (Mk 11:12-21). The nature of Jesus' action in the temple has been the object of great debate. Are Jesus' actions best understood as a simply cleansing the temple (i.e., an attempt to remove unjust and immoral practices from the temple), or are they better understood as an act of symbolic judgment and destruction of the temple institution? While much of this debate has focused on the historical Jesus, our present focus is on the way in which the Markan narrative presents Jesus' actions. The following actions of Jesus are presented in Mark 11:15-18: (1) driving out the πωλοῦντας and ἀγοράζοντας ("the sellers" and "the buyers"), (2) overturning the tables of the moneychangers, (3) overturning the seats of those selling doves, and (4) preventing vessels from being carried through the temple.

Traditionally these actions have been understood in terms of Jesus cleansing a corrupt temple, but there is a growing trend among Markan interpreters to understand these actions as a symbolic judgment and destruction of the temple.[3] In order to adjudicate between these two interpretive possibilities, I will consider three areas of evidence: (1) Jesus' actions, (2) Jesus' teaching, and (3) the intercalation of the fig and temple-action pericopes.

Jesus' actions. If Jesus is understood to be merely cleansing a corrupt temple, then many of his actions are difficult to understand. Particularly difficult is the detail of Jesus driving out both those who are selling and those who are buying. For most interpreters who support a reading in which Jesus is cleansing the temple, the sellers are driven out because of corrupt economic practices, such as defrauding those who buy from them. But Timothy Gray astutely asks, how would such a motive explain the Markan Jesus driving out the buyers with the sellers? If economic corruption is the problem Jesus seeks to solve, then the buyers can only be victims in this ring of corruption. Presumably the buyers have not acted corruptly, so why then are they kicked out of the temple along with the sellers? Such an interpretation might fit with the Lukan parallel, as the Third Gospel omits the buyers and only depicts Jesus driving out the sellers (Lk 19:45). But the inclusion of buyers along with sellers in Mark's narrative conveys the termination of all activity in the temple, as without buying and selling animals for sacrifice there can be no sacrifices! Thus Jesus' action of driving out both buyers and sellers is more consistent with a symbolic act of destruction than it is with a cleansing.

After driving out the buyers and sellers, Jesus turns over the tables of the moneychangers and the seats of those who sold doves. E. P. Sanders, followed by others, has argued that both the changing of money and the buying of animals (such as doves) were services necessary in order for pilgrims to participate in the cultic activity of the temple.[4] As such Jesus' actions impede the ability of pilgrims to purchase and offer sacrifices, actions necessary for these pilgrims to receive the expiation of their sins. These actions that obstruct cultic practice seem more consistent with a symbolic destruction of the temple institution, one

---

[3]For Markan interpreters who understand Jesus' temple action as a cleansing of the temple, see Vincent Taylor, *The Gospel According to St. Mark* (London: Macmillan, 1952), 460-61; J. Marcus, *Mark 8–16: A New Translation with Introduction and Commentary*, AB 27A (New Haven, CT: Yale University Press, 2009), 781-95; France, *Mark*, 442-47; Craig A. Evans, *Mark 8:27–16:20*, WBC 34B (Nashville: Thomas Nelson, 2001), 181-82. For those who understand the same action as a symbolic judgment, see Moloney, *Gospel of Mark*, 222-26; Gray, *Temple in the Gospel of Mark*, 25-43; J. R. Daniel Kirk, "Time for Figs, Temple Destruction, and Houses of Prayer in Mark 11:12-25," *CBQ* 74 (2012): 509-27.

[4]See E. P. Sanders, *Jesus and Judaism* (Philadelphia: Fortress, 1985), 61-65, and Jacob Neusner, "Money-Changers in the Temple: The Mishnah's Explanation," *NTS* 35 (1989): 288-89.

that would bring the cessation of its cultic activity, than with the mere cleansing of a corrupt temple. Yet, proponents of a "cleansing" reading have proposed that these actions were not aimed at cultic activity and the cessation of it but rather at the moneychangers and dove sellers who were price-gouging pilgrims. Some argue that such a reading is supported by Jesus' identification of the temple as "a den of robbers," a description that comes from a citation of Jeremiah. While I will address this citation of Jeremiah shortly, I contend here that Mark's use of the word καταστρέφω, a word that more often refers to "destroying" rather than "overturning," is determinative.[5] This violent description of Jesus' actions toward those who sold doves and the moneychangers is more consistent with an intended symbolic destruction and the termination of essential temple activity than it is with the eradication of price gouging or other such corrupt economic activity within the temple.

Finally, the text says that Jesus prevented people from carrying vessels (σκεῦος) through the temple. Within this context, σκεῦος likely refers to cultic vessels that were used in the daily operations of the temple; such vessels would have included items used to carry the gifts and offerings of temple worshipers.[6] If Jesus' intent is simply the cleansing of a corrupt temple, the prevention of such actions is difficult to explain, as the movement of cultic vessels through the temple would have been unrelated to any type of corruption. Kelber astutely notes the significance that such actions would have had: "The obstruction of the vessel's transport effects the cessation of the temple's cultic function. In the view of Mark, therefore, Jesus not only puts an end to the temple's business operation, but he also suspends the practice of cult and ritual. At this point, the temple no longer operates. It is shut down in all its functions."[7] Through halting temple operations, including the offering of sacrifices, Jesus' actions are far more consistent with a prophetic act that signals the *permanent* end of temple operations, an end that would have been consistent with the imminent destruction of the temple itself.

Jesus' teachings. While E. P. Sanders concluded that the actions of the historical Jesus in the temple are a symbolic destruction of the temple, he further concluded that the Scripture citation in Mark 11:17 is a redactional move made by the Evangelist

---

[5]See Gray, *Temple in the Gospel of Mark*, 27.
[6]See ibid., 29; Moloney, *Gospel of Mark*, 223; W. H. Kelber, *The Kingdom in Mark: A New Place and a New Time* (Philadelphia: Fortress, 1974), 99-102; William R. Telford, *The Barren Temple and the Withered Tree: A Redaction-Critical Analysis of the Cursing of the Fig-Tree Pericope in Mark's Gospel and Its Relation to the Cleansing of the Temple Tradition*, JSNTSup 1 (Sheffield: JSOT Press, 1980), 93n102.
[7]Kelber, *Kingdom*, 101.

to present the act as a cleansing rather than a symbolic judgment.[8] Many subsequent interpreters have followed Sanders's lead, concluding that this Scripture citation supports reading the temple activity of the Markan Jesus as a cleansing rather than a symbolic destruction of judgment.[9] Recent studies, however, have persuasively argued the opposite—that Jesus' Old Testament citation, when the cited texts are understood within their original context, is strikingly consistent with interpreting the temple action as a symbolic destruction.

The citation itself fuses two Old Testament texts together, Isaiah 56:7 and Jeremiah 7:11. Regarding the first text, Daniel Kirk correctly identifies Isaiah 56 with an eschatological vision of God's salvation and deliverance.[10] The cited text is part of this vision, as God declares that his house, the temple, "shall be called a house of prayer for all peoples" (Is 56:7). But within the context of Isaiah, such a declaration does not match the current state of the temple (the first temple) due to the current failings of its leaders.[11] According to Isaiah, these leaders are blind sentinels (Is 56:10) and shepherds having no understanding (Is 56:11). According to Kirk, this passage significantly shapes Israel's eschatological expectations for a new and restored temple. Such expectations of a new temple, one to which all nations would be drawn, can be seen in Tobit 13:8-11; 14:5-7; 1 Enoch 90.28-39; and the Temple Scroll from Qumran (11QT^a[11Q19] 29.7-10).[12] Thus through the citation of Isaiah 56:7 the Markan Jesus is pointing out that the current, second temple is no better than the first and that it cannot be identified with the eschatological temple envisioned in Isaiah 56:7, as it has not become a house of prayer for the nations. Like the "blind guides" of the first temple, the current temple leadership has failed, and the current temple has fallen short of eschatological expectations. If this temple is not the eschatological temple envisioned by Isaiah, then a clear conclusion can be drawn—this corrupt temple must be destroyed and replaced by the envisioned Isaianic temple.

While the citation of Isaiah 56:7 might be consistent with interpreting Jesus' actions as symbolic destruction over against a cleansing, does the citation of Jeremiah 7:11 swing the pendulum toward a cleansing? Such is Sanders's contention, as he sees the reference to a "den of robbers" as an indictment on corrupt

---

[8]Sanders, *Jesus and Judaism*, 66.

[9]See Marcus, *Mark 8-16*, 788, and Adela Yarbro Collins, *Mark: A Commentary*, Hermeneia (Minneapolis: Fortress, 2007), 526.

[10]Kirk, "Time for Figs," 515.

[11]See Gray, *Temple in the Gospel of Mark*, 33-34.

[12]See ibid., 33-34, and Kirk, "Time for Figs," 515-16.

financial practices of the temple's leadership. Timothy Gray responds to Sanders by arguing that in both the citation of Isaiah and of Jeremiah the temple itself is in focus rather than the temple's leadership. In Isaiah the *temple* itself functions as a "house of prayer," and in Jeremiah, it is the *temple* itself that has become a *den* where "robbers" dwell or hide. Certainly temple leadership is critiqued by the larger context of these passages, but in the cited texts it is the temple rather than the leadership that is in focus. Kirk keenly argues that the identification of the temple as a den of robbers or bandits has long been misunderstood by interpreters.[13] In identifying the temple as a den of robbers, Jeremiah is not describing the corrupt behavior that takes place in the temple; rather, he is describing a misguided belief that the temple will function to protect all within it regardless of their behavior. Thus the "robbing" described by Jeremiah does not take place within the temple but without, and the temple has become a place where those who have committed robbery outside the temple believe they can find a safe haven within. For this presumptuous attitude, Jeremiah 7 predicts the destruction of the Jerusalem temple. Thus this citation of Jeremiah 7:11 is best understood not as a critique of corrupt financial practices in the temple but an indictment of those who trust in the temple for protection, even when they are not living in accordance with their identity as leaders of God's people outside the temple.[14]

When these Markan Scripture citations are read within the proper Old Testament context, they favor understanding Jesus' action as a symbolic destruction rather than a cleansing. They seem to support the notion that Jesus is condemning both the present temple and its leadership. Through his teaching Jesus is claiming that the present temple is not the eschatological temple promised by Isaiah but rather like the former temple, because its leaders misguidedly believed the temple would protect them regardless of their evil ways. For such failings the former temple was destroyed by the Babylonians, and Jesus' teaching seemingly implies that the present temple awaits the same fate.

The cursing of the fig tree. The strongest evidence for understanding Jesus' temple action as a symbolic judgment or destruction rather than a cleansing is Mark's intercalation of the cursed fig tree pericope with the pericope of Jesus' temple action. Such intercalation, often referred to as a "Markan sandwich," is a common redactional technique of the Markan Evangelist.[15] By merging the

---

[13]Kirk, "Time for Figs," 518-20.
[14]Ibid., 519.
[15]For a thorough treatment of this interpretation, see Telford, *Barren Temple*.

stories together in this way, the Evangelist is inviting the reader to understand these two pericopes as mutually interpretive. Thus the cursed or withered fig tree pericope offers the reader an interpretive lens for understanding the significance of Jesus' temple action. In light of such an intentional literary device, the connection between the two pericopes becomes quite obvious. Jesus finds both a fruitless fig tree and a fruitless temple (the fig tree was a common symbol in the Hebrew Bible for Israel and its temple), which intentionally parallel each other. Thus the cursing of the fig tree parallels the subsequent cursing of the temple.

Just as Jesus' words declare that the fig tree will be eternally barren, so also should Jesus' actions in the temple be understood as a declaration of its eternal barrenness. The barrenness of both the fig tree and the temple is confirmed when Jesus finds the former withered to the root. The reader can be assured that in Jesus' temple action he is predicting the same future as that of the withered fig tree. It must be noted that this intercalation loses all meaning if Jesus' temple action is understood as merely a cleansing. Since there is no way that the cursing and subsequent withering of the fig tree can be understood in terms of "cleansing" or "purification," such a reading cannot be followed without rejecting what appears to be an obvious intercalation by the Markan Evangelist.

In light of this evidence I conclude that Jesus' temple action is best understood as a symbolic destruction of the Jerusalem temple. The fig tree pericope not only supports this interpretation but also functions as a symbolic presentation of the temple's fruitlessness, a fruitlessness that brings about the temple's destruction.

Again, it must be noted that while the focus of this pericope is on the failure of the temple and its authorities, the pericope also depicts Jesus as a powerful and authoritative figure, one who exercises God's judgment over the so-called leaders of Israel. Such a pericope reminds the reader that the powerful Jesus still exercises the same authority he wielded in the first half of the Gospel.

Jesus' teaching on faith, prayer, and forgiveness (Mk 11:22-25). Immediately following the intercalation of the fig tree and temple action pericopes are teachings from Jesus that at first glance seem completely unrelated to the preceding events or to the temple and its destruction. But recent narrative-critical studies have argued that a strong connection exists between this teaching and Jesus' condemnation and symbolic destruction of the temple. The first part of Jesus' teaching seems to be about faith, as Jesus says that if the disciples have faith, they can say to "this mountain, 'Be taken up and thrown into the sea.'" Any connection to the Jerusalem temple and its destruction seems opaque at best.

But the connection becomes clearer when one considers what mountain Jesus is talking about. Traditional interpretations have understood "this mountain" as a generic reference to any mountain, but recent interpreters have proposed that the text has a specific reference in mind—specifically, Mount Zion, on which the temple sat.[16] By identifying the mountain in this way, the narrative flow of the passage improves significantly, and a clear connection between Jesus' temple action and this teaching on faith becomes evident. While certainly faith is a theme of the passage, so also is the destruction of the temple. In essence Jesus responds to his disciples' amazement at the fig tree's destruction by assuring them of access to even greater power. With faith, even they themselves could bring about the destruction of the temple that Jesus has prophesied.[17]

The following teaching on prayer (Mk 11:24) can also be tied to Jesus' prophecy of the temple's destruction. The reader has just been reminded of the eschatological purpose of the temple, namely, that it is meant to be a house of prayer for all nations. Here Jesus promises the disciples power and effectiveness in all prayer that is accompanied by faith. Thus one might conclude that it is among the disciples and the eschatological community they form that the "house of prayer for all nations" will truly be manifest. Here the Evangelist might be claiming that where the physical temple failed, the new temple, the eschatological people of God, will succeed.[18]

The final teaching on forgiveness (Mk 11:25) also finds a thematic connection to the Jerusalem temple. The temple was the place where the atonement and forgiveness of sins was facilitated through sacrifices and offerings. But if the temple is destroyed as Jesus prophesied, the end of the sacrificial system seems to be implied. Thus, just as the eschatological community of God's people will be the locus of prayer for all nations, so also Jesus' teaching on forgiveness may signal that this same community will be the new locus of atonement and forgiveness of sins. If Mark is read in this way, it seems the Evangelist is making a bold claim—that the forgiveness of sin is no longer tied to the temple but to the community's willingness to forgive the sins of others.[19]

---

[16]Ibid., 58-59; Gray, *Temple in the Gospel of Mark*, 48-53.

[17]See John Paul Heil, "The Narrative Strategy and Pragmatics of the Temple Theme in Mark," *CBQ* 59 (1997): 79; Kirk, "Time for Figs," 522-23.

[18]See Gray, *Temple in the Gospel of Mark*, 54; Kirk, "Time for Figs," 523-27; Heil, "Narrative Strategy," 79-80.

[19]See Gray, *Temple in the Gospel of Mark*, 54-55; Kirk, "Time for Figs," 523-27; Heil, "Narrative Strategy," 79-80.

In summation, the focus of Jesus' teaching on faith, prayer, and forgiveness, teaching long seen as disparate in relation to the surrounding pericopes, could actually be directly related to his judgment of the temple. In these teachings one can perceive Jesus as establishing the new messianic community as a replacement for the temple itself.

The question of Jesus' authority (Mk 11:27-33). While entering the temple on the following day, Jesus is confronted by the temple authorities, "the chief priests, the scribes, and the elders." The mention of these three groups reminds the reader of Jesus' first passion predictions, where the reader is told that these three groups will be responsible for Jesus' death (in the third passion prediction only the chief priests and scribes are referenced). Thus the reader knows that those confronting Jesus here will be those responsible for his death, a death that they began plotting after Jesus' action in the temple (Mk 11:18).

In confronting Jesus, they asked him, "By what authority are you doing these things? Who gave you this authority to do them?" (Mk 11:28). Within the narrative it seems quite clear that they are questioning Jesus' authority to challenge the temple and their leadership of it. The answer to the question is obvious to the reader, as the Gospel has demonstrated Jesus wielding the very power of God (e.g., Mk 2:5; 4:39; 5:35-43; 6:48). As such the question functions to highlight the temple authorities' opposition to God and to demonstrate that the stewards of God's temple and people stand in opposition to God's authority. In response Jesus offers his own question about the authority of John the Baptist. The temple leadership is unwilling to answer the question, as it puts them in a difficult predicament, either denial of John's authority, which will be unpopular with the crowds, or condemnation of themselves for not following John. The question functions to further highlight these leaders' ongoing opposition to God's messengers and authority.

The parable of the wicked tenants (Mk 12:1-12). This question regarding Jesus' authority is immediately followed by the parable of the wicked tenants, an allegorical parable that harshly critiques the leadership of Israel both past and present. In the parable a landowner entrusts his vineyard to tenant farmers. When the time comes to collect his portion of the produce, he sends servants to his tenants, but the tenants mistreat each servant that is sent, even killing one of them. The master finally sends his son, anticipating that his son will be respected and thus successful in obtaining the produce. But with the hope of receiving the inheritance of the landowner, the tenants kill the son as well. Jesus concludes the parable by stating that the tenants will certainly be destroyed and that the vineyard will be given over to others.

The meaning of the allegory is easily discernible. The landowner is rightly identified with God, the vineyard is Israel,[20] the tenants are the leadership of Israel both past and present, the servants are the prophets (no doubt including John the Baptist), and the son is Jesus himself, whom the current leadership of Israel will soon kill. Unlike other parables in Mark, this parable is no mystery, as the reader is told that the temple authorities "realized that he had told this parable against them" (Mk 12:12). The parable has two clear functions, closely related to each other: (1) to indict the temple authorities for their opposition to both God and his messenger, and (2) to prophesy the resulting destruction for such opposition.

Questions for Jesus (Mk 12:13-34). The parable of the wicked tenants is followed by three successive stories in which the temple authorities present Jesus with a question, all of which attempt to undermine Jesus' authority. All of these questions are posed to Jesus while he is in the temple precincts.

The first question is brought to Jesus by the Pharisees and the Herodians, though the reader is told that it is the temple authorities who send them with the ultimate goal of trapping Jesus with his words. The question is about paying taxes to Caesar, whether it is lawful for a Jew to do so. There are numerous interpretive issues related to this passage, but for my purposes it is only necessary to note that the answer Jesus gives avoids the trap and successfully thwarts the efforts of the temple authorities leaving them amazed. The next question is presented to Jesus by the Sadducees, the sect to which the temple authorities largely belong. In an attempt to thwart Jesus' authority and credibility, they ask Jesus a question about the resurrection, one that seeks to illustrate the folly of such a belief. But Jesus' response not only thwarts his opponents but also both demonstrates Jesus' authority as an interpreter of Torah and highlights the temple authorities' failure in this regard.

Finally, one of the scribes, a group closely associated with the temple authorities in Mark, asks Jesus which of the commandments is the greatest. Jesus responds to the question with the double love commandment (Mk 12:29-31). Here Mark breaks with the previously established pattern. Instead of disagreement or

---

[20]The clear allusions to the vineyard song of Is 5:1-7 make this identification obvious.

tension between Jesus and his opponent, the two agree regarding the answer. But it is the scribe's response that is remarkable and provides the true import of the final question in the sequence. Not only does the scribe agree with Jesus, but he claims that the love of both God and neighbor is "more important than all whole burnt offerings and sacrifices." Thus the triadic questioning of Jesus by the temple authorities finds its climax in a statement made by one of Jesus' opponents that radically marginalizes the temple's primary function!

In summation, these three questions move Mark's temple motif forward in the following ways: (1) they present the temple authorities as opponents of both God and his messengers, (2) they further demonstrate Jesus' superior authority over that of the temple authorities, and (3) they culminate in a statement that marginalizes the sacrificial system that is central to the temple's purpose.

Jesus and the son of David (Mk 12:35-37). In this section Jesus raises the question of the Messiah's relationship to David. After quoting from Psalm 110, Jesus asks how David can call the Messiah "lord" if he is his son. In chapter two I addressed the interpretive issues of this passage, which have long vexed Markan interpreters. Here I will only briefly summarize the results from what I argued above. The psalm in question has the historical figure of Solomon in mind, as it is Solomon to whom Yahweh says these things. The reason David can call Solomon "my lord" is that David appointed Solomon as king before his death in order to secure succession through Solomon. Thus Jesus is presenting the crowd with a riddle that he knows they will be able to answer. But it is the answer that is significant for Jesus' purposes. By offering the answer Solomon, Jesus is creating an important link between Solomon, who built the Jewish temple, and the Messiah, who Mark is claiming has Solomonic authority over the temple.

The episode therefore is not about whether the Messiah can be a "Son of David" but the authority over the temple that is associated with being a Son of David. This passage fits quite well in Mark's antitemple motif, as it offers scriptural justification for Jesus' authority over the temple. But the passage also functions to further establish Jesus' messianic identify and the scope of Jesus' messianic power, which is that, Jesus is the messianic "Son of David" who, like the previous sons of David, wields authority over Israel's most sacred religious institution and even has the authority to condemn it.

The temple and the poor (Mk 12:38-44). Following Jesus' establishment of his Solomonic authority over the temple, he harshly rebukes the scribes, condemning their ostentatious self-presentation, their impure motives for righteous behavior, and their devouring of widows' possessions. While the temple authorities present themselves as righteous and devout representatives of Yahweh, the Markan Jesus claims that they are quite the contrary. Underneath a veneer of righteousness lies a wickedness that is evinced in the oppression of widows, acts that stands in stark contrast to the Torah-prescribed protection of widows (see Ex 22:21-24; Deut 24:17, 19-22; 27:19). For such acts the leaders of Israel will be recipients of "excessive" divine judgment. The temple authorities are again presented as enemies of God and thus recipients of God's impending judgment.

This scathing critique and condemnation of the scribes is followed by an episode in which Jesus observes various people giving money to the temple treasury. In this episode the large gifts of the affluent are contrasted with the extremely small gift of a widow. In response to these incongruent gifts, Jesus declares that the woman has given more than the wealthy donors because she has given out of her poverty, while they have given out of their wealth. Jesus' words indicate that this woman has in fact given what would be necessary for sustaining her very life. The traditional interpretations of this pericope focus on the sacrificial giving of the woman as a model to be followed, with the accompanying implication that it is not the size of one's gift that matters but rather the attitude of the heart in the act of giving. But these traditional interpretations fail to pay proper attention to the immediate context of this pericope—that is, the preceding denouncement and condemnation of the temple authorities for devouring the possessions of widows.

Seizing on what appears to be an undeniable connection between these two pericopes (if they really are indeed two separate pericopes!), recent interpreters have proposed a radically different interpretation of the woman's gift. Rather than illustrating an ideal for true giving that should be imitated by others, the story actually functions to illustrate the wicked behavior of the scribes. The pericope presents in living color what Jesus has just accused the temple authorities of doing—devouring the possessions of widows.[21] Thus the story illustrates the perversion of God's will (i.e., the care of widows outlined in the Torah) by the very people who have been established by God to enforce his will.

---

[21]For examples, see Addison G. Wright, "The Widow's Mites: Praise or Lament?—A Matter of Context," *CBQ* 44 (1982): 256-65; Moloney, *Gospel of Mark*, 246-47; Ched Myers, *Binding the Strong Man: A Political Reading of Mark's Story of Jesus* (Maryknoll, NY: Orbis Books, 1992), 320-22; Evans, *Mark 8:27–16:20*, 284-85.

Tragically, those who are required by God to care for the needs of widows are taking their possessions instead. In this pericope Mark again vividly illustrates the wickedness of the temple authorities and further demonstrates how the stewards of God's people have become God's opponents.

Predicting the temple's destruction (Mk 13:1-2). The narrative function of Mark 13:1-2 is debated. Do these verses begin a new literary unit in Mark, do they conclude the literary unit of Mark 11–12, or do they function as a narrative hinge that simultaneously concludes one unit and opens another? Most recent interpreters favor the third option—that Mark 13:1-2 has a significant literary connection to both Mark 11–12 and the rest of Mark 13. While I agree that such a function is probable, I argue that the emphasis of this hinge is on concluding Mark 11–12 rather than introducing Mark 13, a position that runs against the grain of the majority position. I contend that the connections between the prediction of the temple's destruction in Mark 11–12 are much stronger and more obvious than the connections of the temple's destruction and the rest of Mark 13. Note the strong connections between Mark 11–12 and Mark 13:1-2: (1) Mark 11–12 begins with Jesus entering Jerusalem and coming to the temple for the first time, while Mark 13:1-2 has Jesus leaving the temple for the last time; (2) virtually all the actions of Mark 11–12 take place in or within close proximity to the temple, and Mark 13:1-2 shares this spatial orientation; and (3) Mark 13:2 functions as an excellent summary of the antitemple motif of Mark 11–12, making explicit what has only been implicit throughout the motif—the destruction of the temple.

But while the connection between Mark 11–12 and Mark 13:1-2 is clear and obvious, the connection between Mark 13:1-2 and Mark 13:3-37 is less so. The only certain connection between these two literary units is that between Jesus' prediction of the temple's destruction (Mk 13:2) and the disciples' question "When will this be, and what will be the sign that all these things are about to be accomplished?" (Mk 13:4). The first part of the question seems to be connected to Jesus' prediction of the temple's destruction, but the second part of the question moves from the singular to the plural, that is, "this thing" to "these things." There seems to be a shift in Mark's focus, or at least a broadening of it, from the specific event of the temple's destruction to the events that Jesus will address in the Olivet discourse—namely, the events related to the parousia and eschaton. Thus, beyond being the initial catalyst for the disciples' question about the eschaton, the connection between the temple's destruction and the rest of the Olivet discourse is unclear and tenuous. Certainly many interpreters argue that the reference to the "desolating sacrilege" is a reference to the temple's destruction, but such a conclusion is far from certain. Some interpreters question whether Mark 13:14 is even addressing the Jerusalem temple at all.[22]

I contend that Mark is written after the temple's destruction; as such, might not the reference to the "desolating sacrilege" be looking forward to future eschatological sign rather than one in the past? And even if Mark 13:14-19 is referring to the destruction of the temple, the focus of Mark 13 seems to be the parousia itself, for which the events of Mark 13:14-19 are only the immediately preceding eschatological signpost rather than the chapter's main event.[23] Thus I conclude that Mark 13:1-2 primarily functions to make a climactic statement for Mark's antitemple motif in Mark 11–12, one that makes explicit what has been implicit throughout this literary unit—the destruction of the Jerusalem temple.

THE ANTITEMPLE MOTIF AND THE MARKAN NARRATIVE

The antitemple motif of Mark 11:1–13:2 finds a strong narrative connection to the passion predictions that dominated Mark 9–10. Jesus finally arrives in Jerusalem, where conflict with the temple authorities, those whom Jesus has specifically predicted will be responsible for his impending death, quickly ensues. While Mark 9–10 introduced Jesus' death as well as its significance, the reader has not yet been made privy to the circumstances that will cause Jesus' death, that is, the why of his execution by religious authorities. This question is quickly answered in Mark 11–12, as the reader realizes that Jesus' harsh critique of the Jewish temple and its authorities will be the catalyst for his death (see Mk 12:1-12).

Beyond this basic narrative function of providing the cause of Jesus' death, which was predicted in Mark 9–11, recent narrative studies of Mark 11–12 have made compelling cases that the antitemple motif that dominates these chapters

---

[22]See Adam Winn, *The Purpose of Mark's Gospel: An Early Christian Response to Roman Imperial Propaganda*, WUNT II/245 (Tübingen: Mohr Siebeck, 2008), 70-76; Joachim Gnilka, *Das Evangelium nach Markus*, Evangelisch-Katholischer Kommentar zum Neuen Testament (Zurich: Neukirchener Verlag, 1979), 2:195-99.

[23]While N. T. Wright (*Jesus and the Victory of God* [Minneapolis: Fortress, 1996], 361-65) and R. T. France (*Mark*, 530-40) have argued that Mk 13:26-27 is not describing the parousia but rather the realities that accompanied the destruction of the Jerusalem (note that Wright and France do not agree on all details related to the interpretation of these verses), I and others remain unconvinced of such a position (e.g., M. E. Boring, *Mark*, NTL [Minneapolis: Fortress, 2006], 373; Evans, *Mark 8:27–16:20*, 329-30; Collins, *Mark*, 614-15).

not only communicates the corruption and subsequent destruction of the Jerusalem temple institution but also that it makes a claim about a new "temple" that will replace the old. This temple will truly be a place of prayer for all nations, and it will be the location in which God's people experience the forgiveness of their sins. Unlike the old temple, this temple will not be a physical building but the new eschatological community of God's people, obviously including the Markan community itself. Thus the antitemple motif in Mark functions to teach the readers of the Gospel their identity as the new temple of God that has replaced the old temple. The functions of the old temple find their fulfillment in this new temple.[24]

Additionally, this section also continues to affirm the unity between the Jesus who will suffer death at the hands of the religious rulers and the powerful Jesus who dominated the first half of Mark's Gospel. The Jesus of Mark 11:1–13:2 is clearly a powerful and authoritative figure. He establishes himself as an authority over God's temple and its current leadership, he frequently thwarts his opponents in arguments, he supernaturally orchestrates events, and he boldly predicts the temple's destruction—a reality I have previously argued had already come to pass for Mark's readers. This powerful figure will embrace his divinely ordained future of suffering and death as an act of service for his people.

WHERE THE NARRATIVE MEETS THE READER

Again we come to the question of how this section of Mark's narrative addresses the concerns of Roman Christians living under the shadow of Flavian propaganda. As demonstrated in the introduction, the destruction of the Jerusalem temple was a central piece in Flavian propaganda. Vespasian presented his victory over Jerusalem and the destruction of the Jewish temple as a major military victory and used it as evidence of divine legitimization of his reign. As discussed previously in the introduction, Vespasian gave prominence to this victory through a variety of means, including a massive triumph, commemorating it on coins, and enshrining it on buildings and monuments (see chapter one for a more thorough discussion).

As noted in chapter one, in addition to communicating his divinely appointed rule over the world, Vespasian's victory also communicated the superiority of his gods, the gods of Rome, over the God of the Jews. Thus Flavian propaganda

---

[24]See Gray, *Temple in the Gospel of Mark*, 90-93, 198-200; Kirk, "Time for Figs," 522-27; Heil, "Narrative Strategy," 76-100.

implied a challenge to the power and honor of the God of Israel—the God of the fledgling Christian faith. By destroying his house and defeating his people, the Romans had shamed the God of the Jews. There is clearly precedent in Israel's history for such challenges to God's honor and power. Exilic prophetic literature refers to the mockery and derision of Yahweh that resulted from the Babylonian destruction of Jerusalem, the first Jewish temple, and the resulting exile of God's people. In Ezekiel 36:20 Yahweh himself describes Israel's exile to the nations in the following way, "When they came to the nations, wherever they came, they profaned my holy name, in that it was said of them, 'These are the people of the LORD, and yet they had to go out of his land.'" In Deutero-Isaiah (Is 48:9-11), it is for the sake of Yahweh's name and the profanation of his name that he will deliver Israel from exile. Presumably, such profanation came from Israel's enemies and was directed at their God, who had failed to protect his people. In Isaiah 52:5 Yahweh describes the nations who have defeated Israel by saying, "Their rulers howl . . . and continually, all day long, my name is despised." Given the Roman theology of victory, it seems quite likely that the current destruction of Jerusalem and the defeat of Yahweh's people would have led to similar mockery and derision from the victorious Romans.

Certainly Roman Christians would not have been immune from such mockery, and as noted in chapter one, the destruction of the temple, along with the rest of Vespasian's propaganda, would have created a significant crisis for the Roman church. While the impact of such propaganda on Jewish Christians would likely have been minimal, given their deep monotheistic roots, it would likely have been much greater on Gentile Christians and recent converts from Greco-Roman paganism. Questions of the legitimacy of the Christian faith and Christian God would no doubt have plagued Gentile congregants and have been an obstacle to Christian mission among Gentiles (again, see chapter one).

Up to this point in the narrative, Mark's Gospel has addressed virtually every piece of Flavian propaganda, but it has not yet addressed Vespasian's destruction of Jerusalem and its temple. I propose that Mark 11:1–13:2 finally addresses this piece of propaganda through a carefully crafted narrative. In response to Flavian propaganda, propaganda undergirded by the theology of victory, Mark argues that the destruction of Jerusalem and its temple is not the result of Rome's great power but rather the result of Yahweh judging a corrupt temple and its corrupt leadership for turning against his purposes. In the Markan narrative God's appointed Messiah not only identifies this corruption and but falls victim to it, as he himself is rejected and executed by the temple authorities. Long before Rome turned its attention to a rebellious Judea, God's appointed ruler, Jesus, recognized a rebellious temple institution and prophesied its utter destruction. Thus the Markan Evangelist uses this antitemple motif to dismantle the power of Flavian propaganda and simultaneously transfers that power to Yahweh and his Messiah, Jesus. Through this move the Gospel of Mark redefines Rome and its emperor as mere pawns in the plans of the Yahweh of Israel.

There is strong precedent for such a move by the Markan Evangelist. The Jewish people make similar arguments in response to the destruction of the first temple by the Babylonians. The exilic and postexilic prophets are quite adamant that the reason for the temple's destruction was not Yahweh's inferiority to pagan gods but rather Yahweh's punishment of an unfaithful people. In Isaiah 42:24-25 the prophet states:

> Who gave up Jacob to the spoiler,
>> and Israel to the robbers?
> Was it not the LORD, against whom we have sinned,
>> in whose ways they would not walk,
>> and whose law they would not obey?
> So he poured upon him the heat of his anger
>> and the fury of war;
> it set him on fire all around, but he did not understand;
>> it burned him, but he did not take it to heart.

Lamentations consistently identifies Yahweh rather than Babylon as the source of Judah's destruction, a destruction that is a result of Judah's wickedness:

> How the Lord in his anger
>> has humiliated daughter Zion!
> He has thrown down from heaven to earth
>> the splendor of Israel;
> he has not remembered his footstool
>> in the day of his anger. (Lam 2:1)

The Babylonians are presented by the prophets as mere pawns in the plans of Yahweh. Jeremiah 25:8-9 states:

> Therefore thus says the LORD of hosts: Because you have not obeyed my words,
> I am going to send for all the tribes of the north, says the LORD, even for King

Nebuchadnezzar of Babylon, my servant, and I will bring them against this land and its inhabitants, and against all these nations around; I will utterly destroy them, and make them an object of horror and of hissing, and an ever-lasting disgrace.

Similarly in Ezekiel 21, Babylon is depicted as a sword that Yahweh uses to punish his people. I contend that the Markan Evangelist is following the precedent of Israel's prophets and that the Markan antitemple motif is thus a narratival attempt to explain the current destruction of the temple in the same way the prophets explained the first destruction.

There is even precedent for Jews contemporary with Mark making similar arguments to explain this destruction of the second Jewish temple. Such a response can be found in 2 Baruch, a late first-century apocalypse. In 2 Baruch the response is coded as a response to Babylon's destruction of the first temple, but in actuality it is addressing the Roman destruction of the second. Second Baruch presents God as orchestrating foreign powers and using them as pawns in the destruction of the temple.[25] Similarly, the Apocalypse of Abraham (a late first- or early second-century CE text) attributes the Roman destruction of the temple to Yahweh himself, who uses Rome as a tool for punishing Jewish infidelity (Apocalypse of Abraham 27).

However, for my purposes perhaps the most significant explanation of the temple's destruction is provided by Josephus.[26] For Josephus the destruction of the temple was in fact the will of God, and it was ordained by God as an act of judgment against a small group of rebellious Jews.[27] Like the prophets of Israel, 2 Baruch, and the Apocalypse of Abraham, Josephus presents Rome as an agent of God used to bring about God's will, but an agent who wants no part in such destruction.[28] This agency of God is perhaps best illustrated in a quotation, no doubt a creation of Josephus himself, from the Roman general and future Flavian emperor Titus: "God indeed has been with us in the war. God it was who

---

[25]For discussion see Philip F. Esler, "God's Honour and Rome's Triumph: Responses to the Fall of Jerusalem in 70 CE in Three Jewish Apocalypses," in *Modelling Early Christianity*, ed. Philip F. Esler (London: Routledge, 1995), 235-38.

[26]For the following arguments I am greatly indebted to work of Steve Mason ("Figured Speech and Irony in T. Flavius Josephus 1," in *Flavius Josephus and Flavian Rome*, ed. J. Edmondson et al. [Oxford: Oxford University Press, 2005], 260-65) and Jason Whitlark (*Resisting Empire: Rethinking the Purpose of the Letter to "the Hebrews,"* LNTS 484 [London: T&T Clark, 2014], 175-76).

[27]Josephus, *J.W.* 7.358-360; 1.10-12.

[28]Josephus, *J.W.* 1.10.

brought down the Jews from these strongholds; for what power have human hands or engines against these towers."[29]

If Mark's temple motif functions to communicate the replacement of the old temple with a new temple—namely, Mark's reading community—then the motif might go a step beyond simply countering Flavian propaganda. Not only would the motif defend the community (and the God it serves) from shame, but it would also empower that community through giving it a new identity. According to the Markan antitemple motif, a new temple, the Markan community itself, has already been created and was occupied by Yahweh long before the Jerusalem temple was destroyed by the Romans. As such, in destroying the temple, Rome simply destroyed an empty shell, the former house of Yahweh that had long been abandoned. Yahweh's true home, the place where atonement for sins can be found and the true house of prayer for all nations, is indeed the people who follow Jesus, God's appointed world ruler. The words of Mark 11:23 take on greater meaning when read in the context of Flavian propaganda. With these words Jesus communicates the power that his readers possess in light of their new identity, a power greater than that of Roman legions, as in faith his readers are able to cast the entire temple mount into the sea. Thus, far from being a sign of divine favor on Rome, the destruction of the Jerusalem temple is presented as a sign of divine favor on the Markan community, establishing it as the true dwelling place of God and divine power.

---

[29]Josephus, *J.W.* 6.410-411, trans. H. St. J. Thackeray, LCL, vol. 3 (Cambridge, MA: Harvard University Press, 1928).

SEVEN

JESUS IN MARK'S
PASSION NARRATIVE

THE MARKAN PASSION NARRATIVE has played a significant role in the assessment of Mark's Christology. For the redaction critics the passion narrative is the ultimate statement against the Markan opponents who promoted a Christology of power and glory. For Kingsbury the passion narrative is the moment to which Mark's messianic secret was building, and he concluded that only after Jesus' crucifixion could Jesus be rightly and openly identified as God's Son. For narrative critics the passion narrative is the culmination of the Markan narrative, and thus it must play a significant role in shaping the Christology of the entire Gospel. While many narrative critics are willing to see a tension between power and suffering in Mark's Christology, the passion narrative plays a pivotal role in leading many to privilege the suffering Jesus over the powerful Jesus in their assessment of Mark's narrative Christology.

In light of such assessments of Mark's passion narrative, it must be considered whether my presentation of Mark's narrative Christology not only fits with Mark's climactic passion narrative but can be advanced by it. Does Mark's passion narrative necessarily privilege the suffering of Jesus in Mark's Christology, or might it fit with my proposal that Mark has brought Jesus' power and suffering together through the use of Roman political ideology? Additionally, how might Mark's passion narrative be read in light of Flavian propaganda? Are

there features of Mark's passion narrative that might advance the Markan po-
lemic against Vespasian that I have outlined to this point? To these questions I
turn in this final chapter.

THE CHRISTOLOGY OF MARK'S PASSION NARRATIVE: CONSIDERING THE ENTIRE PICTURE

The christological conclusions that the above-mentioned interpreters have
drawn from Mark's passion narrative are not surprising given the general
content of this distinct literary unit, content that contains details that magnify
suffering, shame, humility, and death. The Markan Jesus is betrayed, abandoned,
and denied by his closest followers. He is lied about, mocked, beaten, and spit
on by Jewish authorities. Roman soldiers beat and mock him. Finally, he is
crucified, during which he is mocked even further. Some even argue that
through the quotation of Psalm 22 Jesus proclaims that he has been abandoned
by God himself. In light of such a stark picture of pain, rejection, and abandonment, it is no wonder that many interpreters have concluded that the climactic part of the Markan narrative tips the christological scales in the direction
of the suffering Jesus over against the powerful one.

Certainly interpreters who have reached such conclusions have done so for
good reasons, and any attempt to transform Jesus' death from one largely characterized by shame to a death characterized by honor or power would be mistaken.[1] The death of Jesus is a shameful death, to be sure. But in reaching such
a conclusion, I again stress that the reader should pay attention to the entire
narrative in assessing the christological import of this final climactic literary
unit. It must be remembered that this shameful death has been foretold by Jesus
explicitly on three separate occasions, and, as I have previously argued, Mark
has cast this death in terms of Jesus embodying, perhaps to the extreme, Roman
political ideology. If one accepts my previous arguments, then this death is not
a negation of the powerful Jesus who dominated the first half of Mark's Gospel,
a Jesus who is in fact quite present until (and through?) the passion narrative.
Rather, this death is the proper outcome for the true ruler of the world. He must
embrace this shameful death as an act of service for his people—an act that
Mark has used to highlight his greatness rather than to mitigate it.

---

[1] I note my own such attempt to do this exact thing (see Adam Winn, *The Purpose of Mark's Gospel:
An Early Christian Response to Roman Imperial Propaganda*, WUNT II/245 [Tübingen: Mohr Siebeck, 2008], 127-35), and I am thankful for the critics who guided me away from such an extreme.

In fact there seem to be numerous factors within the passion narrative itself that confirm what I have argued to this point—that Mark presents a unity rather than a tension between the powerful Jesus, whom God has appointed as his ruler of the world, and the suffering Jesus, who experiences pain, shame, and death. In the Gospel's narration of Jesus' shameful death the author is consistently weaving details into the narrative to remind the reader that this suffering figure is truly God's appointed ruler and that his suffering is actually consistent with such an identity. These details and their significance for the Christology of the passion narrative have often been either ignored or marginalized by Markan interpreters. I will consider these details here.

PROPHETIC FULFILLMENT AND THE SO-CALLED CRY OF DERELICTION

The role of prophecy and fulfillment in the passion narrative, that is, prophecy correctly made by Jesus and prophecy Jesus himself fulfills, functions to remind the reader of Jesus' great power and significance, even in the face of his shame and suffering. The entire narrative itself is a fulfillment of the passion predictions made by Jesus in Mark 8–10; thus the entire episode illustrates Jesus' prophetic power. As noted previously, the ability to predict one's death and the details surrounding it would have been regarded as a sign of divine power. It must always be remembered that the passion narrative in Mark fulfills Jesus' prophetic word and thus conveys his divine power. But even within the narrative Jesus predicts numerous events that come to pass, including Judas's betrayal, Peter's triple denial, and the desertion of his disciples. Placing these events within the context of Jesus' prophetic voice not only emphasizes his divine power but also removes some of the shame and embarrassment associated with the failure of his followers. This failure and betrayal does not surprise Jesus, and thus he is distanced from the shame related to it.

While the Markan passion narrative does not explicitly claim that Jesus' death fulfills Jewish Scripture, Mark seemingly implies such fulfillment. Psalm 22 plays a pivotal role in Mark's passion narrative, and it is undeniable that the Evangelist sees the psalm as in some sense a prophetic voice that prefigures Jesus' suffering and death. The psalm is explicitly referenced in Mark 15:34, as Jesus' cry from the cross, "My God, my God, why have you forsaken me?" is a citation of the psalm's first line. Much has been made of this citation by Markan interpreters, with many reading the line as communicating the culmination of Jesus' abandonment on the cross—that is, the abandonment of God himself.[2] Such a reading of Jesus' cry from the cross often plays a prominent role in interpretations of the passion narrative that promote suffering over power as Mark's primary christological orientation. This cry of dereliction is seen as the culmination of a narrative Christology that is crucicentric and eschews any dimension of power and glory.[3]

While such a reading is currently in vogue among Markan interpreters, it is not the only possible reading of Jesus' cry from the cross. Jesus' citation of the first line of Psalm 22 may very well function to invoke the entirety of the psalm, with the intention of providing a prophetic background for the entire crucifixion narrative. That the Gospel intends for the citation of the psalm to function in this way is strongly supported by unmistakable parallels between the details of the psalm and those of the crucifixion narrative itself. Psalm 22:7, "All who see me mock at me; they make mouths at me, they shake their heads," finds a strong parallel with Mark 15:29, "Those who passed by derided him, shaking their heads and saying . . ." Psalm 22:18, "They divide my clothes among themselves, and for my clothing they cast lots," parallels Mark 15:24, "and divided his clothes among them, casting lots to decide what each should take." Finally, Psalm 22:15, "My mouth is dried up like a potsherd, and my tongue sticks to my jaws," parallels Mark 15:23, 36, "And they offered him wine mixed with myrrh; but he did not take it . . . and someone ran, filled a sponge with sour wine, put it on a stick, and gave it to him to drink." It seems clear that the Evangelist intends for Jesus' death to be understood as a prophetic fulfillment of the suffering righteous one described in Psalm 22, as readers are seeing the fulfillment of Psalm 22 described before them. Thus it seems quite likely that Jesus' citation of the first line of the psalm functions to draw the reader to this conclusion.

But if the Gospel is using Jesus' cry to invoke the entirety of Psalm 22, the invocation has significant implications for the christological significance of the cry itself. Many interpreters have noted that Psalm 22 does not end in suffering and death but rather ends in deliverance and vindication of the suffering righteous one. Thus it only seems reasonable to conclude that Jesus' cry from

---

[2] See Matthew S. Rindge, "Reconfiguring the Akedah and Recasting God: Lament and Divine Abandonment in Mark," *JBL* 130, no. 1 (2011): 755-74; Francis J. Moloney, *The Gospel of Mark* (Peabody, MA: Hendrickson, 2002), 326-27; Sharon Dowd, *Reading Mark: A Literary and Theological Commentary on the Second Gospel* (Macon, GA: Smyth & Helwys, 2000), 160-61; et al.

[3] See Moloney, *Gospel of Mark*, 326.

the cross, a cry that invokes the entirety of Psalm 22, not only looks back to the details of his suffering that fulfill the psalm but also looks forward to the details of his resurrection that also fulfill the psalm.[4]

Surprisingly, narrative critics who see a strong connection between Jesus' cry from the cross and a crucicentric Christology eschew any such attempt to connect the cry with Jesus' future vindication—even interpreters who are willing to see Psalm 22 as an intentional background to Mark's passion narrative. But such a refusal to recognize the clear connections between a suffering righteous one who is vindicated in the psalm that Mark is invoking and the suffering Jesus, who will be vindicated through resurrection in the Markan narrative, seems to be a refusal to see the obvious. It seems the motive driving such a denial is the rejection of attempts to make Jesus' cry from the cross simply a forward-looking claim to God's future vindication without any appreciation or recognition of his present suffering. I stand in agreement with these interpreters in concluding that such a move would be to swing the pendulum too far, but I disagree with their refusal to recognize any connection between Jesus' cry from the cross and his recognition of future vindication. Such a refusal simply ignores obvious aspects of the Markan narrative. Already in the Markan narrative, Jesus has thrice foretold of his future suffering as well as his future vindication (Mk 8:31; 9:31; 10:33-34). It seems narrativally illogical to then conclude that the crucified Markan Jesus perceives in his citation of Psalm 22 nothing but suffering when he has already predicted that his suffering will be followed by the vindication of resurrection. That the Markan narrative ends in resurrection only further strengthens the claim that Jesus' citation of Psalm 22 intends to look both backward and forward, to his suffering and to his vindication as realities that fulfill Jewish Scripture.

Thus I contend that in the Markan Jesus' citation of Psalm 22 we see the very unity that I have proposed for Mark's Christology—namely, a unity between Jesus as both a powerful and a suffering figure. While not denying the suffering communicated in Jesus' cry from the cross, one should not deny that the same cry looks forward to the glory and vindication that awaits Jesus on the other side of suffering, and that it also sees both Jesus' suffering and vindication as realities

---

[4]For similar conclusions see Joel Marcus, *Way of the Lord: Christological Exegesis of the Old Testament in the Gospel of Mark* (Louisville: Westminster John Knox, 1992), 182; Kelli S. O'Brien, *The Use of Scripture in the Markan Passion Narrative*, LNTS 384 (London: Bloomsbury T&T Clark, 2010), 152-54.

that fulfill Jewish Scripture. Presenting Jesus' death as a fulfillment of Scripture ultimately functions to remind the reader that Jesus' suffering is not antithetical to his position as God's powerful ruler; this suffering was ordained by God for just such a powerful figure.

SIGNS OF GREATNESS AND POWER

The death of the Markan Jesus is accompanied by two supernatural signs, which communicate to the reader the greatness and power of Jesus. The first sign is the darkness that covers the whole land during Jesus' crucifixion (Mk 15:33). The darkness comes in the sixth hour, or noon, the time at which the sun should be the highest in the sky. Yet at Jesus' death the brightest hour of the day is consumed by darkness. Such cosmic signs were a common trope in the deaths of great and powerful men. Diogenes claims that the death of the philosopher Carneades was accompanied by a lunar eclipse.[5] Both Plutarch and Virgil claim that the sun hid its face at the death of Julius Caesar.[6] Similar darkness seems to have been associated with the deaths of both Alexander the Great and the founder of Rome, Romulus.[7] Mark's Roman readers would no doubt have read this darkening of the sun as a cosmic sign that Jesus was indeed a man of great importance, despite his shameful death. This detail of "darkness at noon" also finds a strong parallel with Amos 8:9 and thus further links Jesus' death with a fulfillment of Jewish Scripture, demonstrating again that this death of Jesus is in accordance with God's divine will and does not undermine Jesus' identity as God's powerful world ruler.

The second sign is the tearing of the temple veil from top to bottom at the death of Jesus (Mk 15:38). The significance of this event is debated, yet regardless of one's interpretation of the specific significance of this event (e.g., a symbolic destruction of the temple, the first step of its destruction, or the end of the Jewish sacrificial system), the event attributes great significance to Jesus' death as well as to Jesus himself. Again the reader is reminded that this Jesus, despite his suffering and death, is a figure of great importance and power. The latter does not mitigate the former. Through these signs Mark brings together a Jesus of both great power and great suffering.

---

[5]Diogenes Laertius, *Lives and Opinions of Eminent Philosophers* 6.64.
[6]Plutarch, *Caesar* 69.3-5; Virgil, *Georgica* 1.463-468.
[7]See Robert Gundry's discussion of the competing traditions on darkness related to Romulus's death (*Mark: A Commentary on His Apology for the Cross* [Grand Rapids: Eerdmans, 1993], 963). On Alexander the Great, see *Alexander Romance* 3.33.5.

A UNIQUE CRUCIFIXION

Death by crucifixion was generally slow and painful, a death that could take days to complete. Thus that Jesus' crucifixion only lasts for six hours is a rather remarkable detail. This detail might suggest to the Roman reader that Jesus held control over his own death, that he chooses to lay his life down after a short time on the cross. The Gospels of both Luke and John communicate such control (Lk 23:46; Jn 19:30) and are stating explicitly what perhaps is implicit in Mark. The brevity of Jesus' crucifixion would have been noteworthy to the Roman reader and would have led to the perception that Jesus' death was anything but ordinary. Another unique detail in the narration of Jesus' crucifixion is his loud cry from the cross. Given that crucifixion was essentially a death by suffocation (as victims slowly lost strength, they were unable to keep their own body weight from restricting their lungs), the ability of the victim to cry out loudly from the cross would have been surprising to the ancient reader and would have evinced the significant strength of the victim.

In light of these two details, one might conclude that while Jesus experiences the shameful death of crucifixion, he experiences it unlike others before him. In the midst of this shameful death, he is able to cry with great strength from the cross. And unlike others Jesus does not languish on the cross but rather seems to give up his own life after a relatively short six hours. These details, combined with the signs noted above, signal to the reader that this death is far from ordinary, as is the one experiencing it. In this way Mark is able to continue to hold together both Jesus' greatness and identity as God's appointed ruler with his shameful suffering and death.

JESUS' PASSION AS A ROMAN TRIUMPH

To this point I have sought to demonstrate that the Markan passion narrative does not solely favor Christology that is crucicentric but that even in the passion narrative Mark holds together his presentation of Jesus as a figure of both power and suffering. These two sides of Mark's christological coin remain present in Mark's passion narrative. But I have yet to consider the fusion of these two christological images within the context of Roman political ideology, which I have previously argued is the bridge that brings these two apparently contradictory images into unity. I have also not yet considered the way in which Mark's passion narrative might function to address the crisis of Flavian propaganda that faced Mark's readers. The work of T. E. Schmidt, which draws parallels between Mark's passion narrative and a Roman imperial triumph, provides a way forward for both of these unresolved issues.[8]

A Roman triumph was essentially a massive parade that functioned to honor and celebrate a victorious Roman general or emperor for military success.[9] While no two triumphs were created equally, many features were common to most triumphs. Schmidt notes that a significant number of these features find striking parallels in Mark's passion narrative.

The first point of comparison is Mark's use of the word *praetorian* to describe the Roman military headquarters in Jerusalem as the location of Jesus' trial (Mk 15:16). While the word *praetorian* could certainly have described this military compound in Jerusalem, it also was a word that described the personal body-guard of the emperor, who would have been present at a Roman triumph. Schmidt proposes a double purpose for this word—both the identification of a physical location for Jesus' trial and the use of a reference that would have drawn the reader's mind to the Roman imperial world.[10]

In the same verse Mark also references the presence of an entire cohort of Roman soldiers—a military unit numbering approximately six hundred. Many interpreters have noted that such a detail seems historically implausible, as it would be unlikely for such a large number of soldiers to be present for the trial of a single Roman criminal.[11] While some have countered that, at a time such as Passover and with the arrest of a popular "messianic" claimant, such a larger number is reasonable. That Jerusalem itself only had one permanent cohort in the entire city throughout the year and perhaps two at the time of Passover makes it unlikely that even these events would have required the presence of such a large percentage of the available military strength of the city. In light of such an implausible historical detail, Schmidt argues that Mark has added (or exaggerated) this detail for the sake of creating a parallel with a Roman triumph, at which an entire cohort of Roman soldiers would have been present.[12]

---

[8]T. E. Schmidt, "Mark 15.16-32: The Crucifixion Narrative and the Roman Triumphal Procession," *NTS* 41 (1995): 1-18.

[9]For discussion of Roman triumphs see H. S. Versnel, *Triumphus: An Inquiry into the Origin, Development and Meaning of the Roman Triumph* (Leiden: Brill, 1970).

[10]Schmidt, "Mark 15.16-32," 6.

[11]See C. E. B. Cranfield, *The Gospel According to St. Mark*, Cambridge Greek Testament Commentary (Cambridge: Cambridge University Press, 1959), 452; Morna D. Hooker, *The Gospel According to St. Mark*, Black's New Testament Commentaries 2 (Peabody, MA: Hendrickson, 1991), 370; R. T. France, *The Gospel of Mark*, NIGTC (Grand Rapids: Eerdmans, 2002), 637; et al.

[12]Schmidt, "Mark 15.16-32," 6.

In the following verse (Mk 15:17) we again find a detail that strains historical plausibility but also finds a striking parallel with a Roman triumph—that is, Jesus' adornment with a purple garment. Purple garments were incredibly rare in the ancient Mediterranean world and extremely expensive. Schmidt argues that no one below the rank of equestrian would have been allowed to wear such a robe. As such Schmidt argues that it is highly implausible that such a robe would have been placed on the criminal Jesus. That Matthew changes the color of the robe to scarlet, the color of a Roman soldier's cloak, suggests that the first Evangelist perceived the historical implausibility of this Markan detail. But while this detail might be out of place in a historical remembrance of Jesus' passion, it finds a plausible home in an intentional Markan parallel of a Roman imperial triumph. Before the triumphal procession began, the Roman triumphator would have been adorned in just such a purple garment. Schmidt proposes that Mark has created the detail of a purple robe in order to further a parallel between Jesus' passion and a Roman triumph.[13] In addition to the adornment with a purple robe, a crown of thorns is placed on Jesus' head. This detail again finds a parallel in Roman triumph, as the triumphator would have worn a laurel crown on his head.

In Mark 15:18-19 Jesus receives mock praise from Roman soldiers, as they salute him, verbally recognize his position, and prostrate themselves before him. Such actions parallel the homage Roman soldiers paid to the triumphator at the outset of a Roman triumph. Certainly Mark portrays these actions as mockery, but even such mockery continues the parallels between an actual Roman triumph and Mark's creation of an "antitriumph."[14]

The detail of Simon of Cyrene carrying Jesus' cross (Mk 15:21) creates a further parallel with a Roman triumph. In a triumph a bull that was to be sacrificed was led in the procession. Next to the bull walked a Roman official who carried a double-bladed ax, the instrument of the bull's death, over his shoulder. In the Markan parallel Jesus replaces the sacrificial bull as Simon caries the instrument of death over his shoulder.[15]

The parallels continue with Mark's description of the place at which Jesus' procession ends, Golgotha, Aramaic for "the place of the skull." A Roman triumph ended at the temple of Jupiter, the Capitolium, a Latin word derived from the word

---

[13]Ibid, 7.
[14]Ibid, 8. For others who have noted similarities between this veneration and royal veneration, see Winn, *Purpose of Mark's Gospel*, 131n123.
[15]Schmidt, "Mark 15.16-32," 9-10.

caput or "head." The name finds its origins in a legend about a skull that was found during the construction of the temple's foundation. Thus the processions of both Jesus and the Roman triumphator end at the place of the skull.[16]

In Mark 15:23 Mark offers a detail that is unique in the canonical passion narratives. Jesus is offered wine mixed with myrrh, but he refuses the wine. This detail finds a striking parallel in Roman triumphs, as at the end of the procession the triumphator would have been offered wine, which he would have refused. Immediately after he had refused the wine, the bull would have been sacrificed. Strikingly, immediately after Jesus refuses the wine, the Markan text reads, "and they crucified him."[17] While this detail finds a parallel in Matthew (it is absent in both Luke and John), the tradition is modified. Jesus is offered wine mixed with gall, but unlike the Markan Jesus, the Matthean Jesus tastes the wine before rejecting it. Again it seems plausible to conclude that Mark has intentionally created a parallel with a Roman triumph that the Gospel of Matthew has obscured.

The final parallel noted by Schmidt is that of Jesus being crucified between two thieves, with one on his right and one on his left.[18] At the end of a Roman triumph the triumphator was often elevated above the ground. While at times the triumphator was alone, many examples exist in which he was flanked by two men, one on his right and left. The emperor Tiberius was seated between his two consuls.[19] Claudius was seated between his two sons-in-law.[20] And Vespasian was seated between his sons, Titus and Domitian.[21]

In addition to the parallels offered by Schmidt, I propose that the confession of the centurion might offer an additional parallel to a Roman triumph, or at the least fit quite well with the conclusion that Mark has presented Jesus' death as such.[22] There has been much debate regarding the nature of the centurion's confession, with much of the debate considering whether the confession is an authentic confession of Christian faith or simply a generic recognition of Jesus' greatness (i.e., his greatness ranks him as a son of god among many others). I want to set that debate aside for the moment and address a secondary but often related issue: the catalyst for the confession.

---

[16]Ibid., 10-11.
[17]Ibid., 11-12.
[18]Ibid., 14-16.
[19]Suetonius, *Tib.* 17.
[20]Cassius Dio, *Roman History* 60.23.1.
[21]Josephus, *J.W.* 7.125.
[22]While Schmidt sees significance in the confession of the Roman centurion, our understandings differ. For Schmidt on the Roman centurion see "Mark 15.16-32," 16-17.

The reader is told that the centurion's confession comes after he "saw that in this way he breathed his last" (Mk 15:39). Thus it seems the manner of Jesus' death is the catalyst for the centurion's confession.[23] Various theories have been proposed as to what about the manner of Jesus' death triggers the centurion's recognition and declaration of Jesus' divine sonship, including the portents of darkness and the tearing of the temple's veil, the loud and perhaps impressive cry from the cross, or simply that the death itself mysteriously turns blindness into sight.[24] While such views have varying degrees of merit, I contend that Mark's reference to the manner in which Jesus died is directly tied to Mark's presentation of Jesus' death as a Roman triumph. It references the entirety of the triumph, beginning with the mockery from the Roman soldiers at the praetorian (which the centurion presumably witnessed) and culminating in Jesus' death. Thus I propose that what the centurion recognizes is the "triumph" that Jesus has received at the hands of the Roman soldiers themselves, and such recognition elicits from him a confession that a centurion would normally have offered to a triumphant Roman emperor, "son of god."

The confession of the centurion is thus a narrative feature of Mark functioning on both the micro and macro level. On the micro level the confession signals recognition of the passion turned "triumph" in the Markan passion narrative. On the macro level the confession functions as a narrative fulfillment of the Markan incipit, which challenges Vespasian's propagandistic claims and presents Jesus rather than the Roman emperor as the true Messiah and Son of God. The debate as to whether or not the centurion offers a genuine confession reflecting Christian faith (the Son of God) or a generic confession of Jesus' greatness (a son of god) misses the confession's narrative function entirely. For the Markan Evangelist the confession is a true one, to be sure, as Jesus is indeed Son of God. But more importantly, Mark presents a Roman soldier offering allegiance that would normally have been reserved for the Roman emperor alone to Jesus—to the Roman reader, the centurion's declaration would have represented a change in allegiance.

Thus I contend that again the Markan Evangelist uses Roman political ideology and imagery to unify two sets of seemingly disparate christological

---

[23]For a similar conclusion see France, *Mark*, 658-59.

[24]For a thorough discussion of these various interpretations, see Brian K. Gamel, "The Centurion's Confession as Apocalyptic Unveiling: Mark 15:39 as a Markan Theology of Revelation" (PhD diss., Baylor University [currently in press with T&T Clark and forthcoming in the LNTS series]), 99-134.

pieces—namely, those pieces related to power and those related to suffering. The unity of these christological pieces articulated in Mark 10:42-45 finds narratival embodiment in Mark's presentation of Jesus' death as Roman triumph. As argued previously, Mark 10:42-45 uses Roman political ideology to boldly claim that Jesus' identity as God's powerful appointed ruler finds its truest expression in service and self-sacrifice, particularly in the act of giving up one's life for the sake of others. This teaching clearly finds its fulfillment in the passion narrative, as it is enacted by Jesus—the powerful ruler of God indeed gives up his life for his people. But in a stroke of narrative brilliance, the Markan Evangelist presents this enactment of Jesus' teaching in Mark 10:42-45 as a Roman triumph. Thus the Markan Jesus is ironically honored in a traditional Roman way for living out, granted in a radical and extreme way, cherished Roman political ideology. But Mark is able to use this motif of a Roman triumph not only to enact the Roman political ideology of Mark 10:42-45 but also to form an inclusio with his incipit, one that brings to narrative fulfillment the challenge to Vespasian that is found in Mark's opening verse.

Such a creative narrative move finds a clear and significant payoff for Mark's Roman readers living in the shadow of Flavian propaganda. The death of Jesus, likely perceived by some of Mark's readers as a weakness on Jesus' résumé (particularly in comparison to that of Vespasian), is transformed into a strength. Jesus' death is an act of extreme benefaction for his people and embodies the political ideals that were deeply ingrained in Mark's readers. Roman imperial power is both mocked and undermined, as in their attempt to crucify Jesus, Roman soldiers have unwittingly given him a triumph.[25] As we have seen throughout this treatment of Mark's Gospel, the pieces of Mark's passion narrative fit well with the reconstructed context of Mark's Gospel and yield a coherent reading of the latter.

---

[25]Such an attempt to understand Jesus' death in terms of a Roman triumph would not be without precedent in the first-century Christian movement. The letter to the Colossians uses triumph imagery when describing the victory accomplished through the crucifixion (Col 2:15). For discussion see Paul Foster, *Colossians*, Black's New Testament Commentaries (London: Bloomsbury T&T Clark, 2016), 275-77; Peter T. O'Brien, *Colossians, Philemon*, WBC 44 (Waco, TX: Word, 1982), 128-29.

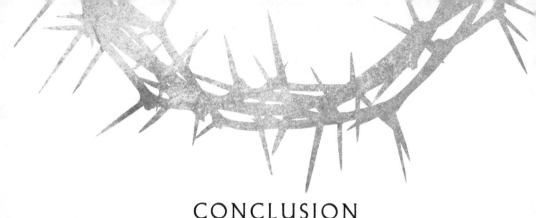

CONCLUSION

FROM THE OUTSET OF THIS BOOK my goal has been to assemble into a coherent whole the christological pieces found within and shaped by the Markan narrative. Under the conviction that Mark's Christology is embedded in and thus inseparable from a narrative, my method has been to read the Gospel as a literary whole. But contra many recent narrative studies of Mark, I have read the narrative in light of a historical reconstruction of the Gospel's intended audience—specifically, Gentile Christians living under the shadow of Flavian propaganda in post–70 CE Rome. While this method of reading Mark's Gospel has shaped many of my interpretive conclusions throughout, here I briefly summarize the three major conclusions of the book.

1. I conclude that the pieces of Mark's Christology that emphasize a powerful Jesus as well as those that emphasize a suffering Jesus are of equal importance in the Markan narrative, and as such it is mistake to privilege one set of pieces over another in the reconstruction of Mark's Christology. To privilege either set of pieces violates realities that are clearly present in the Markan narrative and forces one part of the narrative to cannibalize another. In the Markan narrative it is undeniable that Jesus is God's messianic agent in terms of tremendous power, honor, and glory. To deny such a conclusion would be to deny a strand that I have demonstrated runs through the entirety of Mark's narrative. But Jesus is equally God's messianic agent in terms of

tremendous suffering and shame, which ultimately culminates in his death. To deny such a conclusion would be to deny an obvious literary and theological conviction of the Markan Evangelist.

2. While the two christological poles of suffering and power may seem to stand in tension with each other when the Markan narrative stands alone apart from any particular context, they find a coherent unity when they are read in light of my reconstructed historical setting for the Gospel, one in which Roman political ideology would have been prominent. If Mark was writing for Roman Christians who held to or were at least familiar with this political ideology, then Mark 10:42-45 can be understood as a bridge between the powerful Jesus and the suffering Jesus. Quite in line with Roman political ideology, Jesus the powerful world ruler serves rather than dominates and ultimately sacrifices his life on behalf of his people—an ideal ruler indeed from a Roman perspective!

3. In addition to arguing that Mark's Christology strongly affirms both Jesus' power and suffering and that the two find unity in the realm of Roman political ideology, I have also argued that from beginning to end Mark presents a thoroughgoing response to the claims of Flavian propaganda. From the opening incipit Mark challenges the claims of Vespasian by boldly claiming that Jesus rather than Vespasian is the true Messiah and true Son of God. This claim is supported throughout the Galilean ministry as Mark offers a counter-résumé to that of Vespasian, including Jesus as a superior healer, benefactor, commander of legions, and master of the winds and waves. At the same time, Jesus outdoes Vespasian in the realm of imperial humility, as he regularly resists public honor (contra the common reading that Jesus seeks to keep his identity a secret). Through the central section, Jesus even outdoes Vespasian in embodying Roman political ideology, as he is willing to give his life for his people. Mark even demonstrates that Vespasian's greatest military achievement, the destruction of Jerusalem and its temple, was orchestrated by the God of Israel and was prophesied by the true Messiah and Son of God, Jesus. In so doing Mark strips Vespasian of his powerful victory and places the victory into the hands of Jesus. And even in death, as Roman soldiers attempt to mock, shame, and ultimately defeat Jesus through crucifixion, they unwittingly honor him with the Roman triumph he deserves. The climactic declaration of the Roman centurion parallels the incipit and declares Jesus, rather than Rome's emperor, to be Son of God.

APPENDIX

YAHWEH CHRISTOLOGY
IN MARK'S GOSPEL

A FTER READING THIS BOOK, some readers might be surprised to find that in a book devoted to Mark's Christology there has been no discussion of what seems like a widely popular topic in the field of New Testament studies: whether Mark's Christology should be understood as "high" (Jesus as in some way divine or the Yahweh of Israel) or "low" (Jesus as God's Messiah but ultimately human). To be sure, recent studies on Mark's Christology have raised this very question, with some adamant that Mark's Christology is high and others equally adamant that Mark's Christology is low.[1] Because I have said

---

[1]For examples of those who promote a low Christology in Mark, see J. R. Daniel Kirk, *A Man Attested by God: The Human Jesus of the Synoptic Gospels* (Grand Rapids: Eerdmans, 2016); Donald Juel, *Messiah and Temple: The Trial of Jesus in the Gospel of Mark*, Society of Biblical Literature Dissertation Series 31 (Missoula, MT: Scholars Press, 1977), 78-82, 108-14; Frank J. Matera, *The Kingship of Jesus: Composition and Theology in Mark 15*, Society of Biblical Literature Dissertation Series 66 (Chico, CA: Scholars Press, 1982); Jack Dean Kingsbury, *The Christology of Mark's Gospel* (Philadelphia: Fortress, 1983), 32, 65, 142; Paul Achtemeier, "Mark, Gospel of," *ABD*, 551-53; D. Rhoads and D. Michie, *Mark as Story: An Introduction to the Narrative of a Gospel* (Philadelphia: Fortress, 1982), 105; E. Broadhead, *Teaching with Authority: Miracles and Christology in the Gospel of Mark*, JSNTSup 74 (Sheffield, UK: JSOT Press, 1992), 125-26. For those who promote a high Christology in Mark, see Timothy J. Geddert, "The Implied YHWH Christology of Mark's Gospel: Mark's Challenge to the Reader to 'Connect the Dots,'" *Bulletin for Biblical Research* 25, no. 3 (2015): 325-40; D. Johansson, "*Kyrios* in the Gospel of Mark," *JSNT* 33, no. 1 (2010): 101-24; Paul Owen, "Jesus as God's Chief Agent in Mark's Christology," in *Mark, Manuscripts, and Monotheism: Essays in Honor of Larry W. Hurtado*, ed. Dieter T. Roth and Chris Keith, LNTS 528 (London: Bloomsbury T&T Clark, 2015), 40-59.

nothing about a "high" Christology in Mark and have argued that Mark presents Jesus as God's Messiah, as expressed through titles such as "Son of God," "Son of Man," and "Son of David," some might conclude that I favor those who see a low Christology in Mark. But such a conclusion would be overly simplistic.

The focus of the present study is the Christology of Mark's Gospel as expressed through both Mark's explicit christological pieces and my proposed historical reconstruction of Mark's setting. If one is only looking at the explicit christological pieces in Mark, then I would conclude, as I have in this book, that those pieces present a "low" Christology rather than a "high" one. However, like many arguing that Mark does indeed present a "high" or Yahweh Christology, I contend that if one pays close attention to certain implicit aspects of Mark, a surprising high Christology can be perceived.

It is not my intention to make an exhaustive case for such a position here, but a few examples of such an implicit Christology could be noted. One possible example of an implicit high Christology can be found in Mark 2:1-12, in which Jesus not only heals a paralytic but forgives the paralytic of his sins. In this story, before addressing the man's physical ailments, the healing of which was seemingly the intended purpose of those who brought the man, Jesus declares the man's sins to be forgiven (Mk 2:5). This declaration then causes scribes to question whether Jesus is blaspheming, as it is but God alone who can forgive sins (Mk 2:7). After questioning the motives of these scribes, the Markan Jesus provides the climactic statement of the pericope, saying, "But so that you may know that the Son of Man has the authority on earth to forgive sins . . . I say to you [the paralytic], stand up, take your mat and go to your home" (Mk 2:10-11).

As discussed previously, on the explicit level the reader can understand that Mark is attributing to Jesus, the messianic Son of Man, the significant power to forgive sins. The reader need not look further than this reading to find meaning in the pericope. However, the observant reader might find in the text an invitation to further consideration. Why is the Son of Man able to forgive sins? Many presume that it is because God has granted this power to Jesus because Jesus is God's messianic agent—a reading that presupposes a difference between God and Jesus the Son of Man. But no such claim is actually made by the text. Might another option be available to the reader—namely, that the scribes' claim that only God can forgive sin is indeed true, and thus Jesus' ability to forgive sins would lead the reader to identify Jesus in some way with God? Such a reading is certainly possible, and the reader is seemingly invited to consider it.

Another example of such an implicit Christology is found in Mark 6:45-52, in which Jesus walks on the waves. It is certainly possible to read this story in terms of Jesus as God's powerful messianic agent who walks on water, as Yahweh does. However, for the observant reader, one familiar with the LXX, the text offers literary clues that seemingly lead the reader to perceive an implied identity for Jesus. First, Jesus is presented as walking on the sea. Walking on the sea (not through the sea) is a function attributed to Yahweh alone in Hebrew Scripture. In describing the Yahweh of Israel, Job 9:8 (LXX) says, "Who alone has stretched out the heavens, and walks on the sea as on firm ground." With this detail Mark depicts Jesus doing something that Jewish Scripture claims only Yahweh alone can do.[2]

Second, this Markan pericope includes the odd detail that Jesus intended to "pass by" his disciples, a detail omitted in Matthean redaction of this pericope. This language of "passing by" finds striking parallels in theophany narratives of Hebrew Scriptures. In Exodus 33–34, four times the text references Yahweh's intent to pass by Moses on Mount Sinai, with the LXX using the same verb used by Mark in this pericope. Again, in 1 Kings 19:11, Yahweh tells Elijah that he will "pass by" him on Mount Horeb. There seems to be an established tradition in the Hebrew Scriptures of God "passing by" his appointed agents. Here Jesus is depicted as intending to "pass by" his agents, the Twelve, as he walks on the sea.

Finally, after Jesus' disciples see him and are overcome with fear, Jesus speaks to them and identifies himself by saying ἐγώ εἰμι, "I am." While this phrase could be interpreted as a simple means of self-identification (i.e., "it is me"), the observant reader understands that this form of identification is strikingly similar to the way in which God identifies himself to Moses at the burning bush in Exodus 3:14. When these details are taken all together (Jesus walking on the sea as Yahweh does, Jesus intending to pass by his appointed agents as Yahweh does, and Jesus identifying himself with ἐγώ εἰμι), a strong case can be made that the author of Mark intends the observant reader to see Jesus as none other than the Yahweh of Israel. One must at least grant that such a reading of the text would be possible for a first-century Jew.

These are simply two of many examples by which one could understand the Evangelist to be weaving an implicit high Christology into the narrative. Many readers of Mark, both from the first century and the twenty-first, could miss such examples of high Christology. But some readers, particularly those well versed in the LXX, may perceive this implied high Christology.

---

[2]For a similar conclusion, see M. E. Boring, *Mark*, NTL (Minneapolis: Fortress, 2006), 189; Geddert, "Implied YHWH Christology," 332-34.

One potential challenge for those who propose an implied high Christology in Mark is the question of why such a Christology would only be implied and not explicit. If Mark is committed to such a high Christology, why did the Evangelist not make such important christological claims more explicit in the narrative? While an inability to answer this question does not doom this proposed reading of Mark's Christology, an answer to this question might strengthen the case of its proponents or in some way assuage the concerns of its critics. The reading offered by the present project might provide just such an answer.

As I have established above, there were particular ways in which Roman emperors were expected to live, act, and rule. Good emperors showed deference, at least outwardly, to Roman political ideology. For this reason, they dressed modestly, lived in relatively humble homes, rejected excessive honors and titles, lived under the law rather than above it, and presented themselves as servants to the Senate and people. In efforts to distance themselves from the appearance of monarchs, good Roman emperors refused to be identified as gods or to receive cultic worship within the city of Rome.[3] Such identification would have explicitly communicated that the Roman emperor was greater than his fellow Romans and thus would have violated a Roman political ideology committed to self-rule. Such monarch worship was the property of the Greeks and Persians in the East and was to be resisted by Rome's first and chief citizen. In Rome a Roman emperor only became divine upon his death. Only when the deceased emperor had joined the ranks of Roman gods was it acceptable to worship him.

If Mark is presenting Jesus as a world ruler, one who would have appealed to the political sensibilities of Mark's Roman readers, it would stand to reason that no explicit references to Jesus' divinity would be found. Such references could undermine the Markan enterprise of demonstrating Jesus as superior to Vespasian. Thus my proposed reading of Mark's Gospel would adequately explain the restriction of high christological content to the implied level of the Markan narrative.

To be clear, though favorable to readings that perceive a high Christology in Mark, I am not arguing for a high Markan Christology in the present book. I am merely demonstrating the compatibility that such a reading of Mark's Christology has with the present project.

---

[3]As a point of clarification, it seems there was little concern about Roman emperors being worshiped by non-Romans, a practice that was prevalent throughout the empire in the first century. Such worship was likely seen as a sign of allegiance to Rome and Roman power, and thus it did not offend Roman sensibilities.

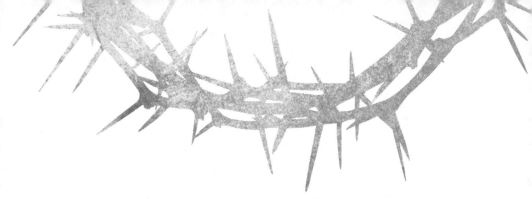

BIBLIOGRAPHY

ANCIENT SOURCES

Aristotle. *Nicomachean Ethics*. Translated by H. Rackham. LCL. Cambridge, MA: Harvard University Press, 1926.

Cicero. *Pro Rabirio Perduellionis*. Translated by N. H. Watts. LCL. Cambridge, MA: Harvard University Press, 1931.

———. *Tusculan Disputations*. Translated by John E. King. LCL. Cambridge, MA: Harvard University Press, 1927.

Dio Cassius. *Dio's Roman History*. Translated by Earnest Cary. 9 vols. LCL. Cambridge, MA: Harvard University Press, 1914–1927.

Josephus. Translated by H. St. J. Thackeray et al. 10 vols. LCL. Cambridge, MA: Harvard University Press, 1926–1965.

Philo. *On the Embassy to Gaius*. Translated by F. H. Colson. LCL. Cambridge, MA: Harvard University Press, 1962.

Pliny the Younger. *Panegyricus*. Translated by Radice Betty. LCL. Cambridge, MA: Harvard University Press, 1969.

Plutarch. *An seni respublica gerenda sit*. Translated by Harold N. Fowler. LCL. Cambridge, MA: Harvard University Press, 1936.

Seneca. *Moral Essays*. Translated by John Basore. LCL. 3 vols. Cambridge, MA: Harvard University Press, 1935.

Suetonius. *The Lives of the Caesars*. Translated by J. C. Rolfe. 2 vols. LCL. Cambridge, MA: Harvard University Press, 1913–1914.

Tacitus. *The Histories and the Annals*. Translated by C. H. Moore and J. Jackson. 4 vols. LCL. Cambridge, MA: Harvard University Press, 1925–1937.

Thucydides. *History of the Peloponnesian War*. Translated by C. F. Smith. 4 vols. LCL. Cambridge, MA: Harvard University Press, 1919.

Xenophon. *Hiero*. Translated by C. E. Marchant and G. W. Bowersock. LCL. Cambridge, MA: Harvard University Press, 1925.

MODERN SOURCES

Achtemeier, Paul J. "'And He Followed Him': Miracles and Discipleship in Mark 10:46-52." *Semeia* 11 (1978): 126-30.

———. "Gospel Miracle Tradition and the Divine Man." *Interpretation* 26 (1972): 174-97.

———. *Mark*. Proclamation Commentary. Philadelphia: Fortress, 1975.

———. "Mark, Gospel of." *ABD* 4:551-53.

———. "Origin and Function of the Pre-Markan Miracle Catenae." *JBL* 91 (1972): 198-221.

Ahearne-Kroll, Stephen P. *The Psalms of Lament in Mark's Passion: Jesus' Davidic Suffering*. Society for New Testament Studies Monograph Series 142. Cambridge: Cambridge University Press, 2007.

Alföldi, A. *Die monarchische Repräsentation im römischen Kaiserreiche*. Darmstadt: Wissenschaftliche Buchgesellschaft, 1970.

Aune, David. *Prophecy in Early Christianity and the Ancient Mediterranean World*. Grand Rapids: Eerdmans, 1983.

Beard, Mary. *The Roman Triumph*. Cambridge, MA: Harvard University Press, 2007.

Bedenbender, Andreas. "Das 'Messiasgeheimnis' im Markusevangelium." *Texte und Kontexte* 27, nos. 3-4 (2004): 1-96.

Béranger, J. "Le Refus du Pouvoir." *Museum Helveticum* 5 (1948): 178-96.

Best, E. *Disciples and Discipleship*. Edinburgh: T&T Clark, 1986.

Bieler, L. *Theios Anⵁr: Das Bild des "Göttlichen Menschen" in Spätantike und Frühchristentum*. 2 vols. Vienna: Höfels, 1935–1936.

Black, C. C. *The Disciples According to Mark: Markan Redaction in Current Debate*. JSNTSup 27. Sheffield, UK: JSOT Press, 1989.

———. *Mark: Images of an Apostolic Interpreter*. Minneapolis: Fortress, 2001.

———. "The Quest of the Markan Redactor: Why Has It Been Pursued and What Has It Taught Us?" *JSNT* 33 (1988): 19-39.

Bolt, P. *Jesus' Defeat of Death: Persuading Mark's Early Readers*. Cambridge: Cambridge University Press, 2003.

Boring, M. E. "The Christology of Mark: Hermeneutical Issues for Systematic Theology." *Semeia* 30 (1984): 143-44.

———. *Mark*. NTL. Minneapolis: Fortress, 2006.

Bringmann, Klaus. *A History of the Roman Republic*. Cambridge: Polity, 2007.

Broadhead, E. *Teaching with Authority: Miracles and Christology in the Gospel of Mark*. JSNTSup 74. Sheffield, UK: JSOT Press, 1992.

Brown, Schuyler. "'The Secret of the Kingdom of God' (Mark 4:11)." *JBL* 92 (1973): 60-74.

Bultmann, Rudolf. *The History of the Synoptic Tradition*. Translated by John Marsh. Oxford: Basil Blackwell, 1963.

———. *Theology of the New Testament*. Translated by Kendrick Grobel. 2 vols. New York: Scribner's, 1951.

Burkill, T. A. *Mysterious Revelation: An Examination of the Philosophy of St. Mark's Gospel*. Ithaca, NY: Cornell University Press, 1963.

Cameron, A. *Circus Factions: Blues and Greens at Rome and Byzantium*. New York: Oxford University Press, 1976.

Carson, R. A. G. "Caesar and the Monarchy." *Greece & Rome* 4, no. 1 (1957): 46-53.

Chilver, G. E. F. "Augusts and the Roman Constitution 1939-1950." *Historia* 1 (1950): 408-35.

Chronis, Harry L. "To Reveal and to Conceal: A Literary Critical Perspective on 'the Son of Man' in Mark." *NTS* 51 (2005): 459-81.

Clark, K. W. "The Meaning of (Kata)Kyrieyein." In *The Gentile Bias and Other Essays*, edited by K. W. Clark, 207-12. Leiden: Brill, 1980.

Clark, M. D. H. *Augustus, First Roman Emperor: Power, Propaganda and the Politics of Survival*. Exeter, UK: Bristol Phoenix, 2010.

Cody, Jane M. "Conquerors and Conquered on Flavian Coins." In *Flavian Rome: Culture, Image, Text*, edited by A. Boyle and W. Dominik, 103-24. Leiden: Brill, 2003.

Collins, Adela Yarbro. *The Beginning of the Gospel: Probings of Mark in Context*. Minneapolis: Fortress, 1992.

———. *Mark: A Commentary*. Hermeneia. Minneapolis: Fortress, 2007.

———. "Mark and His Readers: The Son of God Among Greeks and Romans." *Harvard Theological Review* 93, no. 2 (2000): 87.

Collins, John J. *The Scepter and the Star: The Messiahs of the Dead Sea Scrolls and Other Ancient Literature*. New York: Doubleday, 1995.

Cook, John G. *The Structure and Persuasive Power of Mark: A Linguistic Approach*. SBL Semeia Studies. Atlanta: Scholars Press, 1995.

Cranfield, C. E. B. *The Gospel According to St. Mark*. Cambridge Greek Text Commentary. Cambridge: Cambridge University Press, 1959.

Crossley, James. *The Date of Mark's Gospel: Insight from the Law in Earliest Christianity*. JSNTSup 266. London: T&T Clark, 2004.

Danker, Frederick W., Walter Bauer, William F. Arndt, and F. Wilbur Gingrich. *Greek-English Lexicon of the New Testament and Other Early Christian Literature*. 3rd ed. Chicago: University of Chicago Press, 2000.

Davies, Philip G. "Mark's Christological Paradox." *JSNT* 35 (1989): 3-18.

Dibelius, Martin. *From Tradition to Gospel*. Translated by Bertram Lee Woolf. London: James Clarke, 1971.

Diels, Hermann. *Die Fragmente der Vorsokratiker, Griechisch und Deutsch*. Edited by W. Kranz. 5th ed. 3 vols. Berlin: Weidmann, 1934-1937.

Dittenberger, W., ed. *Orientis Graecae Inscriptiones Selectae*. 2 vols. Leipizig: S. Hirzel, 1903-1905. Reprint, Hildesheim: Olms, 1960.

Donahue, J. R. *The Theology and Setting of Discipleship in the Gospel of Mark*. 1983 Père Marquette Theology Lecture. Milwaukee: Marquette University Press, 1983.

Donahue, John R., and Daniel J. Harrington. *The Gospel of Mark*. Sacra Pagina 2. Collegeville, MN: Liturgical Press, 2002.

Dowd, Sharyn. *Reading Mark: A Literary and Theological Commentary on the Second Gospel*. Macon, GA: Smyth & Helwys, 2000.

Dunn, J. M. D. *Jesus Remembered*. Vol. 1 of *Christianity in the Making*. Grand Rapids: Eerdmans, 2003.

Earl, D. "Prologue-Form in Ancient Historiography." *ANRW* 2:842-56.

Ebeling, Hans Jürgen. *Das Messiasgeheimnis und die Botschaft des Marcus-Evangelisten*. Berlin: A. Töpelmann, 1939.

Ehrenberg, V. "Caesar's Final Aims." *Classical Philology* 68 (1964): 149-61.

Esler, Philip F. "God's Honour and Rome's Triumph: Responses to the Fall of Jerusalem in 70 CE in Three Jewish Apocalypses." In *Modeling Early Christianity*, edited by Philip F. Essler, 233-47. London: Routledge, 1995.

Evans, Craig A. *Mark 8:27–16:20*. WBC 34B. Nashville: Thomas Nelson, 2001.

———. "Mark's Incipit and the Priene Calendar Inscription: From Jewish Gospel to Greco-Roman Gospel." *Journal of Greco-Roman Christianity and Judaism* 1 (2000): 67-81.

Eve, Eric. "Spit in Your Eye: The Blind Man of Bethsaida and the Blind Man of Alexandria." *NTS* 51, no. 1 (2008): 1-17.

Fears, J. Rufus. *Princeps a Diis Electus: The Divine Election of the Emperor as a Political Concept at Rome*. Papers and Monographs of the American Academy in Rome 26. Rome: American Academy in Rome, 1977.

———. "Theology of Victory at Rome: Approaches and Problems." *ANRW* 17.2:736-826.

Ferguson, Everett. *Backgrounds of Early Christianity*. 3rd ed. Grand Rapids: Eerdmans, 2003.

Finney, Mark. *Honour and Conflict in the Ancient World: 1 Corinthians in Its Greco-Roman Social Setting*. LNTS 460. London: T&T Clark, 2012.

Foerster, Werner. "δαίμων, δαιμόνιον." In vol. 2 of *TDNT*, 120.

Foster, George. "The Anatomy of Envy: A Study of Symbolic Behavior." *Current Anthropology* 13 (1972): 165-202.

Foster, Paul. *Colossians*. Black's New Testament Commentaries. London: Bloomsbury T&T Clark, 2016.

France, R. T. *The Gospel of Mark*. NIGTC. Grand Rapids: Eerdmans, 2002.

Gamel, Brian K. "The Centurion's Confession as Apocalyptic Unveiling: Mark 15:39 as a Markan Theology of Revelation." PhD diss., Baylor University, 2015.

Garnsey, P. *Famine and Food Supply in the Graeco-Roman World: Responses to Risk and Crisis*. Cambridge: Cambridge University Press, 1988.

Geddert, Timothy. "The Implied YHWH Christology of Mark: Mark's Challenge to the Reader to 'Connect the Dots.'" *Bulletin for Biblical Research* 25, no. 3 (2015): 329-31.

Gnilka, Joachim. *Das Evangelium nach Markus*. 2 vols. Evangelisch-Katholischer Kommentar zum Neuen Testament 2. Zurich: Neukirchener Verlag, 1979.

Goodyear, F. R. D. *The Annals of Tacitus: Books 1-6*. Cambridge: Cambridge University Press, 1972.

Gradel, Ittai. *Emperor Worship and Roman Religion*. Oxford Classical Monographs. Oxford: Oxford University Press, 2002.

Graf, H. R. *Kaiser Vespasian, Untersuchungen zu Suetons Vita Divi Vespasiani*. Stuttgart: Kohlhammer, 1937.

Gray, Timothy C. *The Temple in the Gospel of Mark: A Study in Its Narrative Role*. WUNT II/242. Tübingen: Mohr Siebeck, 2008. Reprint, Grand Rapids: Baker, 2010.

Grundmann, W. *Das Evangelium nach Markus*. 6th ed. Theologischer Handkommentar zum Neuen Testament 2. Berlin: Evangelische Verlagsanstalt, 1973.

Gundry, Robert H. *Mark: A Commentary on His Apology for the Cross*. Grand Rapids: Eerdmans, 1993.

———. "Richard A. Horsley's *Hearing the Whole Story*: A Critical Review of Its Postcolonial Slant." *JSNT* 26 (2003): 131-49.

Hahn, Ferdinand. *The Titles of Jesus in Christology: Their History in Early Christianity*. New York: World Publishing, 1969.

Hammond, M. "*Res Olim Dissociabiles: Principatus ac Libertas*: Liberty Under the Early Roman Empire." *Harvard Studies in Classical Philology* 67 (1963): 93-113.

Hare, Douglas R. A. *The Son of Man Tradition*. Minneapolis: Fortress, 1990.

Heard, Richard G. "The Old Gospel Prologues." *Journal of Theological Studies* 6 (1955): 1-16.

Heil, John Paul. "The Narrative Strategy and Pragmatics of the Temple Theme in Mark." *CBQ* 59 (1997): 76-100.

Hengel, Martin. *Studies in Early Christology*. Edinburgh: T&T Clark, 1995.

———. *Studies in the Gospel of Mark*. Translated by J. Bowden. Philadelphia: Fortress, 1995.

Henrichs, A. "Vespasian's Visit to Alexandria." *Zeitschrift für Papyrologie und Epigraphik* 3 (1968): 51-80.

Hooker, Morna D. *The Gospel According to St. Mark*. Black's New Testament Commentary 2. Peabody, MA: Hendrickson, 1991.

Horsley, Richard. *Hearing the Whole Story: The Politics of Plot in Mark's Gospel*. Louisville: Westminster John Knox, 2001.

Howard, W. F. "The Anti-Marcionite Prologues to the Gospels." *Expository Times* 47 (1935–1936): 534-38.

Hurtado, Larry. *Mark*. New International Biblical Commentary 2. Peabody, MA: Hendrickson, 1989.

Iersel, Bas M. F. van. *Mark: A Reader-Response Commentary*. Translated by W. H. Bisscheroux. London: T&T Clark, 1998.

Incigneri, Brian. *The Gospel to the Romans: The Setting and Rhetoric of Mark's Gospel*. Biblical Interpretation Series 65. Leiden: Brill, 2003.

Johansson, D. "*Kyrios* in the Gospel of Mark." *JSNT* 33, no. 1 (2010): 101-24.

Juel, Donald. *Messiah and Temple: The Trial of Jesus in the Gospel of Mark*. Society of Biblical Literature Dissertation Series 31. Missoula, MT: Scholars Press, 1977.

Kaminouchi, A. M. *"But It Is Not So Among You": Echoes of Power in Mark 10.32-45*. JSNTSup 249. New York: T&T Clark, 2003.

Keck, Leander. "Mark 3:7-12 and Mark's Christology." *JBL* 84 (1965): 341-58.

Kelber, Werner H. "Conclusion: From Passion to Gospel." In *The Passion in Mark: Studies on Mark 14–16*. Edited by Werner H. Kelber. Philadelphia: Fortress, 1976.

———. *The Kingdom in Mark: A New Place and a New Time*. Philadelphia: Fortress, 1974.

Kim, Tae Hun. "The Anarthrous υἱός θεοῦ in Mark 15,39 and the Roman Imperial Cult." *Biblica* 79 (1998): 221-41.

Kingsbury, J. D. "The Christology of Mark and the Son of Man." In *Unity and Diversity in the Gospels and Paul: Essays in Honor of Frank J. Matera*, edited by Christopher W. Skinner and Kelly R. Iverson, 55-70. Atlanta: Society of Biblical Literature, 2012.

———. *The Christology of Mark's Gospel*. Philadelphia: Fortress, 1983.

Kirk, J. R. Daniel. *A Man Attested by God: The Human Jesus of the Synoptic Gospels*. Grand Rapids: Eerdmans, 2016.

———. "Time for Figs, Temple Destruction, and Houses of Prayer in Mark 11:12-25." *CBQ* 74 (2012): 509-27.

Kolenkow, A. B. "Miracle and Prophecy." *ANRW* 23.2, 1470-1506.

Lacey, W. K. *Augustus and the Principate: The Evolution of the System*. Leeds, UK: Francis Cairns, 1996.

Lane, W. L. *The Gospel of Mark*. New International Commentary on the New Testament 2. Grand Rapids: Eerdmans, 1974.

Lee-Pollard, Dorothy A. "Powerlessness as Power: A Key Emphasis in the Gospel of Mark." *Scottish Journal of Theology* 40 (1987): 73-88.

Levick, Barbara. *Claudius*. New Haven, CT: Yale University Press, 1990.

———. *Tiberius the Politician*. Rev. ed. New York: Routledge, 1999.

———. *Vespasian*. New York: Routledge, 1999.

Luz, Ulrich. "Das Geheimnismotiv und die markinische Christologie." *Zeitschrift für die Neutestamentliche Wissenschaft und die Kunde der Älteren Kirche* 56 (1965): 9-30. ET, "The Secrecy Motif and the Marcan Christology." In *The Messianic Secret*, edited by Christopher Tuckett, 75-96. Philadelphia: Fortress, 1983.

Malbon, Elizabeth Struthers. *In the Company of Jesus: Characters in Mark's Gospel*. Louisville: Westminster John Knox, 2000.

———. "The Major Importance of the Minor Characters in Mark." Pages 58-86 in *The New Literary Criticism and the New Testament*. Edited by Elizabeth Struthers Malbon et al. JSNTSup 109. Sheffield, UK: Sheffield Academic, 1994.

———. *Mark's Jesus: Characterization as Narrative Christology*. Waco, TX: Baylor University Press, 2009.

Malina, Bruce. *The New Testament World: Insights from Cultural Anthropology*. 3rd ed. Louisville: Westminster John Knox, 2001.

Marcus, Joel. *Mark 1–8: A New Translation with Introduction and Commentary*. AB 27. New York: Doubleday, 2000.

———. *Mark 8–16: A New Translation with Introduction and Commentary*. AB 27A. New Haven, CT: Yale University Press, 2009.

———. *Way of the Lord: Christological Exegesis of the Old Testament in the Gospel of Mark*. Louisville: Westminster John Knox, 1992.

Martin, Ralph P. *Mark—Evangelist and Theologian*. Exeter, UK: Paternoster, 1972.

Martitz, W. von. "υἱός." Pages 338-40 in vol. 8 of *TDNT*.

Mason, Steve. "Figured Speech and Irony in T. Flavius Josephus 1." In *Flavius Josephus and Flavian Rome*, edited by J. Edmondson et al., 243-88. Oxford: Oxford University Press, 2005.

———. "Josephus, Daniel and the Flavian House." In *Josephus and the History of the Greco Roman Period: Essays in Memory of Morton Smith*, edited by Fausto Parente and Joseph Sievers, 161-94. Leiden: Brill, 1994.

Matera, Frank J. *The Kingship of Jesus: Composition and Theology in Mark 15*. Society of Biblical Literature Dissertation Series 66. Chico, CA: Scholars Press, 1982.

McCrum, M., and A. G. Woodhead. *Select Documents of the Principates of the Flavian Emperors: Including the Year of Revolution: A.D. 68–96*. Cambridge: Cambridge University Press, 1961.

Metzger, Bruce M. *A Textual Commentary on the Greek New Testament*. 2nd ed. New York: UBS, 2002.

Meye, Robert. *Jesus and the Twelve: Discipleship and Revelation in Mark's Gospel*. Grand Rapids: Eerdmans, 1968.

Millar, F. "Triumvirate and Principate." *JRS* 63 (1973): 50-67.

Moloney, Francis J. *The Gospel of Mark: A Commentary*. Peabody, MA: Hendrickson, 2002.

———. *Mark: Storyteller, Interpreter, Evangelist*. Peabody, MA: Hendrickson, 2004.

Morgan, John R. "Cynics." In the *Oxford Classical Dictionary*, edited by Simon Hornblower and Antony Spawforth, 418-19. 3rd ed. Oxford: Oxford University Press, 1996.

Myers, Ched. *Binding the Strong Man: A Political Reading of Mark's Story of Jesus*. Maryknoll, NY: Orbis Books, 1992.

Neusner, Jacob. "Money-Changers in the Temple: The Mishnah's Explanation." *NTS* 35 (1989): 288-89.

Neyrey, Jerome H., and Richard L. Rohrbaugh. "'He Must Increase, I Must Decrease' (John 3:30): A Cultural and Social Interpretation." *CBQ* 63 (2001): 468-69.

Nicols, J. *Vespasian and the Partes Flavianae*. Historia Einzelschriften 28. Wiesbaden: Franze Steiner, 1978.

Norden, E. "Josephus und Tacitus über Jesus Christus und eine Messianische Prophetie." In *Zur Josephus Forschung*, edited by Abraham Schalit, 27-69. Darmstadt: Wissenschaftliche Buchgesellschaft, 1973.

O'Brien, Kelli S. *The Use of Scripture in the Markan Passion Narrative*. LNTS 384. London: Bloomsbury T&T Clark, 2010.

O'Brien, Peter T. *Colossians, Philemon*. WBC 44. Waco, TX: Word, 1982.

Owen, Paul. "Jesus as God's Chief Agent in Mark's Christology." In *Mark, Manuscripts, and Monotheism: Essays in Honor of Larry W. Hurtado*, edited by Dieter T. Roth and Chris Keith, 40-59. LNTS 528. London: Bloomsbury T&T Clark, 2015.

Percival, John. "Tacitus and the Principate." *Greek & Rome* 27 (1980): 119-33.

Perrin, Norman. "The Christology of Mark: A Study in Methodology." In *A Modern Pilgrimage in New Testament Christology*, 104-21. Philadelphia: Fortress, 1974.

———. "The Creative Use of the Son of Man Traditions by Mark." In *A Modern Pilgrimage in New Testament Christology*, 84-93. Philadelphia: Fortress, 1974.

Pilch, John. "Secrecy in the Gospel of Mark." *Professional Approaches for Christian Educators* 21 (1992): 150-53.

Räisänen, Heikki. *The "Messianic Secret" in Mark's Gospel*. Translated by Christopher Tuckett. Edinburgh: T&T Clark, 1990.

Rajak, Tessa. *Josephus: The Historian and His Society*. Philadelphia: Fortress, 1984.

Reese, D. G. "Demons: New Testament." Pages 140-42 in vol. 2 of *ABD*.

Regul, Jürgen. *Die antimarcionitischen Evangelienprologe*. Vetus Latina: Die Reste der altlateinischen Bibel 6. Freiburg: Herder, 1969.

Rhoads, David, and Donald Michie. *Mark as Story*. Philadelphia: Fortress, 1982.

Rhoads, David, Joanna Dewey, and Donald Michie. *Mark as Story: An Introduction to the Narrative of a Gospel*. 2nd ed. Minneapolis: Fortress, 1999.

Rindge, Matthew S. "Reconfiguring the Akedah and Recasting God: Lament and Divine Abandonment in Mark." *JBL* 130, no. 1 (2011): 755-74.

Roskam, Hendrika N. *The Purpose of the Gospel of Mark in Its Historical and Social Context*. Novum Testamentum Supplements 114. Leiden: Brill, 2004.

Salmon, E. T. "The Evolution of Augustus' Principate." *Historia* 5 (1956): 456-78.

Sanders, E. P. *Jesus and Judaism*. Philadelphia: Fortress, 1985.

Santos, Narry F. *Slave of All: The Paradox of Authority and Servanthood in the Gospel of Mark*. JSNTSup 237. London: Sheffield, 2003.

Saulnier, C. "Flavius Josèphe et la Propagande Flavienne." *Revue Biblique* 96, no. 4 (1989): 545-62.

Schenke, L. *Die Wundererzählungen des Markusevangeliums*. Stuttgarter biblische Beiträge. Stuttgart: Katholisches Bibelwerk, 1974.

Schmidt, K. L. *Der Rahmen der Geschichte Jesu*. Berlin: Trowitzsch und Sohn, 1919.

Schmidt, T. E. "Mark 15.16-32: The Crucifixion Narrative and the Roman Triumphal Procession." *NTS* 41 (1995): 1-18.

Schmithals, W. "Die Worte vom Leidenden Menschensohn." In *Theologia Crucis—Signum Crucis: Festschrift für Erich Dinkler zum 70 Geburtstag*, edited by C. Anderson and G. Klein, 417-45. Tübingen: J. C. B. Mohr, 1979.

Scott, J. M. "Gods, Greek and Roman." In *Dictionary of Jesus and the Gospels*, edited by Joel B. Green, Jeannine K. Brown, and Nicholas Perrin, 328-35. 2nd ed. Downers Grove, IL: InterVarsity Press, 2013.

Seeley, David. "Jesus' Temple Act." *CBQ* 55 (1993): 263-83.

———. "Rulership and Service in Mark 10:41-45." *Novum Testamentum* 35 (1993): 234-50.

Smith, D. E. "Narrative Beginnings in Ancient Literature and Theory." *Semeia* 52 (1990): 1-9.

Smith, J. Z. "Towards Interpreting Demonic Powers in Hellenistic and Roman Antiquity." *ANRW* 16.1, 425-43.

Steichele, H. J. *Der Leidende Sohn Gottes: Eine Untersuchung einiger alttestamentlicher Motive in der Christologie des Markuseangeliums.* Biblische Untersuchungen 14. Regensburg: Pustet.

Sweat, Laura C. *The Theological Role of Paradox in the Gospel of Mark.* LNTS 224. London: T&T Clark, 2013.

Tannehill, Robert. C. "The Disciples in Mark: The Function of a Narrative Role." In *The Interpretation of Mark*, edited by Mark Telford, 134-57. Issues in Religion and Theology 7. Philadelphia: Fortress, 1985.

———. "The Gospel of Mark as Narrative Christology." *Semeia* 16 (1979): 57-95.

Taylor, Vincent. *The Gospel According to Saint Mark.* London: Macmillan, 1952.

———. *The Gospel According to Saint Mark.* 2nd ed. London: Macmillan, 1966.

Telford, W. R. *The Barren Temple and the Withered Tree: A Redaction-Critical Analysis of the Cursing of the Fig-Tree Pericope in Mark's Gospel and Its Relation to the Cleansing of the Temple Tradition.* JSNTSup 1. Sheffield, UK: JSOT Press, 1980.

———. *The Theology of the Gospel of Mark.* Cambridge: Cambridge University Press, 1999.

Theissen, Gerd. "Die pragmatische Bedeutung der Geheimnismotive im Markusevangelium: Ein wissenssoziologischer Versuch." In *Secrecy and Concealment: Studies in the History of Mediterranean and Near Eastern Religions*, edited by Hans G. Kippenberg and Guy G. Stroumsa, 225-46. Studies in the History of Religions 65. Leiden: Brill, 1995.

———. *The Gospels in Context: Social and Political History in the Synoptic Tradition.* Minneapolis: Fortress, 1991.

Tödt, H. E. *The Son of Man in the Synoptic Tradition.* Translated by Dorothea M. Barton. London: SCM Press, 1965.

Twelftree, G. H. "Demon, Devil, Satan." In *Dictionary of Jesus and the Gospels*, edited by J. B. Green and S. McKnight, 163-72. 1st ed. Downers Grove, IL: InterVarsity Press, 1992.

Versnel, H. S. *Triumphus: An Inquiry into the Origin, Development and Meaning of the Roman Triumph*. Leiden: Brill, 1970.

Vielhauer, P. "Erwägungen zur Christologie des Markusevangeliums." In *Zeit und Geschichte. Dankesgabe an Rudolf Bultmann zum 80. Geburtstag*, edited by E. Dinkler, 155-69. Tübingen: J. C. B. Mohr, 1964.

Wallace-Hadrill, A. "Civilis Princeps: Between Citizen and King." *JRS* 72 (1982): 32-48.

Watson, David F. *Honor Among Christians: The Cultural Key to the Messianic Secret*. Minneapolis: Fortress, 2010.

Watson, Francis. "Ambiguity in the Markan Narrative." *Kings Theological Review* 10 (1987): 11-12.

Weeden, Theodore J. *Mark—Traditions in Conflict*. Philadelphia: Fortress, 1971.

Wegener, Mark I. *Cruciformed: The Literary Impact of Mark's Story of Jesus and His Disciples*. Lanham, MD: University Press of America, 1995.

Whitlark, Jason A. *Resisting Empire: Rethinking the Purpose of the Letter to "the Hebrews."* LNTS 484. London: T&T Clark, 2014.

Williams, Joel F. "The Characterization of Jesus as Lord in Mark's Gospel." In *Character Studies and the Gospel of Mark*, edited by Christopher W. Skinner and Matthew R. Hauge, 107-26. LNTS 483. London: T&T Clark, 2014.

Winn, Adam. "'No Stone Left upon Another': Considering Mark's Anti-Temple Motif in Both Narrative and History." In *Christian Origins and the Formation of the Early Church*, edited by Stanley E. Porter and Andrew W. Pitts. Early Christianity in Its Hellenistic Context Series 4. Leiden: Brill, forthcoming.

———. *The Purpose of Mark's Gospel: An Early Christian Response to Roman Imperial Propaganda*. WUNT II/245. Tübingen: Mohr Siebeck, 2008.

———. "Resisting Honor: The Markan Secrecy Motif and Roman Imperial Ideology." *JBL* 133, no. 3 (2014): 583-601.

———. "Son of God." In *Dictionary of Jesus and the Gospels*, edited by Joel B. Green, Jeannine K. Brown, and Nicholas Perrin, 886-93. 2nd ed. Downers Grove, IL: InterVarsity Press, 2013.

———. "Tyrant or Servant: Roman Political Ideology and Mark 10:42-45." *JSNT* 36, no. 4 (2014): 325-52.

Wrede, William. *Das Messiasgeheimnis in den Evangelien: Zugleich ein Beitrag zum Verständnis des Markusevangeliums*. Göttingen: Vandenhoeck & Ruprecht, 1901. ET, *The Messianic Secret*. Translated by J. C. G. Greig. Cambridge: James Clarke, 1971.

Wright, Addison G. "The Widow's Mites: Praise or Lament?—A Matter of Context." *CBQ* 44 (1982): 256-65.

Wright, N. T. *Jesus and the Victory of God*. Minneapolis: Fortress, 1996.

Yakobson, A., and H. M. Cotton. "Caligula's *Recusatio Imperii*." *Historia: Zeitschrift für Alte Geschichte* 34, no. 4 (1985): 497-503.

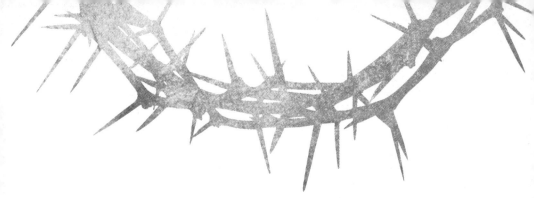

AUTHOR INDEX

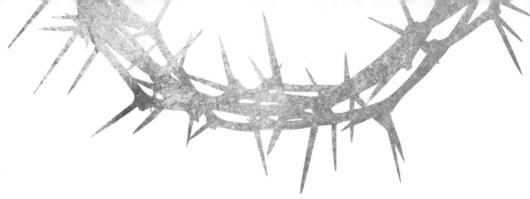

SUBJECT INDEX

SCRIPTURE INDEX

Finding the Textbook You Need

The IVP Academic Textbook Selector
is an online tool for instantly finding the IVP books
suitable for over 250 courses across 24 disciplines.

---

ivpacademic.com